D0849153

Scarlett O'Hara's Younger Sister

Scarlett O'Hara's Younger Sister

EVELYN KEYES

My Lively Life
In and Out of Hollywood

Lyle Stuart Inc.   *Secaucus, N.J.*

Fourth printing

Queries regarding rights and permissions should be
addressed to Lyle Stuart Inc., 120 Enterprise Ave.,
Secaucus, N. J. 07094.

Published by Lyle Stuart Inc. Published simultaneously
in Canada by George J. McLeod Limited, Toronto, Ont.

Manufactured in the United States of America

Library of Congress Cataloging in Publication Data

Keyes, Evelyn, [date -]
Scarlett O'Hara's younger sister.

Includes index.
1. Keyes, Evelyn, [date -] 2. Moving-picture
actors and actresses—United States—Biography.
I. Title.
PN2287. K655A38   791.43'028'0924 [B]   77-5607
ISBN 0-8184-0243-1

to my editor and my publisher

Contents

There are two tragedies in life.
One is not to get your heart's desire.
The other is to get it.

GEORGE   BERNARD   SHAW

BOOK ONE

CHAPTER 1...

> "I want . . . to be . . . hap-py . . . but I
> won't be . . . hap-py, 'til I make you . . . hap-py . . ."

I read all about it in the New York Times. *How Ruby
Keeler had been resurrected, tap shoes and all, and
brought back to Broadway for this 1970 version of an
old musical,* No, No Nanette.

*It didn't have much to do with me. I was living a
couple of hours straight north from that scene. My
house perched in splendid isolation on the side of a
Berkshire foothill, the nearest neighbor a mere dot in the
valley below. Deer traipsed across my lawn every
morning. Raccoons came to rob the bird feeders in the
evening. A little tennis, four hours at the typewriter, the
evening news and bed, this was my day. What did I
have to do with the lunatic world of show biz? Surely it
was a figment of wild imagination (mine) to think I had
ever been on a movie set in Hollywood? Mexico? London? Paris? Was that really my face that showed up
once in a while on the late late late show?*

*I was utterly astonished when the call came.
"Darling! How ever are you?" It was a man I knew who
worked for the William Morris Agency.*

"I'm fine, just fine . . ."

"The Nanette *people are sending out a National
Touring Company, and they need somebody for Ruby's
role. Are you interested?"*

*My heart jumped to racing speed. My God. Did they
want to resurrect . . . me?*

*"Y-yes," I sputtered (keep calm!), "I'm . . . v-very
interested."*

*"They'll want to see you, of course. How's your tap,
kept it up?"*

*I felt ill. I hadn't even thought of tap dancing for
several million years. "Oh sure!" I cried, "You bet I
have!"*

*"Next Thursday, then, three o'clock. Okay, Love?"
He gave me the name of the theater.*

I thought I might faint.

*This was Monday. How could I relearn to tap dance
in three days?*

*"One song will be enough," he said, "and a short
routine. Just to let them know you can still do it."*

*Still do it. I never could do it too well. Mother first
started me with piano lessons—classical music, which
was refined. "You must practice hard each day, " she
told me, "so you'll be good enough to become a teacher
yourself when you grow up."*

I had something else in mind.

I grew up in Atlanta watching my mother scuffling for pennies: bak-
ing pies, selling corsets to overweight women (she herself was a toothpick), raising canaries for a pet shop until she forgot to close the cage
door and seventy birds took it on the lam.

I watched older sisters shoved out to get jobs the instant they
finished high school, dutifully bringing the pay checks home to
Mother, unable to go anywhere, buy a dress, have a date.

I watched my pinch-lipped, humpty-dumpty grandmother, in
whose house we lived, rocking on the front porch, keeping an eye out
for neighborhood sin, chewing snuff, sometimes getting up to switch
my legs when I had sinned. (Like laugh.)

Alone all day, I began to read. Which is how I learned there were
better ways to live. That children had a mother *and* a father. They told
me I had had one, but he died when I was two. They told me I was the
apple of his eye, his precious pet. That I was inconsolable when he
"went away." They told me for the longest time after, I would run
down the street every time I saw a man coming, crying, "Dad-dy!
Dad-dy!"

When I was five I asked my uncle, "Are you my Daddy now?" He
was a man, thin as a wafer, who kept his arms close to his sides and
legs pressed tight together, as if he were fearful of taking up too much
room. He stared at me, breathing through his mouth. I could tell I had
done a sinful thing by the way he answered. "No! Cer . . . tainly not!"

He retreated into the bathroom and quickly closed the door. I peeked through the keyhole to see why, but he slapped a towel over the knob.

When I was seven, I dreamed of being an Indian, living in the forest with the animals; at eight, a nomad riding a camel across the sands.

I was thirteen before I realized the answer to my escape caper.

Become an actress. Actresses weren't stuck with one life, they could have a hundred. Look at Greta, Jean, and Norma. They could even have fathers if they wanted. An actress had it made.

I confided this secret ambition to my music teacher. "You!?" she snorted scornfully. "How could you become an actress? You have no voice! You can't even be heard across the room!"

Driving down to New York I thought of her. I laughed. Her uppity remark of some thirty-eight years ago was heading me toward a rehearsal studio today. "I want to *dance*," I told my mother after that, "I want to *move* with music, not make it." Dancers didn't have to talk, they had only to smile.

Mother's Methodist blood (she was a preacher's daughter) was exhausted at fifty-five from years of struggle, and she had lost her ability to withstand the wheedling of her youngest. She quickly gave in.

Three times a week after high school I went to dance class on Peachtree Street. When I had two routines under my belt—one "oriental," one tap—I began picking up jobs on weekends. Dubbed "Goldie" Keyes, in costumes by Maude Keyes, I danced for the Daughters of the Confederacy, the American Legion, the Masons. Five dollars here, ten there. The money paid my fare to Hollywood.

The odor in the Broadway Dance Studio was familiar: stale sweat from hopeful bodies straining their way to stardom. The same ancient photographs adorned the wall of the reception room: an adagio team, a ballerina au point. The kid tap dancer could have been Goldie. An old lady sat beneath them, white-haired, face painted with stage makeup, cupid's bow lips, circles of scarlet on soft, wrinkled cheeks. She looked up when I came in, and smiled. "I've been a professional since I was fifteen," she told me. Her dentures threatened to slide into her lap.

At least she knew who she was, which was more than I could claim. I went to the mirror in Room 3. Who the hell are you, I asked the image, where do you belong? I checked my teeth. Plenty of fillings, but still intact. Same slim figure. "You look just the same!" exclaimed a woman at the doctor's office the other day. Look closely, lady, those lines around the eyes, along the mouth, they aren't the same. That look in the eye, that's a dead giveaway. They've seen a thing or two.

I raised my arms in a pose. Tried a tentative time step: brush, pull-back, hop-step, brush-step. Ludicrous. Bones creak, unused muscles object. The overhead light beamed down on me. Unflattering as hell. But what does it matter when you're young?

Slow fade . . . Dissolve . . . Fade In . . . To same face, much younger, as Thirties background music creeps in, a Victrola playing "The Lady in Red". . . .

On Monday she stayed after class to work on a new step in the small studio off the main one. Intent on what she was doing, she didn't know Bill was there until he loomed behind her in the mirror. "Oooh!" she squealed, whirling around. She had seen him last Friday coming into the studio as she was leaving, and got goose pimples. He was just darling, reddish curly hair, blue eyes, and taller than she. But, pooh, he was a grown man, over twenty for sure, who wouldn't pay any attention to a sixteen-year-old girl.

Now he smiled, showing really great teeth. "Let me show you how to do that step," he said, glancing at himself in the mirror. His style was loose; he had great legs and knees. She had this thing for knees.

He asked her to a dance. They continued dating. They necked in cars, living rooms, front porch swings. His tongue filled her mouth, he opened her blouse and sucked at her breasts, pulling at the nipples until they rose in hard little knobs and the fire shot down her body. She quivered and ached with longing, juices overflowing. He unbuttoned his fly. "Touch it, touch it," he whispered, "put your hand on it!"

At school somebody had passed around a booklet with Popeye and Wimpy cartoons, both with those enormous objects sticking out of their pants. She didn't think she could stand not knowing one minute longer, not having one of those things sticking in her. Actresses, she told herself, must know everything, feel everything—didn't they hug and kiss and press together on the screen, and in *Red Dust*, Jean Harlow had locked Gene Raymond in the bedroom with her and slipped the key down between her breasts as she lay on the bed. They must have done after the fade-out what Bill was doing to her—and more.

He drove her to a part of Atlanta she didn't know. Its sleaziness bothered her; the electric sign saying "Motel" made her heart start to pound. She waited in the car while he went in to register. Other cars arrived, their headlights flashing across the seat where she cowered, suddenly afraid of the step she had taken.

The jangling key in his hand looked obscene. A bare bulb hung by its exposed wire from the center of the ceiling, spotlighting the bed that took up every inch of room space. The sheets, a dingy gray, were mussed from previous use, a big wet spot in the middle of the bottom one. He wasted no time pushing her down on the bed, falling on top of her. Perhaps one paid by the minute, crossed her mind.

The clash of lips couldn't be called a kiss, jets of hot wet air from his mouth blasted her face. Frenzied hands grabbed at her breasts, tugged at her clothes. The heaving, wriggling mass threatening to squash her was no longer human.

On the wall somebody had scribbled in red crayon, "I entered Mary seven times."

A hand was yanking at her skirt. Somehow he had let it out; she felt its naked hardness against her skin, that very same object that had thrilled her so when she had run her fingers along its velvety surface, when his hand would slide inside her panties, between her legs, and he would whisper, "Oh, Honey, you're ready, you're so-o-o rea . . . dy." She would be so hot, she would die she was so hot. . . .

But now—this was monstrous, *seven times*!? This wasn't what she—

She screamed. "No!" She began to writhe and struggle below him like some demented animal.

"Shhh!" he spat in her ear, "they'll hear you—"

"*Get away from me!*"

"Will—you—be—quiet! You don't want anybody coming in here!" He had stopped moving on top of her.

"I want to go home." She began to cry. "I want to go home, I want to go home, I want to—"

"All . . . right!" he spat, and pushed himself off her and onto his feet. He stood scowling down at her, breathing heavily and buttoning his fly. "You are nuts, you know that, you are really crazy. Let's get out of here!" He turned abruptly and slammed out the door.

There was nothing to do but get up and follow him; she didn't know where they were.

The ride home was terrible. "I'm sorry," she mumbled as they sped along Peachtree Street. She was feeling foolish, and what was worse, childish.

"Jeez." His profile was angry. "You wanted to do it—"

"I know—"

"I paid for the room, too." She supposed that was the last straw.

"I'm really sorry."

"Forget it."

Dis . . . solve. Fade . . . in. . . .

Ho, I said to the older Broadway image, why are you thinking about the good old days?

I watched my efforts in the mirror, and despaired. My feet were heavy clumps of lead, the taps a dull thud instead of that nice clickity-clack Ann Miller sound. Listen, I said to me, maybe it's too late. Earlier, when I had stopped by Capezio's to pick up a pair of tap shoes, the place was overrun by young gypsies readying for some show. When this older person (me) came in, their eyes slid past her as if she didn't exist. You'll see, I silently told them, you're not going to be able to hold on to it either.

By noon I knew that if I was to get it together by Thursday, I needed professional help. The only person I could think of who might know a dance coach was my husband's girlfriend, Marcia. She had been a dancer around New York.

I called her. I knew the number, it was the same as Artie's. He had turned her into his secretary. Artie Shaw could talk people into things like that.

Marcia did know somebody. His name was Victor. I made arrangements to meet him at the rehearsal studio at three o'clock, which would give these quivering muscles time to rest for an afternoon session.

I went out to get some lunch.

CHAPTER 2...

"*You . . . ought to be in pic . . . tures. . . .*"

Hamburger Heaven had no empty stool and a long line waiting, so I ducked out and drank an Orange Julius at the corner stand instead.

The July heat rose from the pavement like a smack in the face. It didn't slow down the crowds scurrying by through the discarded cigarette butts, candy wrappers and dog droppings. I finished the drink and joined them. I had walked a block or so when I noticed ahead of me a trickle of water, steam rising from it, wending its way across the sidewalk into the gutter. Urine, as it turned out, its maker a dingy bundle lying in the doorway of the Winter Garden Theater.

I slowed my steps, wondering what I should do. I was not quite accustomed to these bodies lying about the streets. Somebody bumped me and hurried on, anxious to cross this miniscule river of Jordan. A priest. Nobody else stopped, either. A cop on the corner glanced over, glanced away, the picture of boredom.

I, too, stepped daintily across and went on my way. How quickly we learn indifference. I grew up trusting policemen, dentists and the government, nicely eating my peanut butter and jelly sandwiches, minding my manners and learning my bigot ways in our WASP ghetto. Were those the good old days?

A young couple, boy and girl, dashing around the corner, almost ran me down. With a giggle and a side-step they hurried on, late for something—an audition, I imagined. They wore the uniform: jeans and sandals, shoulder bags undoubtedly stuffed with dance shoes and leotards. It reminded me of my Thursday ordeal, and I grew chill in the afternoon heat.

As a kid, I had missed all that New York audition stuff. Hollywood was where I was headed, where they discovered you on street corners —where you didn't need to be heard across a room. . . . Once finished with high school I was on my way. I was through with fooling around, too; Bill had plowed his way in the second time, and what a disappointment it was. All pain and blood, and not an ounce of ecstasy as promised. I didn't intend to waste my time with that nonsense anymore. I would become a movie actress and go to UCLA in my spare time.

My mother and sisters saw me off on the train, my two cardboard suitcases holding two Maude-made dresses, a pink trimmed in blue, a brown trimmed in white, two pairs of pajamas, and clean underwear (in case of accident). Mother asked the conductor to take care of her little girl. He said he would. He got off in Chicago. So much for the kindness of strangers.

I picked Warner Brothers first, Bette Davis and James Cagney being my idols. The wall surrounding the place was formidable, and I walked the length and breadth of it, some dozen miles, before I saw a sign that made me catch my breath. At last, where the action was! I stepped inside. A large sign in bold red lettering greeted me. WE HAVE 2,894 MEN, 4,703 WOMEN, AND 6,938 CHILDREN MORE THAN WE NEED.

Not exactly a welcome mat. My eager heart plummeted. I turned to go. A voice said, "Can I help you?"

Behind a barred window, a young man was smiling at me. I smiled back. I knew about young men. "Well, I thought I could . . . ask for a job . . . ?"

"It's the wrong day," he said.

"Oh!" I was embarrassed not to know a wrong day. "Then I'll just—"

"Have you ever done anything?"

"I'm a dancer . . . I can, you know, dance. . . ."

"Oh yeah?" He seemed pleased with the information. "Listen, wait here just a second. Joe!" He called to somebody in back of him. "Here," he said to me, "step in here a second." He opened the door next to the barred window.

I was overcome. I was actually inside a studio, just—like—that. Who said it was hard to do? Nothing to it.

An older man sat behind a desk across the room. "Maybe you ought to take a look at this one," the younger one said.

The older one took a look.

No one had ever looked at me like that before. A buyer at the slave market? A wolf viewing a potential meal?

"Yeah," he murmured, "not bad. A hoofer, you say? Get her number, Busby's starting a picture next week." He turned back to what he was doing.

I floated away in a state of euphoria. In one day I had achieved the impossible. Entry. Nothing could stop me now! I was going to be . . . a . . . star!

> *Waiting on Broadway for the light to change, I was smiling at my naïvete—not even the young man had ever called—when someone next to me whispered in my ear. Startled, I looked around. "W-what?" I suppose that was a smile.*
>
> *"Isn't it very warm, I said."*
>
> *"Don't you know?" I snapped, and rushed away. Muggers, I knew, would ease up and stab you in broad daylight.*

Halfway down the block, I slowed down. You nut. That poor lonely, soul, reaching out for human contact. Probably the difference between going on or giving up. When you hear the news tonight how he leaped from the top of the Empire State, you'll know where to lay the blame.

I looked back up the street. Fortunately he wasn't in sight.

But suddenly Barton was. Barton never failed to come to mind along with any reminder of the delicate line we straddle between life and death.

Barton.

Barton Bainbridge.

Classy name? Every one of my husbands (and lovers) had classy names. Not necessarily the original one, but that didn't matter, having it when I came along is what counted. Never, ever, would I have become a Virshup or Goplug or Mertzel, and I shudder to think what kind of snobbishness that came from.

A roommate at the Hollywood Studio Club introduced me to Barton. It was a fine place, the old Studio Club—founded so that young girls with blown-up ambitions and meager allowances had a decent place to live while waiting for the big break. It was cheap—around ten dollars a week for room and board. It was respectable—no men allowed upstairs. It was also crowded: we shared bedroom, dining room and bath. We also shared boyfriends since none of us knew very many.

I thought Barton terribly distingué with his blond hair and blue eyes. And so mature. Twenty-seven is, when you're seventeen. Handsome, blue-eyed older men were my inclination. His deep, rich voice and English accent really got me. I have this thing for accents. He told me he had an ambassador father, that he had gone to school in India. He spoke of maharajas and palaces. Of New Zealand and Maoris. Of Australia and New Guinea. I was very impressed, I, with one train trip under my belt.

Barton introduced me to bars, and I loved them. Loved the low-key lighting, the noise, the happy people having so much fun. He introduced me to sloe gin fizzes, and told me they were just right for somebody who had never drunk alcohol. There had never been any in our house, another item on grandmother's list of sins. There was no way for me to know that Barton drank more than other people; I had no standards. A man who lived next door back in Atlanta used to drink. Every so often he would go on a wild rampage, beat up his wife and daughter who would come running to the safety of our house. I didn't connect any of this with classy Barton, sipping from elegantly tinkling glasses in quiet bars where nobody was beating up anybody. Where would I have learned that an eight-ounce tumbler full of straight whiskey was not necessarily what your average sophisticated world traveler drinks first thing in the morning?

I stayed overnight with him once in a while without much enthusiasm. Besides the discomfort of the overrated sex act, I didn't care for the worry afterward. "Look," I had told Barton, trying to get out of it, "I don't want to get pregnant."

"You can't—not by me, anyway," he told me, "I've had my tubes tied."

He had a small apartment up in the Hollywood Hills, pleasant enough. Once the push-push wham-bam stuff was over, the sleeping part was nice. I was still missing the body warmth of my mother, with whom I had slept until I left home.

There was just one thing I might have noticed had I been wiser. The man's nightly flirtation with death.

Barton left the gas heater burning brightly when we dozed off to sleep—with the windows closed.

CHAPTER 3...

"Pardon my southern . . . accent. . . ."

It was God himself, Cecil B. DeMille, maker of *The Ten Commandments, King of Kings, Sign of the Cross,* who finally signed me to a seven-year contract.

Ushered into the great man's presence at Paramount Pictures by one Jeanie MacPherson, a writer already well into middle age (rumored to have had a fling with DeMille back in the Ice Age), I was awestruck. Even back in Atlanta we knew who Cecil B. DeMille was. Besides his religious spectaculars, he was host on "The Lux Radio Theatre of the Air," a Monday night program chock full of stars doing play versions of hit movies, to which all America tuned in. (I myself later did a few—*Here Comes Mr. Jordan* with Cary Grant, *The Third*

Man with Joseph Cotten, *Whistle Stop* with Alan Ladd, among others.)

To my surprise he wasn't a giant, merely of medium height, a bald man in his fifties, quite grandfatherly, except for eyes like electric drills. "She photographs rather well," Miss MacPherson told him. "Show him your photographs, dear."

Quivering hands presented the three poses made with borrowed money. (Fifteen dollars.) Front. Profile. Smile.

Miss MacPherson spoke again. "Lovely legs, too. Show him, dear, pick up your skirt so he can see them."

I had had a few "almosts" before I got to DeMille's office. I was a pretty enough little thing; my breasts, unfortunately, were only average. America—and movie producers—preferred those blown-up jobs. A test at RKO in a bathing suit—smile, honey, and stick out your chest! A test at Universal—say cheese, sweetie, and stick out your chest! A test for the part Lana Turner got when they put her in a sweater without a bra and let them bounce to fame and fortune.

DeMille, it would appear, was a leg man.

He frowned at MacPherson's remark, however, and looked up from the photographs. I blushed. He smiled. I tried to. Should I, I wondered, do . . . what she said . . . ?

"How long have you been here?" DeMille inquired, watching me.

"A-a-about three months—"

"From where?"

"Atlanta, that's in Georgia—"

"That southern accent must be eliminated *at once!* "His voice was stern. "You don't want to play nothing but southern girls all your life, *do you?*"

"Oh!" I hadn't thought about that. "No no! Certainly not!"

He nodded at MacPherson. "She has possibilities."

She beamed. "I'm so glad you agree, C.B., *I* thought so the moment I—"

"Have your agent get in touch with me," DeMille said, waving a hand in my direction. "Glad to see you don't wear that vulgar red stuff on your nails."

Then God turned back to his desk. Subjects dismissed, exit, walking backwards. Slo-o-ow fade-out!

He wouldn't go broke signing me. Beginning with fifty a week it would take seven years to rise to a thousand, with annual options that allowed him to change his mind and drop me altogether. (My contract had to be court-approved, as I was under age.)

My boyfriend Barton's lack of enthusiasm was evident: "They sign people all the time and drop them the first option."

"Not Mr. DeMille!" I insisted. "He hasn't signed anybody for ten years, and I'm the only one now!"

"Ah. He probably wants your body."

I was shocked. "He . . . does . . . not! How can you say such a thing! He has never—my . . . goodness!"

Barton was wrong. DeMille never wanted my body. But no one warned me that someone else might.

My movie star education began on the Paramount lot in the fall of 1937. Tap dancing was out, considered by my mentor as vulgar as red nail polish. The southern accent was exorcised, and acting lessons begun. We contract players did scenes from plays in the small Paramount Theatre to learn our trade and give filmmakers an opportunity to take a look at us.

Which is how I met Anthony Quinn.

Tony was a tall one. His height, his startling black eyes and intense manner were impressive as hell. Aztec and Irish, he told me he was, plain Mexican wouldn't do for romantic Tony. And he was that. Quoted Shakespeare and poetry at the drop of a hat, sent me Gibran's *The Prophet,* and gave himself the code name of Mr. Christian so that he could call me any place, any time, and it could be our secret.

I was thrilled to know such a good actor. Here, at last, was where I belonged! Tony proposed marriage and said we would be an acting couple like Lynn Fontanne and Alfred Lunt. He was gentle and thoughtful and tender, and he gave it all an aura of sweet Jane Austen romance. But not so much so that he didn't want to consummate our beautiful relationship.

So I tried the thing again.

And was disappointed—again.

The earth stood perfectly still. There was simply too much of Tony (yes, there too). Legs and arms too long and miles of male body trying (and succeeding) to invade my limited space. He explained the beauty of this physical endeavor, though, and the necessity for it. How else could we reach nirvana? He said our bodies were beautiful, and that if we could only do our scenes naked as well, we would find total freedom of expression at last.

I might have tried it again had not DeMille called me into his office and told me in no uncertain terms to "stay away from that half-breed."

I backed away instantly. God had spoken. I could see my career ending before it began. (Nice retribution, I thought, when the half-breed married DeMille's daughter and gave him little quarter-breed grandchildren.)

Mister DeMille. A tyrant, a man of temper, a despot in his own world where so many people, wanting something (success) and willing to do almost anything to get it, trembled at his disapproval, had an orgasm when they were praised. He made splendid entrances, whether it be the Paramount commissary or the set, with his staff trailing at a respectful distance. One son-in-law's job was to follow him on the set with a high stool ready to slide under the royal ass should Mr. DeMille want to sit. And when he did, he never looked around, knowing it would be there. (It was.)

I was immune—I thought—to the Chief's displeasure. Was I not teacher's pet, grand-daddy's darling "baby," as they called me around the DeMille office, signed for my "perfect profile and ethereal, ladylike qualities," as the newspapers said? I had seen others get it. One day his cutter, a middle-aged, gray-haired woman, had brought him some film he had asked for. But she had erred and brought him the wrong piece. In a fit of rage, he yanked the entire reel out of its can and left it in a disorderly heap on the floor for her to pick up as best she could. The costume designer got it for her choice of dress for my screen debut. Didn't she know a light color didn't set off blonde hair and fair skin?

I got mine in front of two hundred extras, the crew, the cast, and a horde of visiting firemen.

DeMille was beginning a picture, *The Buccaneer,* the story of Jean Lafitte, the pirate, starring Fredric March. I was to have my first part, three lines in toto, but I got the star treatment just the same, as DeMille's new find. Three days were spent selecting the right gown and hairdo for the auspicious launching of this new speck of light in the galaxy.

In an approved Empire gown of pale green, a yellow taffeta petticoat rustling beneath, green beaded slippers on my feet, I arrived on the sound stage for the big day.

The set, a re-creation of the bayous around New Orleans, circa 1800, took up an entire stage. Real trees dripped with real Spanish moss; actual streams wended their way through flowering shrubs, while live pelicans, cranes, and assorted exotic feathered creatures splashed about on their surfaces. The two hundred costumed extras strolled about through it all.

DeMille, perched high above on a giant boom, gave his orders through a microphone whose projection filled every corner of the stage. My scene was with Fredric March himself, nervous-making enough. I also had to *walk* with him, through the trees, the streams and the people.

For a novice, doing a scene standing still is bad enough, but to have to *move,* to walk and talk and find a mark and stop in a certain light at the same time—was too horrendous.

I became addled. The bright lights, the hubbub of voices, the boom through the microphone, rattled me completely. I couldn't see, couldn't hear. Someone tugged at my dress, straightening a wrinkle, the makeup man powdered my nose. He handed me a lipstick. "Here," he said, "put some of this on." I grabbed the familiar tube like a drowning person for a life raft.

A mighty roar descended from on high. *"Forget the makeup and pay attention to the scene! You can look like an old hag as long as you can act!"*

Two hundred (plus) pairs of eyes were looking at me, and it wasn't paranoia. I was humiliated. I began to cry. The more I tried to stop, the worse it got.

Fredric March came to the rescue. He took my elbow and pulled me to one side. "Say your lines," he hissed, *"say your lines."* His fingers dug into my arm. Finally I was able to do what I had to.

Afterwards Mr. DeMille patted me on the shoulder and said it was fine. No apology. Fredric March, though, thought I needed further soothing. He invited me into his trailer dressing room parked just outside the stage. He was so handsome in his elegant, tight white trousers, black boots, and short red jacket. His hair was dark and curly. About forty then, March was in his prime. The Compleat Movie Star.

He told me to sit beside him, and asked where I was from, where I lived, told me I mustn't let DeMille get me down, the old boy could be a bastard sometimes.

And then, in the gentlest way, he took my hand and placed it over the bulge in the front of those tight white pants. My first movie star erection, in person.

I was taken so off-guard that I didn't snatch my hand away. It rested there, a lifeless object, belonging to somebody else.

There was a knock at the door. "Ready when you are, Mr. March," said the voice of the assistant director.

Mr. March picked up my hand and gave it back to me, polite as could be. "Please," he said in a courtly fashion, gesturing around his dressing room, "feel free to rest here." And he left for the set.

I got out, fast.

CHAPTER 4

"Just Molly and me . . .
and baby makes three. . . ."

Mother never pushed matrimony. She never said you'll grow up, meet a nice man, get married and live happily ever after. Neither did her replacement, Cecil B. DeMille. Mother—and the greatest movie producer of them all—surely knew best. So after Tony I took no further chance of Mr. DeMille's disapproval and steered clear of all males on the Paramount lot. No waiting in the corner for a prince to come. Stardom was my goal, and things were popping.

My mentor introduced me to a waiting world between acts on "The Lux Radio Theatre." I bought a special dress for the occasion with my first paycheck: a black crepe with a frilly organdy collar, and a black pancake hat to match. I washed my hair too, and set it in sweet little ringlets.

The sight of me sent DeMille into another one of his rages. *"Where . . . did you get . . . that outrageous garb?!"* he hissed. He ripped off the frilly collar with one yank, sent the hat sailing across the stage. "Get the hairdresser," he spat to the nearest assistant. "Get rid of those ridiculous curls."

On the air his voice dripped with honey. "My first protegé in ten years. Show them, Evelyn, how you must work to lose your southern accent." "Yes, Mr. DeMille. Pet-er-r-r-r Pip-er-r-r-r picked a peck of pickled pep-per-r-r-rs," I sobbed, humiliated once again. There seemed always to be someone around to watch my disgrace. This time it was Leslie Howard, the star for that week.

The path to glory is not without bumps.

Then came the premiere of *The Buccaneer* in New Orleans. Off I went on a plane (my first) in finery borrowed from Paramount's wardrobe department. A ball gown of Dorothy Lamour's. A sable jacket of Jean Arthur's. I didn't know how to call room service, or tip, so I never ate unless I was taken somewhere. Fortunately there were enough official gatherings. Oysters Rockefeller! (First.) Shrimp Jambalaya. (Ditto.) Autographs! (First.) Applause! (First, other than my family.) A gay joint in the French Quarter. (First but not last.)

On to a triumphant return to Atlanta. ATLANTA'S OWN, cried the headlines, my name up there on the marquee (first) right alongside Mr. March's.

These jaunts became a way of life, and in those pre-television days a way to build up name and face. To give me something to talk about and to plug, they stuck me in things. I stood around one day as Marie Antoinette in a tall white wig and pink feathered gown, not moving, not speaking, in *Artists and Models,* starring Jack Benny (never saw him); a Roumanian peasant girl in something starring Bing Crosby (never saw him); played "the girl" in *Sons of the Legion*—meaning the American one. I was made honorary colonel of that organization and for a few months there as the Legion's darling I combed the country. Back and forth I went, up and down, Seattle, Chicago, Salt Lake, a Tuesday-it-must-be-Cleveland kind of existence, whisked in and out always by police escorts with sirens blazing—getting to *expect* it, and irritated when it wasn't there—seeing nothing but airports, hotel rooms (soon learning how to order and tip), radio stations and photographers snapping pictures.

If it was trying for my secret boyfriend, Barton Bainbridge, he never said so. (We picked up again after I broke off with Tony Quinn.) He professed not to like motion picture people and never had anything to do with them. Mr. DeMille need never know about him. It was nice to have somebody between trips to have a bite with, see a movie. If he insisted on doing "that thing" once in a while, oh well, it was over quickly, and at least he was safe. I never had to worry about a troublesome pregnancy the way the other girls around the Studio Club did.

Or so I was convinced.

Before I had left California, I had been assigned a good role with actual scenes. A big break. I was to play a snotty rich girl in *Say It In French* starring Ray Milland. When I arrived in New York the company was there, shooting at the Waldorf-Astoria, where I was staying too. I had come a long way, Baby. The director, Andrew Stone, smallish man, big nose, close-together eyes, thought I might as well be in the shots since I was so handy. I couldn't have been happier about it.

For my good work he took me to dinner one night. Dinner in New York City with a man! Leon and Eddie's, and the fellow with the chain around his neck coming round, and Mr. Stone drinking almost a bottle of wine all by himself. Afterwards he said to come to his suite so we could go over the next day's scene.

Any female would know that ploy except a silly eighteen-year-old with half a southern accent. The man—oh really, it's too absurd—*chased* me around the room. A foolish scene, he with eyes red from drink, trying to grab me, and I dodging behind sofa and chair. Older by some twenty-five years, he tired before I did, and I managed to escape.

I was queasy on the plane on the way back to the Coast. I actually hadn't felt too hot the entire trip. But I attributed it to the then mad pace, the endless hours in the air: prop planes lurched and skittered about the skies a great deal.

The condition didn't improve on my return. Every morning I felt like throwing up, which is odd for somebody who never had a stomach ache in her life. My period skipped a month too, but I didn't put the two together. Barton, with his tied tubes, was perfectly safe, and my brief interlude with Tony had been a good six months before. But something was clearly amiss, and I knew I had better find out what.

Barton, worried, took me to his doctor, a friend of his, the one who had performed the vasectomy. He looked at me with a jaundiced eye. "If you are pregnant," he said nastily, "it can't be Barton."

"Well!" I flushed, "If I am it certainly can't be anybody else!" I disliked the man. I disliked his poking around inside me as I lay in that vulnerable position females have to assume for examination. From the corner of my eye I saw him pick up a monstrous instrument.

"If you *are* pregnant," I heard him say somewhere beyond my knees, "this will fix it."

Wha-a-ap! Pain like hot fire shot through me as the good doctor went to work. It felt as if he were ripping me apart. As if he had shoved an elephant into a space the size of a dime. And it grew and grew and I couldn't stand it and began to shriek—until he mercifully jabbed a needle into my arm, and a soft peace floated over me, and I slept.

Some time later, Barton took me home, both of us considerably shaken.

I rested over the weekend, and Monday morning started *Say It In French.*

And all at once I was living in a nightmare.

Andrew Stone wasn't going to let some upstart would-be actress turn him down. He was going to show her where the power lay.

In the middle of my first scene, he called, "Cut!" with great disgust. Eyes of ice cubes turned to me. *"I can't hear you! Speak up!"*

A tremolo began just beneath my skin as my bones turned to water. We started again, but I knew he was going to do it again, as sure as I was standing there. This time his eyes turned up to heaven. "Why?" he asked his deity. "It is beyond me, *why,* with all the talent in this studio, I am burdened with amateurs." His eyes dropped to me as if he had found a maggot in his soup. "We will just have to stop shooting," he sighed, "until you learn to speak up."

For one entire hour, while the cast and crew waited, and the production remained at a standstill, the dialogue coach stood on one side of the stage reading all the other actors' lines, and I stood on the other, shouting out my lines to him.

I shivered with shame, and what little of acting I knew went out of my head, which gave Mr. Stone further reason to vent his spleen.

The agony was repeated daily in one form or another. I was afraid to tell Mr. DeMille, afraid for him to know a director didn't like me, afraid he might think he had erred in signing me. And, too, perhaps anger was a director's prerogative. Didn't DeMille have his fair share of explosions?

I went home, sick with nervousness. I couldn't eat, I couldn't sleep, I had lost ten pounds in three days. I began to loathe the Studio Club for the very things I had adored before, the late night chitchat, the buzz of friendly voices. Barton suggested I move in with him; he had taken a house in North Hollywood, a sweet little place with a garden.

The pains started on the set. At intervals. I couldn't imagine what it was.

One night, at Barton's house, when the pain had become sheer agony, the dam burst. Two (or more) months of accumulation in my womb spewed all over the bed, the floor, the room. When I tried to make it to the bathroom, I left a crimson trail behind me, my insides flowing out in a river of blood.

I collapsed.

My pulse, Barton told me later, disappeared. He picked me up, lay me on the back seat of his car, and drove like a demon to the nearest hospital. A quick transfusion saved my life.

Mr. DeMille never knew. Barton had the good sense to use his own name to register me. I told DeMille it was appendicitis. He bought it. But I was very sick in those pre-penicillin days and couldn't return to work. I was replaced in the picture and lost my first decent part. But —the one bright spot—I was rid of Andrew Stone.

I read about myself while I was recovering. "DeMille directs his protegé's every move: what she wears, how she does her hair, where she can go, what she can do. . . ."

CHAPTER 5

"I'm a dreamer . . . Aren't we all . . . ?"

During my convalescence, Barton went off to an office he had in Florida, leaving me for company a little collie puppy and a Siamese cat —who promptly popped out seven kittens. Nine frisky animals and the radio helped keep my spirits from sagging too far. I listened to the "Lucky Strike Hit Parade": "A-Tisket, A-Tasket," "One O'Clock Jump," "Flat Foot Floogie." I heard a Roosevelt Fireside Chat: "We will never go to war." Orson Welles' famous broadcast, *War of the Worlds*, that caused many people to panic. I heard H. V. Kaltenborn tell us/me that Chamberlain was going over to talk to Hitler about the Czechoslovakia situation. "Hitler is a man of moods," Mr. Kaltenborn said, "I've noticed that each time I've had personal contact with him. . . ."

He would have to get in line in Hollywood, I thought. The industry's concern was whether he would foul up the lucrative foreign market. My concern was *Gone with the Wind.*

GWTW bulletins far outnumbered those from Europe. Production would start soon, and who would play Scarlett O'Hara and Rhett Butler was the concern of the entire country. Every actress and actor in Hollywood (and the rest of the world) had been out to Selznick International in the last year to see about a part, except me, who was *from* Atlanta.

I was depressed. Nobody wanted me. I was through. This physical catastrophe had done me in. DeMille was starting another picture, *Union Pacific,* with Barbara Stanwyck and Robert Preston, and there was nothing in it for me. Mr. DeMille was losing interest; I knew it.

I clung to Barton, calling him in Palm Beach almost daily. "Oh, Barton, please, *please* come back!" I would cry.

"Now now," the deep voice purred, "you know I can't do that."

"But I miss you terribly!"

"Darling," he murmured, "I love you very much, you know that."

"Well, you're the only one who does," I pouted.

Then one day I received a call from my agent and Barton was tucked away in the back of my mind once more.

The *Gone with the Wind* makers had finally gotten around to me.

David O. Selznick's office was a cheery place, with overstuffed chairs and sofas, drapes in chic chintz, sun streaming through a large bay window behind his desk. My life had evolved into entering men's offices to sell my feminine wares. In other situations it's called something other than "actress."

I was very jittery. I had read the book and had had this wild dream —knowing it couldn't possibly come true—that I would star in this grand movie-to-be-made about my home town.

Dozens of stars had been tested and retested. Talent scouts, including director George Cukor, had scoured the South for the right girl to play Scarlett O'Hara. Drama students, debutantes and Junior League types had been sifted through and discarded. Streams of girls in bustles and hoopskirts arrived daily at the Selznick portals pleading to be tested. Every studio in town, including Paramount, had sent over their roster of stock players, neglecting this Atlanta girl who was under personal contract to Cecil B. DeMille.

On that first day of November 1938, when finally it was my turn to be seen, the role of Scarlett still hadn't been cast. I wasn't much older than the sixteen-year-old Scarlett who begins the story. I knew I couldn't play her in later years, after three husbands and three babies. And my eyes were hazel, not green.

But still . . . one's imagination runs wild. . . . What if . . . what if . . . I thought as I entered the door.

Selznick was a tall man, with black curly hair (that turned white later), shaggy in appearance, his tie awry, cigarette ash on his sleeve. He wore thick-lensed spectacles. George Cukor was in the office too, shorter, more stocky. He also wore spectacles. As they rose and turned toward me, the sun caught all four lenses so that both men looked at me with flashing lights instead of eyes. It was disconcerting to a nervous wreck.

"How do you do?" "How do you do?" "From Atlanta? No accent? Can you get it back?" "Oh goodnes' gra-shus, shu-ah ah ca-yun."

"Thank you for coming." (That means, get the hell out, we've seen all we want of you.)

I left without ever seeing their eyes. Hope plummeted. The moment I had dreamed of, come and gone. "Oh, Barton," I cried on the phone that night. "Nobody wants me! Nobody wants me!"

"I want you," Barton said, "Come to Florida."

DeMille stuck me in *Union Pacific,* in the briefest of roles. "Help! Help!" I cried. "Indians are attacking the railroad!" (And who could blame them.) Paramount stuck me in *Sudden Money,* a dumb picture with Charles Ruggles and Broderick Crawford.

It was an anticlimax when the Selznick people called. They were interested in me for Scarlett's sister, Suellen. I didn't believe them for one minute, they fooled around with everybody.

I rehearsed a scene with George Cukor, and told myself the privilege of working with a master was enough. David Selznick chased me once around his office, in a rather obligatory fashion, as if his heart wasn't in it. (Perhaps the new drug, benzedrine, that he was swallowing like popcorn had urged him on.) I met Alfred Hitchcock there too, freshly arrived in America to film *Rebecca.* (Laurence Olivier too, who had arrived with a companion destined to make history herself.) Hitchcock said to me, in that slow English voice, "I have one pa-ht left to cah-st, the vil . . . lage i . . . di . . . ot. Wou . . . ld you li . . . ke to play it?" Ha Ha.

The suspense was unnerving. Leslie Howard had been set for Ashley Wilkes. Olivia de Havilland was given the role of Melanie. Mr. DeMille said if I didn't get Suellen he would shoot me at sunrise, or something worse, whatever that could be.

On January 2, 1939, I was told the role was mine—depending on who played Scarlett. A salmon going upstream against the rapids.

Later that month, Vivien Leigh, a stranger to Hollywood, was signed. Which was fine—the local would-be Scarletts could still face each other at parties, rejects together. And I was in.

I was happy, Atlanta was happy—one of "their own" was to be a part of the proceedings (my blonde hair darkened to brown to be nearer to Vivien's color). Ann Rutherford joined us as the third sister. There were costume fittings, learning to walk in hoops, hair styles chosen, rehearsals upon rehearsals and more tests made. Endless, endless—Selznick was a nut for detail.

For a good six months I would be traipsing to some GWTW set, going to balls, picking cotton, sobbing when Scarlett took my fiancé for herself, working with all three directors who made the film, first with George Cukor, replaced by Victor Fleming, and when Fleming suffered a nervous breakdown, with Sam Wood, who took over.

But for all the troubles, everyone was so pleased to be in this most publicized flick of all time that the atmosphere around the set was almost partylike, especially since our dialogue was constantly being handed to us at the last minute, as if our host, Selznick, was thinking up some charade for us to play. One time the fun started as early as 2:30 in the morning, when we had to be made up and driven out to location at Lasky Mesa in San Fernando Valley in time to catch the sunrise for Scarlett's scene at the end of Part One. She had just returned to Tara to find utter devastation. "As God is my witness," she vowed, "I'll never go hungry again. . . ."

Later she whacked me, Suellen, because I complained. And she didn't pull her punches. My cheek wore the imprint of Vivien's fingers for the rest of the afternoon.

To say that I knew *Gone with the Wind* would become the lasting classic it has would be a lie. It was certainly a super-production. But I wasn't impressed by Selznick's attention to each stitch, design, color, shoe buckle, down to using thorns for fastening clothing during the Civil War period (when buttons would have disappeared) and importing Georgia red dust to stain our shoes and skirts. DeMille, too, was a stickler for detail.

I never thought one way or the other about black actors sitting among us, that Hattie McDaniel even had a chair of her own, that they were earning more than I (easy to do). They were playing slaves, which made it all right, kept them in their place. (It never occurred to me that there was anything unnatural in there not being a single black face at the big premiere held later in Atlanta.)

Barton's return trips usually caught me working. My blinders firmly in place, our subject matters were constantly at variance. "It looks as if there's going to be a war," he said in March. I shook my head impatiently. I was far too wrapped up in Selznick's Civil War to pay much heed to Hitler's invasion of Czechoslovakia. I said crossly, "Just when I might get enough money to take a trip to Europe, he's going to spoil it. Hey, guess what, they may use one of my kittens for Bonnie Blue to play with in the picture, oh, and you know what a cruel thing they did to that poor child yesterday? They wanted her to cry for a sound track, so her mother told her she had to take some medicine, and after she cried they gave her some ice cream instead! What a terrible business!" I giggled.

"And you can bet," Barton said, "that her mother is collecting the money they pay the kid."

"Oh. I hadn't thought of that. I sure wish I could have helped my mother out like that, she always has had to work so hard to make ends meet. All I did was . . ." I remembered something.

"What are you thinking?"

"Boy. You know what happened to me when I was about that child's age? Sometimes I got lonesome being by myself so much and then I would trail along after my big brother and his friends, see, and this day they went down in the basement, a real scary place, with an earthen floor, very dark and rat-infested, you could hear them rustling in the corners. Well, when the boys darted behind a pile of crates, and I was trying to scramble after, an arm reached out to stop me. 'Hey!' One of the boys had stayed behind. 'Where you goin'?' He was about fifteen years old and tall for his age. He picked me up so suddenly it scared the breath out of me. I couldn't make a sound. The space was narrow, and his one step forward pressed my back against the scrapy wall. I hung there in midair, my five-year-old legs dangling loosely in space." I shook my head, remembering.

"Is that it?"

"Oh no! He—you know I didn't understand what he was doing—he fumbled with his pants, and out shot this . . . *thing* shaped like a . . . like a cucumber from Mother's garden. Well, he shoved it against me so hard my head snapped back against the wall, and boy, that jarred my breath back into place and I began to howl bloody murder!" I laughed. "My brother came flying back to see why I was crying, and so did my mother, and of course the boy ran—and fast! I never did see *him* around there again!"

"Well, well," Barton said, "that explains a great deal about you."

"Oh? What?"

"You're not very fond of . . . doing it, are you?"

"Oh pooh. How you talk!"

But he was right.

CHAPTER 6...

*". . . Tomatoes, to-mah-toes, potatos,
po-tah-toes . . . let's call the whole thing off. . . ."*

I had to be the world's lousiest lay. But then, so was Barton. Perhaps he knew it. Perhaps that's why he stayed around and put up with my indifference. With my preoccupation with myself and my career. I didn't even know his business was going badly. If he told me, I didn't hear. What did I know about business, or care? What were his little Mickey Mouse affairs next to mine!

On Easter Sunday, wearing a blonde wig to cover my dyed-brown locks—DeMille preferred me blonde—I was at Paramount all day being photographed with twelve other players who the powers-that-be decided would be the "stars of tomorrow." We were called "The Golden Circle," and a larger number of us actually made it than most of those yearly lists. There were William Holden, Susan Hayward, Robert Preston, Betty Field, Patricia Morrison, Ellen Drew, and, uh, the wigged one, who thought she had arrived.

I then left Barton *and* the GWTW set behind, after finishing what I believed was my last scene in that picture to join DeMille in Omaha, Nebraska, for the premiere of *Union Pacific*.

Mr. DeMille and his party had gone on ahead by train (Union Pacific, I assume), and I had to fly to make it. The flight took from midnight to 11:30 the following morning—with a mad dash from the airport, with police escort, to meet the train as it pulled into the station.

That 200,000 strong were waiting in period costume to see this Hollywood bevy, that the streets were jammed as we rode through in carriages, that confetti filled the sky and people hung from every window, that bands played at each corner and voices screamed and cheered as we passed, we took in our stride, as our due. Was not this same excitement always engendered when the gods and goddesses of make-believe descended to the hinterlands? That they may have cheered Barbara Stanwyck and Robert Preston a little louder than they cheered me made no difference whatsoever. I was also one of God's chosen.

In the midst of the festivities—at a dinner for ten thousand, with ten thousand more paying for the privilege of watching us eat—I received a wire from Selznick: RETURN AT ONCE FOR ADDED SCENE. A race to the airport followed, sirens screaming, crowds gathering to wave farewell. Back to the Civil War and the company of Vivien and Clark and Leslie and Olivia. A steady whirlwind of attention, applause, and love (of sorts).

Imagine my shock when my option was dropped the following month.

I couldn't believe it. Baby's rug was yanked from under her. Granddaddy's darling was pushed out into the cold from whence she came.

I went to say good-bye to Mr. DeMille. On this, the last day I would ever see him, his eyes were most gentle. "I still have faith in you," he said, "but I am unable to give you your raise just now, since your illness was such a serious setback—" (He didn't seem to count GWTW, which was at another studio) "—nor do I have anything for you in my next picture, *Northwest Mounted Police.*"

I nodded vigorously, close to tears. "Oh, I do understand, Mr. DeMille, and . . . and I'm going out there into Hollywood, and prove you are right to have faith in me!"

He smiled. "I believe you will."

"But Mr. DeMille," I said earnestly, "achieving success without you—it won't have the same meaning—" I started to cry.

"My dear—" he patted my hand, "of course it will, and I shall be very proud of you—"

"You said—" a lip trembled, "—when you introduced me on the air, that you had made three mistakes in selecting people. That I could be your fourth. Well!" I cried passionately, "I am going to prove to you that I am not your fourth mistake!"

The gentle eyes softened even more. "With such a positive attitude, I'm sure you will," the great man told me.

It was a grand scene. We both did it well.

He shook my hand, and wished me luck.

Outside, the sun shone as if it were a normal day.

My salary ended August 31. Hitler invaded Poland the next day, German submarines began to steadily sink British merchant ships, and by September 3, Britain, France, Australia and New Zealand declared war on Germany.

War. Just as Barton and everybody else had predicted. Newspapers, radio, newsreels in theaters were all full of it. Even I could hardly fail to notice. Would we get sucked into it? How was it going to affect the motion picture industry? But most of all, how was it going to affect *me,* adrift once more, with no money, not an anchor to my name. Except Barton.

I had two more runs at pushing through reluctant doors, both for Hal Roach. I was tested for the girl in *Of Mice and Men.* Roach had me work with a coach, to see if I could learn to act tough enough. Betty Field, my fellow Golden Circler, got it. I was tested for *1,000,000 B.C.* D. W. Griffith, himself, directing, on a comeback bid. Thought I had that one too. Griffith was my champion—all that ethereal lady stuff was down his alley. Hal Roach, though, thought I looked too frail to toss a few dinosaurs around, and would I work out in a gym for awhile. I lost that one to Carole Landis, who had three more inches in height and a bigger bosom. (I have often wondered what would have happened to me if I had needed a size 38 bra instead of my modest 34.)

I got one job. Two days' work in a Walter Wanger–Broderick Crawford mystery. I earned one hundred and fifty dollars. Hardly enough to soothe a worried, single female. The future was bleak.

Barton couldn't have come to town at a better time. I was delighted to see him. We drove to the beach for a reunion celebration. He made me laugh so when he was happy and told jokes. "There were these two queers—" (he had explained) "—and one of them said to the other —(Barton's voice went into falsetto). . . ."

Barton didn't think much of "queers," labor unions, income tax, Jews, radicals and dark-skinned people. Like everybody else I had ever known. Only I was beginning to be puzzled. David O. Selznick was a Jew and so was George Cukor, and they were just swell. And it was rumored Hattie McDaniel, a person about as dark as you can get, would win an Academy Award.

As spirited as the evening was, it took a nose dive during the drive home. We turned on the car radio. War, war, nothing but war. Germany and Russia were dividing up Poland without asking the Poles.

"Oh Barton," I said, "do you really think the United States will have to go to war?"

"It looks more that way every day," he answered soberly.

"Well then," I said, "maybe you'd better marry your wife again. I won't mind, honest I won't, because with her and your three children as dependents, surely you won't be drafted."

His head whipped around, and he gave me a peculiar stare. "You are incredible," he muttered, "you are . . . really incredible." He stepped heavily on the gas. The car jerked forward and began to pick up speed.

I was startled. What a funny way to take my offer of self-sacrifice. "Wha—what's the matter!"

"Nothing is going to interfere with that goddamned career of yours, is it, that precious—"

"Barton! Please slow down!" He was driving like a maniac.

"—career comes first, and nothing is ever going to get in its way—"

"*Please!*"

"Even if I go back to my wife, you wouldn't care one whit—"

"Of course I would care!" I cried, "I would care terribly. Slow down!"

"It doesn't even occur to you that you and I could marry, does it? *Does it?*"

"Oh." I was taken aback. "Oh sure. We could do that." I suppose it actually was my responsibility to save him. The father of my almost child.

That was it. We set out immediately for Yuma, Arizona, where a marriage ceremony could be performed in an instant. Took a wrong turn, lost civilization entirely and ran out of gas in the middle of the desert around three o'clock in the morning.

While Barton went off to search for fuel, I waited in the freezing cold, the stars chunks of ice above me, coyotes howling mournfully. If I could have thought of a way out of the mission we were on, I would have done so.

But no. He returned with a can of gas. We found a Justice of the Peace. You take her, you take him, I-pronounce-you-man-and-wife.

One down. A few to go.

I immediately felt trapped, fettered. "Don't tell anybody," I said to Barton, "this marriage must be a secret until I make it big." I got fitted for a diaphragm even though Barton had had another vasectomy. I was deathly afraid of getting pregnant again. "Do we have to, tonight?" was my constant protest when he reached out for me. When he was drinking he wasn't interested in sex, so I encouraged him to drink.

How happy I was to be called back for yet another added scene in *Gone with the Wind*. ("Scarlett's had three husbands, and I'm going . . . to . . . be . . . an old maid!") It was early November, and the premiere was set for December 15. And of course I would leave my new husband and go off to that one.

It was the premiere to end all premieres.

All of Atlanta was taken over. On the big day an extra million people swarmed into a town of 300,000. The Atlanta *Constitution* ("Covers Dixie Like the Dew") devoted the entire day's edition to *Gone with the Wind*. Confederate flags flew everywhere. Store windows were filled with GWTW displays in Confederate colors. Scarlett and Rhett dolls and candies were on sale. The theater front was made over to look like Tara. We were paraded through the city in open cars, one for each of us, from the airport to the Georgian Terrace Hotel in the center of Atlanta, Clark Gable (the pièce de résistance) the last in line—having arrived in a separate plane with *Gone with the Wind* emblazoned across its side. Women screamed and fainted at the sight of him. The streets, from the suburbs all along the length of Peachtree Street, were packed solid with humanity, many of them in their ancestors' Civil War uniforms or hoopskirts and pantaloons. The Georgia National Guardsmen and State Police were out in full force to keep a little order. Bands played "Dixie" every few yards, rebel yells filled the air, confetti floated from rooftops and windows like snow. And there were some survivors of the native holocaust itself, ancient men in their late nineties, in wheelchairs and faded gray uniforms, willing to give out faint "YAAA-YEEES!" if called upon. I was to feel in later years, as they dragged those of us still living back to Atlanta from time to time for yet other "premieres," that we survivors of GWTW had taken the venerable old warriors' places.

Back in North Hollywood the tiny house on Aqua Vista looked pitifully trashy next to the sumptuous hotel suites I had grown accustomed to, the cans opened for dinner seemed *dreck* after caviar and steak Bearnaise. With time on my hands and no weekly stipend of my own coming in, it was becoming evident just how poorly Barton was doing. Money was doled out for groceries, a dollar here, two there, and none for clothes. The liquor bill, however, was higher than the rent.

"Do you have to drink so much, Barton?" I crossly asked him. "That stuff is very expensive, you know."

"Such a sourpuss," he answered. "It might loosen you up to have a belt or two. Have a drink."

"No! It gives me a terrible headache afterwards."

"The hair of the dog—best thing in the world."

His out-of-proportion gaiety had begun to annoy me; it was empty and false. Propped up by booze, he went off somewhere in his head to an unreachable place. My resentment was festering. My big break had come along, and I blew it. Barton blew it. Misled me with his talk of tied tubes.

The winter of my discontent. I began to stay away from home as much as possible. Visited the girls at the studio Club. I had made friends with Sam Wood's daughter, K. T. Stevens, who had a house at the beach, a fine place to go. Movies. Anything. Any excuse.

In January Howard Hughes decided to test some young hopefuls, including me. For no apparent reason. He directed mine himself, a scene from *Our Town*. Nothing came of it, I suspected, for the same apparent reason. Hughes, I had been told, preferred *extra* large sizes.

His turn-down, coupled with Hitler's spring invasion of Norway and Denmark, brought me low indeed. I took what the Germans were doing as a personal affront. My whole generation was doomed, I was sure, and me along with it.

Four dreary months of not-so-quiet desperation passed before my agent got an appointment with Maxwell Arnow, casting director for Columbia Pictures. It was Arnow who had combed the South a year before looking for a Scarlett O'Hara among the daughters of Dixie.

A chapter of my life was coming to an end.

I was familiar with the wolf look by then, shivering only slightly. Arnow made the usual scan from top to bottom. "Uh huh," he said, "we're starting a picture might use you in. Let's go see what the director thinks."

The office was a cubbyhole, the desk taking up most of it. A good-looking older man sat behind it. He had a thick head of hair, gray at the temples; blue eyes looked at me over a blue bow tie. No smile. Nobody ever smiled at you when you wanted something from them. "I had her in mind for Aherne's daughter," Arnow said.

The man did the scanning business. "He veel do fine," he said.

"Did he mean me?" I whispered as we left. "What kind of accent is that?"

"Hungarian," said Arnow.

"Fancy that," I said.

"You've got to meet the head of the studio now, Harry Cohn."

So there I was in a plush office, the big desk at the rear, the all-powerful man behind it. Thick rugs, leather chairs, sofas and coffee tables made up the rest.

Harry Cohn was around five feet nine, give or take a little, the beginnings of a pouch, thinning hair, watchful eyes (unsmiling). He looked at this latest piece of flesh from the corners of them.

I was cool. (Almost). I was learning. Hope is a thing to avoid like a deadly poison. He won't want you, either, I said to myself, not believing it. Anxiety seized me. Cohn added to it. "Two years with De-Mille, eh? Why'd he drop you?"

"Aaah, uh—he . . . I—"

"You got a crooked tooth in front."

"I w-w-wear a f-facing when I—"

"This your idea?" Cohn said to Arnow, tilting his head in my direction.

"I took her to Vidor's office," Arnow answered. "He gave the nod."

"That dumb Hungarian," Harry Cohn replied. "What does he know?"

A seven-year contract was decided on, starting at $150 a week. The yearly options meant I could count on a salary for at least that length of time. My utter relief was overwhelming. Like searching for an oasis, and finding it.

Barton took my news with yawning indifference. "Ah. It'll wind up like the other."

"You're no fun, why do you put everything down? It's not like the other, I start right away in a picture, I'm Brian Aherne's daughter, and somebody named Rita Hayworth and Glenn Ford are in it, and a Hungarian named Charles Vidor is directing, and they say he's very good."

The eve of my first working day—when I had to get up at six—Barton brought home drinking friends. Retiring at nine, trying to sleep, I could hear their chatter and drunken guffaws through the thin walls. I lay there staring into the dark, stewing. I couldn't blow this opportunity. How many more could I get? Barton himself stumbled to bed, sodden, around three. Bleary-eyed after a few hours' sleep, I determined to do something about it. He brought home a couple the next night. Angrily, I took him into the bedroom. "Barton," I whispered, "you can't do this to me!"

"Don't like my friends, eh, you never did like—"

"It's not that!" I was furious. "It's—Barton, we can't go on this way, you don't care about what I'm doing. I think I should move to the club while—"

"You've just been waiting, haven't you, waiting for an opportunity to get out—"

"That's not so—"

He stormed out of the room. I heard him say, "C'mon, kids, we're not welcome here."

"Barton, maybe we had better—"

"No no. None of that. Come along, come along, there's a place on Ventura. . . ."

The quiet was heaven. Exhausted, I dozed off thinking what a wonderful day it had been. Vidor was making my part into something that wasn't in the script. I never walked, but hopped skipped and jumped in every scene. I was happy. He was so attractive too, a darling accent, and a twinkle. . . .

I was awakened by the cold steel of a revolver jammed against my head.

Barton was sitting on the edge of the bed, pressing a gun sharply into my temple. "You think," he whispered in the dark, "you think you are going somewhere without me, but you're not."

"No, I didn't. I only thought that—"

"You are not going to think anymore. Ever."

"Barton—"

"*Ever.*"

I shut up then. He had been drinking heavily, I could smell it. When he was drunk and got some idea in his head, nobody could talk him out of it. So now he was playing this silly gun game, straight out of a "B" movie. If I were silent, maybe he would lose interest and I could get back to sleep. I didn't believe for one minute that he meant to shoot me. Nobody ever shot anybody that I knew.

Barton sat there for close to a half-hour, the gun never wavering, while I secretly vowed I was going to get out of there the next day. He began to weep. "I can't," he blubbered, "I can't do it, I can't do it, I can't!" The gun dropped down on the bed. He too soon dropped down alongside me and fell into a deep sleep.

The next morning, while he still slept, I packed my few things and checked back into the Studio Club.

CHAPTER 7...

> *"I fell in love with you . . . first time I looked into . . . them—there—eyes. . . ."*

Charles Vidor was the answer to my every girlish prayer: physically attractive and with a most bewitching foreign accent, hinting of drama, intrigue, and Orient Express. He smelled heavenly too. Bathing himself generously with cologne, he left a spicy trail of Woodhue everywhere he went.

Director is God's perfect occupation. On a movie set, his is the Word, make no mistake. Whereas DeMille leaned toward the wrathful, no-other-gods-before-me style, Charles was more subtle, more compassionate. But in charge, nevertheless. He was making a gem out of a tiny role, and I, the eternal Daddy-seeker, was eager to worship at his altar.

My heart ached for him too. He was the only person I knew with relatives and friends in the path of Hitler's army. We gathered around the radio on the set for daily bulletins as Belgium succumbed, Mussolini declared war, the Germans entered Paris.

Barton and his downbeat despondency were out of place on all counts. The straw was the Sunday that a friend of his called me to say that Barton was threatening to kill himself, that I had better come fast.

I was disgusted. What a play for sympathy. Nobody goes around killing himself, for Pete's sake! Only the week before, we had had dinner at his insistence. He wanted to try again. "Barton, there isn't anything to say," I had told him. "You want one thing, I want another. It's best we stay apart, for a while anyway."

He had slammed off in his car, shouting out the window, his voice harsh, "All right! *I'll show you!*" Tires screeched as he drove off, going through a red light. I had lain awake for hours, trembling at the sound of every siren, sure he had had a terrible accident.

And now this. I didn't want any part of it. But I went out to Aqua Vista anyway. I wanted to be friends. I didn't want him feeling badly.

But when I got there he was lying on the couch, listless, staring up at me with dead eyes. Some couple I had met once or twice were there too, watching with mournful eyes. All of them irritated me. But especially Barton. "For heaven's sake, Barton," I snapped crossly, "this is too silly. Get up. Sit up, at least."

He didn't answer.

I took a deep breath and blew it out angrily. "You ought to be ashamed to act like this. Why don't you act like a *man*," I said righteously, "so that I can respect you? Then maybe I'll come back. But not like this I won't." And I walked out. (I had seen enough movies to know how to behave.)

The woman came flying after me. "You can't leave," she whispered hoarsely, "he'll do it for sure! I grabbed the gun away from him once already!"

"You're crazier than he is," I answered, and got into my car.

I moved from the Club to an apartment in the Hills, underneath the Hollywoodland sign. I didn't leave a forwarding address. These shenanigans of Barton's must not interfere with the new shape my life was taking. I wasn't asking anything of him, not even a divorce; he could still use me to avoid being drafted, but he must leave me alone now. Because something was happening between Charles Vidor and me. The undertones, the vibrations spoke entire libraries. He told me he had stepped to the door of his office the day I came in, to watch my legs as I walked away. "They had spirit," he said, more important to a Hungarian than shape.

I was smitten. The sight of him excited me. The tantalizing fragrance issuing from him had a direct line to my pulse. The fact that it was all wrapped up in my career, that under his guidance my work was actually *good,* was mind-blowing. When he whispered huskily one day, "I must see you outside the studio," I breathed, "Yes," without thinking twice.

I didn't know what to expect. Hope was slim that a man past forty might be through with sex. The way he hinted that Hungarians knew more about women—whatever that meant—told me differently. Who knows, I thought, perhaps this bliss business would finally come my way. Perhaps the fragrance alone would see me through. "You are virginal," he said to me. "Ah, well, no-o-o, not exactly, I'm married, you know—"

"That makes no difference. You are not awakened, I can tell. . . ."

It was titillating. Flirtation always was. And who can tell where make-believe leaves off and reality begins when fantasy is your business.

The restaurant was in Glendale, tucked away discreetly where Charles was unlikely to run into anybody he knew. Nobody in Hollywood *ever* went to Glendale. Muzak wafted over the dimly lighted Scotch decor of plaid tablecloths and curtains. As we took a booth a waitress stepped briskly up clad in kilt and tam o'shanter, pad and pencil at the ready.

"Two martinis, please," Charles told her, "very cold. With vodka."

Her eyes slid over to me. Her pencil jabbed the air. "She don't look old enough to me."

"Then bring me a double," Charles said quickly. "That will fix it."

When the waitress had left he smiled at me and reached for my hand. "You do look like a baby," he murmured. His fingers slipped under my sleeve and up my arm. "Your skin is the smoothest I ever touched."

Tingling inside, I tried not to shiver nor smile. I lost on both counts.

The drink came in a big snifter. Charles slid it toward me. "Drink," he said. The innocent-looking liquid almost blasted my head off. I recoiled, coughing.

"It gets better, take another sip. Drink, drink," Charles urged. He lifted the glass and handed it to me.

He was right. The restaurant took on a lovely haze and receded to a faintly tinkling backdrop for the two of us. There was nobody else in the world. He ordered steaks. We nibbled at them. "Drink," he said, handing me the big glass. He ordered another.

His hand touched my knee, slid down between the two of them to rest there. My body shuddered to life. As if I, a puppet, had been plugged in and the current had swept through arms and legs to fill sawdust and straw with the flush of animation. It was almost too much to bear.

In the car his mouth brushed mine; he touched my cheek. On the way home he talked of other things: of the picture, of the night.

We sat together on the couch. He kissed me and I responded. He touched me lightly, my thigh, ear, brushed my hair back, his hand never lingering but moving on so quickly I was not afraid.

I hardly realized he was unbuttoning my shirt. "No," I said.

"Yes," he whispered, "I must see. . . ."

"Oh please. . . ." I was excited. "I . . . you . . . you. . . ." I knew I should stop him. I didn't seem to be able to. . . .

I don't know how it happened. He was suddenly on his knees before me, his mouth on the inside of my knee. It was climbing. . . .

The sensation struck with shuddering impact. It swept through my body in fiery spasms. I was blinded, out of control. Buzzing rockets burst in brilliant explosion and shot me out into space with them.

When I came back, I hardly understood what had happened to me.

Charles' blue eyes were tender. He looked pleased. "Twenty-three!" he exclaimed. "I counted."

I stared at him. "*Counted*! C-c-counted—what?"

"Times for you. I am sure that is a record." Was that pride I detected in his voice? "Was it good?" he whispered huskily.

"Oh Charles," I breathed, stunned to incredulity, "I never knew it could be like this."

"Of course not," answered he, "you have never known a Hungarian before. . . ."

For the four years until Charles and I went our separate ways, I believed that particular act of lovemaking belonged exclusively to Hungarians. I believed everything Charles told me. Any man who could make me feel like that, I never wanted to lose. All other idols faded. I was hooked.

But then, so was he.

He never intended me to be more than one more little fling. Charles, I was to learn later, saw his role in life as a ladies' man. Though he liked being married (four in all, I was the third), he got his best kicks by having sly little affairs behind his current wife's back.

He didn't reckon on unleashing a conflagration lying dormant in this little caper. Imagine his surprise and delight. Here's this fresh young thing, a pushover, so tender, so young, buttocks smooth as marble, who responds to his great lover doings, his bag of Hungarian tricks, like the violin to Heifetz's fingers, and proves to him beyond a shadow of a doubt that he is indeed the world's greatest lover!

He's not going to leave the cause of that discovery to lie about for some other man to grab off, right? First he insured my unavailability by warning me that certain men in the studio made passes at all new girls. He told me how they would go about it, what they would say. When each one did and said exactly as Charles cautioned, I was impressed with his magical insight. I didn't know then that they discussed these matters among themselves in Harry Cohn's private dining room. Which dame looked like an easy lay. A hot lay. Who had a nice fistful of tit, of ass, who might have a tight little cunt, or mouth of a good cocksucker. We females were first considered for our fuckability. Acting talent came second. "Never, never let a man pat you on the behind," Charles said, "unless he is your lover. It is a sign of disrespect." I never did. Not to this day.

Our togetherness remained the back street variety in those first months. I was married. He was married. His wife, Karen Morley, was back east with their young son trying a separation, Charles told me. I tried not to think about that.

One day he told me he was a Jew. I tried not to think about *that*. Seeing my shock, he hastily added he was only half, on his father's side (a lie). That of course made me feel better. Half a Jew is preferable to a whole Jew, right? It was too late to back out, though; he was the most important man in the world to me. If he was that queer thing, a Jew, well, so be it. You can't have everything. I came up with the happy thought that perhaps "Hungarian" was just another word for "Jew." Hungarian sounded glamorous, all that gypsy music and goulash paprika and Buda . . . pesht divided by the romantic Blue Danube. Even the pogroms—a new word to this gentile—that Charles told me he experienced as a boy sounded glamorous. Nothing like that happened in Georgia.

By the time the Germans sent the British scuttling back across the Channel, rolled on into Paris, and endless communiqués came through of the torture and killing of thousands of people in their path, from newborn babies (even unborn) to ancients on their last legs, simply because they happened to be something called Jew (halves, too, even quarters), I was beginning to catch on that there was a terrible thing loose in the world, a blind, unreasoning antipathy.

Fortunately I would be saved, it appears, from eternal exile in Bigotdom by Adolf Hitler and a riproaring, first-class orgasm.

Barton had left me alone. He could have found me. I knew that. But he hadn't and I was grateful. I made two more movies after *The Lady in Question*. Quickies, both. I played Boris Karloff's daughter, standing around among a bunch of bubbling bottles in Daddy's laboratory. The other was a western, with Wild Bill Hickock. I stood around a bunch a horses.

The afternoon Barton did call, he sounded perfectly fine. Neither too pepped up nor down in the depths. He said that he was off to South America to start a business there. Since he wouldn't be seeing me for a very long time he would like to come and say good-bye.

A pleasant Barton entered the apartment. The harsh anger was gone. A gentle, half-smile was on his lips as he said quietly, "It's good to see you again, Evelyn, you look very well."

"So do you." He did too, dressed immaculately in a neatly pressed dark blue suit, shined shoes and sparkling white shirt. "Will you be gone long?"

The little smile. "A very long time. I thought perhaps you would like my car?"

"Oh Barton!" I cried. He had a blue convertible Packard that I adored, so suitable for California, and I had never had one. "Can I really have it?"

"I'll leave it with you, then, and take yours."

I didn't care what he did with that old Pontiac of mine. I didn't care if I never saw it again. "Gee, Barton, you are the dearest thing to think of this."

He looked at me the longest time from what seemed, looking back, a very peaceful place. "I will think of you, Evelyn," he said, "as long as I live."

The way he said it made me want to cry. "Oh Barton, I'm so sorry it didn't—we didn't—you know, work out. . . ."

The little smile, almost rueful. "May I kiss you good-bye?"

His lips on mine, I will always remember, were soft as rainwater; they hardly brushed mine at all. And then he was gone.

It was eleven o'clock that night when the police called.

They had found him out on Ventura Boulevard in the San Fernando Valley, still holding the shotgun that had spewed his brains all over the inside of my old white Pontiac.

The note said it was because I had left him.

I never left a man again.

I made them leave me, instead.

BOOK TWO

CHAPTER 8...

"You brought a new kind of love . . .

to . . . me. . . ."

Barton's act of death and nature's glorious demonstrations of life were forever locked together in my mind. On the way to his funeral I looked out at the tall palms swaying majestically against a blue California sky. I looked at the myriads of blooming flowers along the way, the green grass, dogs, moving cars with people in them, laughing, animated. And I thought, I will never see these things in the same way again.

My brother and a sister, come to comfort me in my time of stress, sat on either side of me. They cried. I didn't. Guilt had a stranglehold. I wouldn't look at the casket. Some woman did, though, sank down and sobbed by it. I've never known who it was. I have hoped it was somebody who loved Barton very much, and that he knew it.

My mother wanted to come out too. I said no. I didn't want to have to cope with her too. We were already far apart, only she didn't know it. She thought I must feel the way she did when her husband died, a man to whom she had been married for twenty years and for whom she had borne five children.

ESTRANGED HUSBAND OF ACTRESS KILLS SELF, the headlines said.

Harry Cohn called me in. He looked at me sideways. "What did you do to kill a man?" he said. I began to shake, out of control. "Can't you take a joke?" he asked.

My brother thought I ought to get out of town. He took me down the coast and deposited me at a motel near the ocean. He managed a restaurant nearby. He worked all day. I was alone in a strange place. With my grief and my guilt.

Charles appeared. "This is ridiculous," he said, "you mustn't hole up like this."

"I don't know what to do."

"I'm going to take you away."

"Where?"

"Never mind. Pack your things."

"I can't—"

"You can." He threw my things into the suitcase. Then he began to make love to me. I didn't want to. I felt I should never be permitted to have any pleasure again as long as I lived. But I had no will to resist.

"We will leave this dreary place," Charles said when it was over.

"My brother—"

"I will tell her." (Half the time Charles got the his and hers backwards.)

We went to the desert, a lovely place surrounded by yucca trees and rolling sand dunes. We took a sweet little bungalow with a fireplace and knotty pine paneling. My guilt grew. Not only had I caused a man's death, I didn't have the decency to mourn him properly. Here I was in bed with another man in only a matter of days. A married man. I had the morals of a pack rat.

"You must not feel responsible," Charles kept telling me. "If a man is going to take her life, it is not one thing that pushes him to do it." He tried, at that time, to heal my guilt. It was only later that he played upon it for his own ends.

Barton's company went through bankruptcy. I had to pay the funeral expenses. I did so eagerly, grateful to pay in some way. Anything, anything at all to assuage the guilt that wouldn't let go its suffocating grip. "Never will I strive so desperately for anything again," I wrote my mother.

Fiery ambition had suffered a serious setback.

But the beat does go on. The name of the game: survival. I left my apartment and moved to another. I traded in the blue Packard and the blood-stained Pontiac for a green convertible Buick. It helped. It helped a little.

Charles helped the most. I clung to him in the aftermath of tragedy. He became the focal point around which I revolved. He was my sun, moon and stars.

Then one day in early September, he drove me to the top of Mulholland Drive, to a hill overlooking the sweep of San Fernando Valley. On the way up he had been strangely silent. We got out of the car and sat on a rock with the valley spread out below us. The wind tossed our hair about in best movie tradition. Charles' blue eyes rested on me.

They were solemn. "Karen," he said, "is coming back. We are going to try again."

My heart plummeted down into the valley. My chest caved in. I couldn't speak.

He took my hand in his. "Promise me," he whispered, "you will not fuck around. I know you will want another man, but—" His blue orbs bore into my hazel, "—*you* do the choosing. You decide who you want. Not the other way around. Any man would be happy to go to bed with you. Why not? You are young and appetizing, and he has nothing to lose. But you—"

"More Molnar?" I muttered, feeling sick.

Ferenc Molnar was a Hungarian playwright of the twenties, beloved of his intellectual countrymen for his wit and profundity. Every Hungarian I met (then) told Molnar stories, and quoted him. Charles often used him to get over certain points. Most particularly to help me understand a woman's place in this society of ours. "There must be a double standard," Charles had told me.

"Double standard?" said I, "what's that?"

"Men and women, they are different—"

"Vive la difference!" I snickered with my newfound sophistication.

"—therefore, it is necessary to have different standards of behavior for the two sexes. As Molnar has said, 'it is easier to get the mud off the *outside* of the boot than from the *inside* of the boot.'!"

He leaned closer. "Will you miss me?" he whispered softly.

I think I nodded dumbly. I was paralyzed. My life had come to an end. He put his arms around me, slowly eased me to the ground. And there, behind a rock on the top of Mulholland, the wind running its fingers through our hair, thistle and loose pebbles digging into my back, Charles made love to me. What you might call a farewell fuck.

CHAPTER 9...

"*Ma—he's makin' eyes at me. . . .*"

Our separation and his and Karen's togetherness lasted two days. It was my suspicion that she only came back to explain in person why she wanted out. I was so relieved to get him back I didn't care what the terms were.

Our relationship out of the closet, Charles and I became a gossip column "item." "The Charles Vidors are phttt! and Charles is squiring Columbia starlet Evelyn Keyes these days." By his side, I became a fringe member of the Hollywood Hungarian colony. For such a small nation, there were an inordinate number of them in motion pictures: directors, writers, producers, set designers—the three Korda brothers alone covered every possible angle.

A favorite hangout for all refugees from Hitler's rampages was a restaurant on the Sunset Strip called The Players, created by director Preston Sturges. One might see Marlene Dietrich, candlelight flickering over those perfect cheekbones, huddled in a corner with perhaps Jean Gabin leaning across the red-checked tablecloth. Or Charles Boyer, Charles Laughton and Elsa, Paul Lukas. Hedy LaMarr. Peter Lorre.

I was happy. I felt at last I was becoming an integral part of the establishment. Charles, however, was rather embarrassed by our affair. His dignity, he felt, was endangered by being in love—or whatever he was—with someone who looked more like his daughter than his paramour. "Listen," he said, "in public I'm not going to pay to you too much attention. It looks foolish for an older man to be infatuated with a young girl. But the other way round, ah, it is adorable if she runs after him." He encouraged me to kiss him in public, fondle him, reach for his hand at every opportunity.

I went along with it. I adored playing Little Girl to my Daddy. I attributed his attention when nobody was around, his constant jealousy and keen watchfulness, as his way of showing care and devotion.

Nothing escaped his attention. My car had a loose sunshade on the righthand side which would work its way downward during the course of a day. Charles noticed it one evening. "Why is that shade pulled down," he asked, "was somebody in the car with you?"

"No, no. It's loose, the screw needs—"

"Somebody was with you."

"I just told you—"

"You are lying to me!"

"How dare you! I am not—"

"It was a man, wasn't it?"

"Oh honestly. You think—"

"Tell the truth"

"I *am* telling the truth—"

"Who was it?"

"Stop it!"

Conversations of this sort were our daily fare, although I was utterly faithful. Once, though, I really shook him up. Once, he almost had a legitimate beef.

One Sunday Charles was spending the day with his son, and planned to play klabias, a Hungarian card game, with some Hungarian cronies in the evening (or so he told me). Left on my own, I went down to K. T. Stevens' beach house at Malibu for the day.

Late afternoon some of us were lying about, talking, sunning ourselves, Van Heflin among them. Who should show up but Errol Flynn and Lily Damita, to whom he was still married. God, were they good-looking. She had an extraordinary figure that fairly undulated across the sand and to the sea. And Errol Flynn. He was so beautiful it stopped my breath.

I was just the right age for the Flynn taste. He made it clear too, with eyes for me and nobody else, in spite of Lily's presence. I went all fluttery.

He invited us all to go along with them to a party at Big Boy Williams' house. I had my car, and Van, who didn't, came with me. My unstable behavior had obviously been noted, because he said, "Stay away from Errol, Evelyn, he's bad news for dames."

"Well!" I flushed. "I certainly have no intention of having the slightest thing to do with Mr. Flynn! That is *Mrs.* Flynn with him!" said the phony little prig, me.

We arrived after dark. A big bonfire was going, people milling about it. No one was introduced. I recognized the hefty frame of Big Boy in the flickering light, and also Lupe Velez, known as the Mexican Spitfire. She seemed rather subdued. I couldn't see how she had earned her reputation, until Errol started teasing her. "Come on, Lupe, show us how you do it."

She tossed her head. "Oh, Errol, *siempre la misma cosa—*"

"Oh come on, Chiquita, you know you like to do it."

She grinned. *"Para ti."* The firelight played across her face, and across the pale blue blouse she wore. With her eyes on Errol, her breasts began to move beneath the pale soft material. Round and round they went, in circles, faster and faster, round and round.

Errol whooped. "Did you ever see anything like that? Isn't it the damndest thing?"

No, I hadn't ever seen anything like it. It made me uneasy. I was out of my league.

Errol phoned me the next day. "Hey, come on over to my place." Charles was sitting right there. "Ah, u-u-uh, well, I-Idon't think—"

Charles grabbed the phone from me, listened long enough to hear a man's voice, slammed down the receiver and slapped me across the cheek.

He got the whole story out of me, of course. He never would believe I never intended to go further. I'm not sure whether I believed it either.

Meanwhile my career inched slowly forward. I was put in a Peter Lorre flick. He played a nice refugee turned wicked gangster because he was shunned by the world, his face having been burned dreadfully. I played a blind girl who couldn't see the mess.

But the studio could see me and liked it well enough to cast me opposite Robert Montgomery in *Here Comes Mr. Jordan.*

That was the good luck.

The bad luck was, I was coming along in Rita Hayworth's wake. The various departments, believing her image to be the winning one, tried to make me over into a blonde replica. Hairdressing added tons of hairpieces, including one of Otto Kruger's old toupees pasted to my forehead. Wardrobe padded my breasts to match Rita's more generous proportions. My thin frame and small face couldn't take the added weight. I looked absurd and felt worse. It was devastating to my self-confidence.

And Robert Montgomery was a cold fish. With eyebrows lifted insinuatingly he said, "I hear you're running around with a married man."

Perhaps he meant it as a joke. But I, guilty as hell, and humorless, snapped, "What business is it of yours?"

He didn't have much humor, either. He never spoke to me again. Fortunately our scenes were over. But the still photographs, always made after shooting, were not. We posed together an entire day, hugging, kissing, smiling, and Mr. Montgomery never said a word to me.

Charles, my still married lover, cast me in his next—*Ladies in Retirement.* Harry Cohn visited the set one day. Louis Hayward and I were doing a scene in which we discover an old Dutch oven by the fireplace has been closed off. "Coo," I say (I'm Cockney), "it's all bricked up!"

"You can't say that line," said Harry our boss. "Sounds too much like 'prick.'!"

Harry's speculative glance in my direction was gone. By then I was known around the lot as Vidor's property in best male-chauvinist-pig tradition. Harry invited us to sit at his table at the Academy Awards dinner. The occasion was an intimate affair, attended only by members of the motion picture industry, and held in the famed Coconut

Grove. The event was covered by the miracle of radio. We sat at tables around the dance floor where microphones were set up and the presentations made. The fellow from Price Waterhouse arrived with the sealed envelopes the way he does on TV today. The voice of our beloved president, Franklin Delano Roosevelt, boomed out at us via long distance, congratulating us for our fine work. Bette Davis thanked him. Cary Grant was at our table. So were William Holden and Rosalind Russell. Oh, I was moving in top-notch society. No more hamburgers at drive-ins for me.

We were often invited to the Cohn home for dinner and a movie later in his private projection room. Hollywood elite sat around his table: stars, writers, producers, directors. The conversation was often out of my reach. "Call me *pischer*, I still prefer Picasso's blue period!" "Let's put the Macbeth theme in Harlem, he's head of the numbers racket, and she's got his number. . . ."

An avid reader from childhood, I redirected my input with Charles' help, trying to catch up. *War and Peace! Madame Bovary! The Red and the Black! Desire Under the Elms!*

None of my increasing education prevented a gut reaction when we went to a party where Katherine Dunham, the black dancer and choreographer, was a guest.

I was shocked. I grabbed Charles' arm. "Look at that!" I whispered hoarsely.

Charles was startled. "What's the matter—"

"Don't you see that . . . nigra over there!?" Even my southern accent reverted to its true form.

"Hush!" hissed Charles, "somebody will hear you."

"Why she's sitting down on the couch, just like she—"

"Shut up!" His fingers bit through the flesh on my arm.

"I can't stay here in the same room with a nigra acting like—"

"That's enough!" He took me firmly by the elbow and propelled me out the front door. He was livid. "Wait here," he told me, "I will make excuses." Not for me, he told me later, but because he was afraid our hosts might notice my disgraceful reaction, or worse, Katherine might. He returned, and practically threw me into the car.

"I told them you are ill," he fumed, "and you most certainly are. Have you no humility? You have learned nothing—"

"Well, see, where I come from—"

"Don't—tell—me about it!" he spat, "a southern nazi is what you are. What is the difference in your stupid reaction and the one Hitler is propagating—blind, unreasonable prejudice toward someone you know nothing about. You don't know Katherine Dunham, and now you never will, and it will be your loss."

I had never seen him angry like this. The jealous kind I could understand, I knew jealousy myself, but this was . . . like he didn't like me, and oh, God, I couldn't take that. If he left me I would die.

"Oh Charles. Please. I'm sorry, listen . . . all my life, it was—I never heard—no one ever said to me what you . . . They always said—"

He turned quickly and put his arms around me. "It is I who must be sorry. Poor baby. This is not the way to do this thing. To jump on you. Of course you never heard these things, all of us are guilty of it in some way. But we must be aware, we must fight it."

"Oh, I will! I will! I'll fight it, I promise!"

He laughed. "What a funny little girl. Come on home. I want to fuck you."

CHAPTER 10 . . .

"Praise the lord . . . and

pass the ammunition. . . ."

Charles laughed again when I decided to go to college. But since he had told me that my type of beauty would fade by the time I was thirty, I figured I'd better become an intellectual as soon as possible. I hied myself to UCLA and enrolled in three courses: Shakespeare, English Drama from 1660 to the present (had to start somewhere), and Contemporary Drama.

The studio found it a joke too. All they wanted to do was photograph me around campus. My higher education lasted three months. Then I was sent off on yet another publicity trek for *Here Comes Mr. Jordan* and Charles' picture *Ladies In Retirement.* This time Chicago, Detroit, catching up once more with the American Legion in Milwaukee. I rode in parades in yellow convertibles and dodged beer bottles thrown by overindulgent legionnaires—a form of higher education not taught on campus.

I was at Charles' house in peaceful Beverly Hills when the word came. Japanese planes had bombed Pearl Harbor? Ah, some crazy plot dreamed up on a Sunday to be shot Monday morning. But the radio said that boys were rushing to the nearest enlisting centers. I was sick. All the young men of my generation were going out to get themselves killed. I looked at Charles and thought, "Oh, thank God, he's too old." Immediately I was ashamed.

We clung to the radio—until all stations went off the air with the frightening announcement that Japanese planes were approaching San Francisco. Then we clung to each other.

The newspaper headlines next day were five inches high, and framed in black. "U.S. AT WAR!" Inside was a photo: "Evelyn Keyes, film actress, models swimsuit to be featured in Spring fashion show."
The world might be crumbling, but leg art lives on!

We expected the West Coast to be bombed. Not Beverly Hills, of course, but who could see well that far up in the sky—particularly if your eyes slant?

I was awakened that night by shouts in the streets. I tried to turn on a light. There was none. The main switch of the city had been pulled. Cars had all pulled over to the side. Total darkness was everywhere. It was an eerie feeling. Perfect strangers huddled together in the streets. I went out to join them. We Americans had never experienced anything like it.

War became a background for America's way of life. Everybody was given gas rationing cards, we in the studios were fingerprinted and given identification cards as if we were defense workers. We made training films ("Loose lips sink ships!").

Fan mail began swooping in from all corners—Australia, India, England, somewhere-in-the-South-Pacific. It was our patriotic duty to answer the gallant servicemen, preferably with pin-up pictures— the nakedest the Hays Office would allow. Presumably to encourage masturbation in the armed forces. We females spent hours posing in bathing suits, negligees and shorts, jumping out of candy boxes for Valentine's Day. Posing with turkeys for Thanksgiving, sleighs for Christmas. We donned our sexiest threads and visited army camps, always with a photographer present who had elected us "girl of the week—month—year." "The one-to-be-with-on-a-deserted-island." (I was elected "Miss Tastiest Dish.") Soon we went to hospitals (with photographer) to cheer up returned veterans who had left pieces of themselves behind somewhere—arms, legs, eyes, even faces. We went out into the fields—a photographer recording our "war effort"— to pick tomatoes rotting on the vines due to the absence of proper labor, men busy somewhere losing their arms, legs, eyes, etc. Oh, it made us feel like such good Americans!

Motion picture companies prospered during the war. Movies were the "free" world's number one entertainment. All the boys "out there" had to be entertained, too. I worked steadily the entire four years—doing nothing noteworthy, but working. Two in '42 with Glenn Ford again: one a Jack London story, another an army air corps tale. Pat O'Brien played my father. The men wore uniforms. I stood about to wave hello and good-bye.

In the summer Charles and I went off to Kanab, Utah, to make a western together. Glenn again. Plus Randolph Scott. Claire Trevor got to play the whore with the heart of gold. I never did. I was always the "nice girl."

I took the role seriously. It bothered me that Charles and I had gone together for so long without getting married. That was the culmination of romance. Marriage. Everybody said so, and in Hollywood everybody got in the act. Especially columnists. "When are you getting married?" Hedda Hopper would ask. "Aren't you two getting married?" Louella Parsons would want to know.

I asked the question too. "Charles, aren't we ever going to get married?"

"I still am married."

"Well, when are you getting a divorce so we can, for heaven's sake?"

"Karen doesn't seem to be in any hurry."

He wasn't either, it would appear. And wouldn't he be, if he loved me?

I was embarrassed to live with him openly on location in front of the movie company. He wanted me to stay in his cabin with him, as we always did when traveling. "I can't," I moaned, "I can't do that in front of—"

"Oh for heaven's sake! They know—"

"They don't have to know—everything."

But I was also ashamed of my reluctance. I had seen Vivien Leigh living openly with Larry Olivier without pretense. Why couldn't I be more sophisticated and honest. After all, I *was* doing it.

This cowardly donkey-carrot struggle, these warring emotions, caused me acute distress. And that in turn brought about the most ridiculous reaction. I began to sneeze when my horse came near me. And what is a western without a horse? They had given me a palomino mare to ride, with a brand new foal. What a sweet photographic sight: the blonde girl sitting straight in the saddle, her horse's blonde mane and tail streaming in the wind, the little leggy colt of the same coloring prancing along after.

CUT!

The leading lady is sneezing her silly head off. Get rid of the horse.

It wouldn't be, I was to learn, that easy to get rid of the reaction.

We finished our western with the required stampedes, fistfights in bars, bucking horses and plenty of shoot-outs. They used phony caps. Other shooting was going on in Africa, Russia and steamy little islands in the South Pacific. There they used real bullets. Some of the men couldn't get up and walk away after a take the way our actors did.

As the months rolled by, we got used to reading lists of casualties, maimed and dead: ours, 365; theirs, in the thousands (theirs always more). We even cheered burning falling planes, if they were theirs, clapped at the explosion of a sinking submarine—theirs, of course.

I became a flaming, righteous liberal, with my keen ex-bigot eye and ear stretched out to catch the merest nuance of prejudice. My tight rein on the morals of my fellow man most emphatically included my own predicament. I would not tolerate the sinful arrangement I had fallen into much longer. I nagged, I wheedled, I threatened to pull a Lysistrata, if we were not soon legally wed.

He soothed me with jewels (rubies), a beaver coat for Christmas (what did we know of endangered species?), a full-length silver fox for a birthday. We worked all the time too. Things easily got postponed. When was there time? He did *Cover Girl,* with Rita and Gene Kelly. I did one good comedy (*Dangerous Blondes,* with Allyn Joslyn) and one piece of junk that shall be nameless. After which the studio threw every female under contract into a murder mystery called *Nine Girls,* with Ann Harding as den mother.

Then I had him. He was stuck. He had this physical thing for me. "You are a fish hook in my side," he told me. He hated it, but I had my way. We were married at the end of February 1944 at the home of Mr. and Mrs. William Pereira. The only regular stand-up wedding I ever had, with flowers, something blue and borrowed, tears, and a matron of honor, Jennifer Jones, who had become a friend.

We had a month's vacation for a honeymoon and took a house in Palm Springs. Charles brought his six-year-old son along. It soon became apparent that this jaunt was a get-together for the two "men." Father would supply the patriarchal element in the boy's life missing since Charles and Karen had parted ways. Shotguns were brought along, the ultimate in machismo. Immediately upon arrival, the two he-man types, a forty-four-year-old Hungarian intellectual and a six-year-old lad, grabbed up the manly instruments and rushed out into the desert, their weapons at the ready. Some fifty yards from the house they began blasting away at a jackrabbit who happened to be hippity-hopping by. Bang! Bang!

Between them they managed to clip the poor devil. It shot straight up in the air, one hind leg hanging loosely, blood dripping from it. It hobbled off, its hippity-hop destroyed, dragging its mutilated limb behind it.

Charles soon found an excuse to go back to Los Angeles. I spent the only honeymoon I ever had with a six-year-old. As good a way as any.

CHAPTER 11...

"Love and marriage . . . love and marriage . . . go together like a horse and carriage. . . ."

The boy took up residence with us during the first few months of wedded bliss. If my knowledge of marriage was limited, it shrank even more when it came to parenthood. I simply joined the child and made Charles our bogie man. "Take a bath, study your lessons," I would tell him, "or your father will kill us both." I knew enough not to recoil in horror when he stepped into the shower to check out my odds and ends against those of his mother.

Charles and I ourselves were most careful not to increase the population, although I almost succumbed when I gave Rita Hayworth a shower (studio arranged) when she was expecting her first—by Orson Welles. She looked so beautiful in basic black and big jeweled cuff-links, with everybody hovering about, that I flirted with the idea of joining the motherhood club.

Instead I followed *her* flirtation with politics.

D-Day had come around, the invasion of Normandy was underway, and Roosevelt was coming up for reelection for the third time. All Hollywood was taking sides. It seemed vital for some of us that he stay in office; for others just as vital that he get kicked out. I heard Rita, Olivia de Havilland and others giving blurbs on the radio *for*. I was jealous. I wanted to get in the act too. I also wanted to show Charles he had married something more than just a piece of ass.

So I joined the Hollywood Democratic Committee. That it would be later called "subversive" and get me in hot water would come as a big surprise.

The Committee was a bona fide branch of the Democratic Party, its aim to reelect an already seated president of the United States. If talking about how to get money to run a political campaign is subversive, then the epithet was deserved. That is just about all they ever talked about at meetings. I was bored to tears. At one gathering I almost gave up my blossoming liberalism altogether when a black fellow sitting next to me insisted on talking three inches from my ear with a breath like poison gas.

The highlight of my political career arrived when I was asked to fly to Seattle to make a speech—which would be written for me—before the Longshoremen's Union. Another subversive character, Harry Truman, was on the bill too. He was running for vice-president. "Clare," I cried in passionate tones, "isn't the first Booth to stab a president in the back!" (She had said unkind things about our beloved F.D.R.)

I received a standing ovation from fifteen thousand strong. Heady stuff. But that's show biz.

The third speaker on the panel was Walter Huston. We flew back to Los Angeles together. I loved him in movies. He was as warm and comfortable in the flesh. He told me about a splendid son named John, who was off to war.

When Charles' boy went back to his mother we gave up the housekeeping bit and took an apartment on the fifteenth floor of the Sunset Towers on Sunset Boulevard. We had a smashing view, but we seldom saw it. Allyn Joslyn and I did another comedy (*Strange Affair*); Charles was busy preparing, then shooting *Together Again*, with Charles Boyer and Irene Dunne.

We were not together a great deal of the time, and *were* with the beautiful people. Which presents ample opportunities for fooling around, if one is so inclined. I was a gung-ho tennis player too, and between pictures I went whipping over to the Beverly Hills Tennis Club to get a few whacks in.

Perhaps if I hadn't been blinded by Charles' repeated references to the merits of marital faithfulness, I might have noticed a little something afoot at Harry Cohn's fiftieth birthday party.

There were always a sprinkling of starlets at Harry's gatherings. All gorgeous, but wasn't everybody? There was no special reason to notice that Charles talked to one of them perhaps longer than the others. Or that they spoke Hungarian together. That always happened when he came across a Hungarian, understandably. Other things were going on to keep me occupied, anyhow.

A hundred or so guests were there, stars every one, and some of them began doing skits, performing, music and lyrics written for the occasion, all teasing Harry with great good humor. Phil Silvers impersonated Harry, crooking his mouth in the corner exactly like Harry. Gene Kelly did something. Frank Sinatra sang. My mind wasn't on my husband. Only when the crowd thinned out and I went to look for him did I find he was with the same redhead. "Time to go, don't you think, Charles?" I said.

The girl leaped to her feet and rushed away. "What's with her?" I asked.

"Yes, let us go," Charles said.

Even a few days later, when I went to see him on the set and found the same girl there, no flash of understanding came to me. I thought she was trying to learn her craft and that the unfriendly glance that slid over me was envy for someone who was more established than she. But I did complain rather peevishly to a publicity woman assigned to Charles' picture whom I ran into. "Doesn't that new girl have anything better to do than hang around this set all day?"

A most extraordinary thing happened. The woman turned an angry purple. "That . . . hussy," she spat with such venom that I took a couple of steps backward. "She has no shame, she flaunts their—they kiss and hug right in front of *everybody!* I don't know how you stand it. . . ."

She may have said more. Probably did, she had such a good start. I didn't hear it. My brain grew hot, swelled up and threatened to burst through my scalp. I understood at that moment why the sultan cut off the head of the bearer of bad news. If I had had a sword on me, there would have been one less publicity flack in the world. Some time later I got around to wondering why she was so upset about Charles' little affair and came to the obvious conclusion, but by then it didn't matter if there had been two or a million, the principle was the same.

If what she said was true, then Charles, husband, half of a union of super-love, had lied through his Hungarian teeth. Molnar's double standard, he had said, didn't apply to us.

I didn't just take the publicist's word for it. I hastened back to the set to ask the Hungarian in person.

It worked out nicely. They were together in the dressing room-office he had on the set. I didn't knock. They jumped apart as I walked in. "So it's true," I said, always quick-witted in emergencies.

There was sparkle in Charles' blue eyes, as if he were pleased his arranged drama was moving right along. We all made the standard noises. How could you, I said. Perhaps it's best, you know, he said. I love him, she said. Then he's yours, I said to her, and When are you moving out, to him. (Okay, see, for *him* to move out.) Et cetera. They've written a thousand movies with the scene. It's why we all knew how to play it so well.

I took my broken heart and left. It's True Confession time to say something died in me. I'll say it: it did. Naïveté crashed to earth and broke its goddamned neck. Charles had taught me one more lesson. Never to trust a soul.

I made it to the parking lot across the street before the tears came. They didn't help my vision and I ran smack into a very tall actor I had once worked with. "Hey," he said, reaching out to steady me, "what's wrong?"

"Nothing," I sniffed.

"You look upset," he said, in glorious understatement.

"Who's upset?" I said, and cried some more.

"Listen," said the actor, "you can't drive this way, what you need is a drink. You're coming with me." He put his arm around me and steered me toward his car. I didn't mind. I didn't want to be alone.

"My marriage is over," I sobbed, getting in his car.

"Join the club."

We had a drink in some dark place on Melrose. And that went down so well we had another. Amazing how a few martinis can brighten up the world. The heaviness in my heart floated up and drifted out the window. The terrible pain ceased. The actor had to go home and feed his dog. I went with him. I love dogs!

The poodle was glad to see us both. We had a few more drinks. I swam in a warm pool of euphoria.

I suppose the bed had been there all the while. Finally it was the only thing there. Down we went in a whirlpool of flung clothing, I thinking as I tumbled bedward, fuck you, Mr. Ferenc goddam Molnar and your two sets of boots, what's good for the gander . . .

And I thought, I don't even like actors very much. But once in a while they have come in handy. . . .

CHAPTER 12...

"Aggravatin' Papa, don't you try to two-time me. . . ."

When I got home around three in the morning, Charles' car was in its slot in the garage. Guilt had sobered me up completely. He would know what I had been up to! I drove off to the nearest all-night coffee shop and phoned. "Charles," I said, "What are you doing there? You said you were moving to a hotel."

"Where are you?" His voice was very quiet. Too quiet.

"Never mind. What are you doing there?"

"I wanted to talk to you again before I left."

"Haven't we said everything there is to say?" I didn't want him to see me, he would know by my face—

"Please. I just want to see you once more."

The few stragglers at the counter were glancing my way, curiously. I couldn't hang around at this hour alone. "All right," I agreed reluctantly.

All the lights in the apartment were off except the lamp by Charles' chair. A whiskey bottle and one glass were sitting on the end table in a pool of light. His face was in shadow. Well staged. Neither of us was ever able to do a damn thing without some part of us stepping back to see the dramatic effect. Charles didn't drink, to speak of.

I took a seat on the couch opposite, carefully remaining out of the light, too.

"Where have you been?" he asked softly, his blue eyes infinitely sad.

"Now Charles, haven't you forfeited the right to ask me that?"

"I just want to know that you are all right."

"I'm fine."

He sighed. Deeply. "In this brief time," he said, "I have missed you terribly. I don't think I can live without you."

"I'm sorry."

"I love you very much."

I didn't feel pleased. I didn't feel anything. Feeling was lying dead with a broken neck.

"I want us to try again," Charles continued, in this low, reasonable voice.

I answered in the same vein. "I—I don't think I could, Charles. Not after I saw you with that—"

He sighed again. He rose. Slowly he walked over and stood before me. A moment passed.

I was taken completely by surprise when his open hand whacked against my cheek. "You've been with a man, haven't you," he hissed, suddenly enraged.

"No!" How quickly we learn to lie.

"Yes you have—"

I saw the next one coming, ducked, slid off the sofa and started to scramble across the floor. He grabbed a foot. I kicked, got up and tried to run. He grabbed an arm. I pulled away and headed for the front door. I got it open. Suddenly he started to push me toward the stairwell that circled down fifteen stories. "You—have—been—with—a—man. . . ."

I grabbed the railing and began to scream, terrified out of my wits. The piercing jangle of our telephone interrupted the touching scene. Charles let go of me abruptly. "You better answer it," he said.

Keeping an eye on him, I went to pick it up. It was the manager of the building. "Are you in danger?" her hushed voice whispered in my ear.

Charles reached out as if to stop me. "Please," he said, "don't say anything—tell them it's nothing. I won't touch you again. Please."

"It's okay," I said into the phone, watching Charles warily, "it won't happen again."

I hung up. He stood looking at me, not moving. His pride had gotten into the act. Or his good sense. What would that headline look like? DIRECTOR THROWS WIFE DOWN STAIRWELL. He could possibly see a good career fading into the distance. Louse up his ladies' man image, too.

Tears came into his eyes. "Please tell me you weren't with another man."

"Of course I wasn't," I replied. When my person is threatened with violence, I'll do anything to save myself.

He put his arms around me then. And . . . well, we made out.

I had never had two men in one evening before—or since. Charles finally departed as the sun rose, presumably to meet his new lady love. I didn't feel as honorable as a whore—she does it for an honest buck; I was only saving my skin.

Drink was the answer. I would get drunk, stay drunk for the rest of my life and never have to face the cold truth—that I wasn't worth much. I retrieved the bottle of Scotch, poured out a full glass—as I had seen Barton do—held my breath and drank it down.

The liquid hit my stomach and flew right up again like a bouncing rubber ball. Whoosh! Over and out. With that, my career as an alcoholic ended.

I was soon put to work in an updated version of Aladdin and his lamp called *A Thousand and One Nights,* with Cornel Wilde and Phil Silvers. I was cast as a modern, wisecracking genie—invisible except to Cornel—snapping fingers for instant miracles, dressed in diaphanous Arabian Jean Louis creations. Adorable on the outside, pain and heartache underneath.

I unburdened myself to Phil one cold morning during the ride to location. My hair was still in curlers, to be combed out when we arrived, a heavy coat over my skimpy costume to keep out the chill air.

As the car rolled along, I babbled to Phil, "—the way Charles pretended to be one thing, and all the time, behind my back, he was something else, that's what hurt so, the deception . . ." I went on and on.

Phil listened quietly and finally turned to me with wonder in his eyes. "I don't know how you do it," he said, in an awestruck tone.

I was taken aback. "Do what?"

"I have always been amazed," Phil Silvers said, "at the freedom with which some people are able to tell other people their woes. I've never been able to do that. I am afraid of boring them. Me, I feel I've got to make them laugh."

Another message, loud and clear. From that day forward, I kept my moans to friends to a minimum.

Harry Cohn, however, overlord to us both, insisted on getting into the act.

CHAPTER 13...

"Have you ever been lone . . . ly . . .
have you ever been blue. . . ."

The major studios were each headed by a Big Daddy who reigned supreme. Employees were held with iron-clad contracts filled with moral clauses that held sway over our private lives as well. And since most anybody who wants to be a movie personality is emotionally unstable for starters, we performers succumbed to the system. Though we complained about the obvious inequities (no outside jobs, no raises unless they gave them), the benefits were superb. The system clucked, protected, nursed, arranged for planes, hotels, theater tickets. Soothed us if we were upset, tended to every comfort when we were working. That all this was likely to keep us in a childlike state well into middle age was not foreseen.

Harry Cohn was one of the best Big Daddies, the stern yet benevolent dictator of the Kingdom of Columbia who watched, hawklike, over his little princes and princesses. Very little happened on the lot that he didn't hear about. Now that two of his "properties" were breaking up, he and the studio must mastermind it: supervise the publicity releases, see that neither of us made fools of ourselves. We must come out of it, our dignity intact. Also, we had both just finished pictures. Heaven forbid anything should jeopardize those investments.

Harry phoned me one Sunday. "Charles is calling from New York. He wants to talk to you."

Apparently Charles was calling through the studio switchboard, as I had changed my number since his departure to an unlisted one. "I don't want to talk to him," I told Harry.

"You can't keep avoiding him, you're at the same studio. Talk to him. Only don't let him talk you into anything. Do what you want to do."

A moment later there was Charles' voice, husky, urgent, seductive. "I have been so foolish," he said. "I will never love anybody but you. Please let me come back to you, and we will seal our love once and for all time. I want you to have my baby!"

One could almost hear violins. Who could resist such a touching scene? And I had been lonely. "Oh yes!" I cried, carried away, "Oh yes, oh yes!" All the world travels in twos—and so must I!

Our performances, I was to learn, had not been played for our ears alone. Harry had neglected to hang up.

After *I* hung up, I came to my senses. I didn't want to go back to Charles. I didn't want a baby. But what could I do? I was committed. A reconciliation must be what my boss, Harry Cohn, wanted too, or he wouldn't have insisted I take the call. Who knows? Perhaps a baby would make all the difference. . . .

Charles returned the next day. He didn't smile, he didn't say hello. He put his arms around me and began to execute his plan.

It was all wrong. The Woodhue, the hair on his chest. For some crazy reason I suddenly thought he wasn't tall enough. Was it the thought that the sperm he wanted to inject would turn into a living, growing thing?

Or is there nothing deader than yesterday's . . .?

The lovemaking that had once thrilled me so now had no effect. And when he entered me, it was an invasion by an alien, undesired body. It was all I could do not to cry out and push him away.

He knew it hadn't worked. (Nor, fortunately, had the attempt at impregnation.) Not much was said. He left and never came back.

Two weeks later I went to Las Vegas. Harry Cohn arranged everything: the lawyer ("No alimony!" I cried, "Never!"); a bungalow at the El Rancho Vegas. Gail Gifford from the publicity department was sent along to keep me company the first couple of weeks and tend to whatever press was milling about. Harry gave me his private telephone number and told me to check in every day to let him know if I was all right and what Charles was up to.

Charles started calling every day the minute I arrived in Vegas. "Don't do it," he would say. "Leave that place and come home to me." It was upsetting. I had worshipped this man with something akin to belief in God, and the belief had melted away as if it had never been. This was a stranger on the phone.

"What's the matter with me?" I asked Harry.

"Nothing. When it's over, it's over. It happens. Don't worry about it." God was being replaced.

Then the stranger called around two in the morning. "I do not wish to go on without you," he said. "If you do not come back—" the pause was dramatic,—"I will shoot myself."

I gasped, horrified.

"You destroy men. I understand now, how your first husband—"

I hung up, sick. Angry, too. I knew that he was playing on the guilt I carried. Only . . . I hadn't believed Barton, and look what happened—

I quickly dialed Charles' number. No answer. My heart was pounding louder than the empty ringing.

I hung up, sobbing. Gail had gone home. Should I call Harry?

Then the phone rang and I grabbed it before it finished the first b-r-r. "I want you to know," Charles' faint voice said, "you're not getting away with it, this time. Before I shoot myself—I am going to shoot you." And he hung up.

I was a basket case. It was the weekend, but I called the studio operator and told her she had to put me through to Harry even if it was the middle of the night. My teeth were chattering so I could hardly explain why I had called.

"I'll get a policeman to watch outside your door," said Harry Cohn's reassuring voice, "but you got nothing to worry about. That Hungarian cocksucker hasn't got balls enough to shoot a flea."

Charles didn't call me in Vegas again. Did Harry say something to him? It occurred to me that Charles wanted me back so that it would look like the little girl just couldn't stay away from *him*. My faith had fallen low.

But not so low it couldn't get one more boot downhill. In Las Vegas I learned not only the perfidy of one man, I learned it was true of mankind in general.

Franklin Delano Roosevelt died. The first, the only man I had ever voted for; the president who had been in office the major part of my life. I was shocked. My petty troubles were nothing compared to this tragedy that marked the end of the world. How could we all go on without him?

I rushed to the casino, expecting to find people wailing uncontrollably, gnashing their teeth, beating their breasts.

Nothing of the sort.

In fact, no change at all. The dice were clicking across green felt, the roulette wheels turning, the ladies concentrating over blackjack.

Maybe they hadn't heard the dreadful news. I touched the shoulder of the man nearest me, and cried "Didn't you know? Roosevelt died!"

"Oh yeah?" the man said, and turned back to put another dollar in a slot machine.

That is how I learned that people die—even presidents—and it makes little difference in the scheme of things. Empty gaps are quickly closed, and life goes on.

I certainly went on with mine.

BOOK THREE

CHAPTER 14...

"I won't say I will . . . but I won't say
I won't. . . ."

It is not clear just when Harry Cohn stepped over the line that separated business from something more. Who can notice that little degree more that means—I want to lay you.

It was only natural for Harry to pick up the threads of my shattered life and to concern himself with every detail—only natural that the studio turn over to me the Columbia bungalow at the Beverly Hills Hotel (all four bedrooms) when I couldn't find a place to live in crowded wartime Los Angeles; that I frequently went to the Cohns for dinner. This was my family, the ones who cared. Harry would see to my future, guide me to stardom. It was he I would listen to from now on. "Stay away from that Hungarian prick," he told me, "all he wants is to lay every dame in town."

So who should I run into on the lot almost immediately. His Wood-hue wafted over and encircled me. Always one for quickly launching into what was on his mind, Charles whispered, stepping toward me, "Will you marry me?"

I backed away and fled from my ex-husband. The man I had lived with for four years. At whose feet I had worshipped. Who had single-handedly changed my life by removing my former blinders of preju-dice. My life would be richer for it and I would be forever grateful. But to entrust him with my heart and body again? Never. Harry was the one I would trust from now on. Perhaps not all the way. Never any-body all the way, ever again. But career was the answer, and Harry Cohn would take care of that.

I was instantly put into a picture, *The Renegades,* with Larry Parks and Edgar Buchanan. I was not happy about it and went to Harry to say so. "God," I complained, "another western." I hated working outdoors in the wind and dust. "And I'm allergic to horses, don't you remember?"

"We'll keep them away from you." He stayed behind his desk.

"Aw, Harry, do I really have to—"

"The more you're seen, the bigger you'll get."

"Not if I'm in crap—"

"It's in color. Be patient."

How could I argue? He ought to know best. My big scene was having Larry's baby in the wilds, without medical assistance. (Having babies in dire circumstances became my stock-in-trade: *Mrs. Mike* in the wilds of Canada with a crazy woman in attendance; *The Prowler* in an abandoned mining town with crazy Van Heflin in attendance. It soothed my conscience about not having the real thing.)

When *The Renegades* was in the can, *One Thousand and One Nights* had been released, was a hit, and I was to be sent East to promote it—and myself. Harry told me, "We're gonna build you up."

I was given a raise and Harry and the publicity department spoke of my future in glowing terms. Off I flew around the country again, this time with side trips to hospitals to cheer up the returning wounded. I made speeches too, at every Kiwanis, Rotary and Chamber of Commerce across the country, winding up in New York. I was having a chic lunch at the chic Colony Restaurant when the news came that we had dropped a chic bomb somewhere in Japan, a new and bigger and better kind with a new name. Atomic, whatever that meant, something straight out of science fiction. We were so happy. It would end the war. We had little concept it might end the world, too.

I thought nothing of it when Harry insisted that I check in with him daily while I was on tour. I had come to feel all the attention was my due, just as were the big suites everywhere, with Columbia picking up the tabs. Charge it, please, was all I had to say.

But even such a royal working life ceases to be enjoyable if there is never any play. Back in California I began to go about a bit with Robert Stack or Harry Kurnitz, Peter Lawford once or twice, and others. Nothing serious. We would sometimes go dining and dancing at Ciro's or the Mocambo, the current "in" places where photographers hung around to record your visit for posterity and invariably report it to Louella or Hedda or Sheilah or the columnist for *The Hollywood Reporter,* where it would appear the next day. Life in a goldfish bowl was the accepted norm.

Harry began to call me when he would see one of the items. "Say, what's this?" he would ask.

"Gee, Harry," I would answer, "I can't sit around home all the time."

"The guy's a bum."

"Oh, come on, he is not!"

Then came the pause I got to know so well. "Did you let him?"

I would sigh, "Oh, Harry, of course not, what do you think I am?"

If I made out with one or two, it was none of Harry's business. There were parties, too, at David and Jennifer's, the Jack Warners', the agent-producer Charlie Feldman's, jaunts to Palm Springs, and lots of tennis.

And, in between, the phone calls from Harry. "I'll bet you let that guy fuck you."

"Harry, Harry. There are other things to do besides that," I answered primly.

Zap! Into another flick—yet another remake of *The Front Page,* this time turned into a musical called *Thrill of Brazil* (and don't ask me why). Keenan Wynn was borrowed from Metro, Ann Miller got out her dancing slippers.

But the one I really cared about was *The Jolson Story.* It was high up on the Columbia agenda. I wanted to play the first Mrs. Jolson, Julie Benson in the script, who had been Ruby Keeler in real life. I told Harry I could tap dance like Ruby, and couldn't I play the part, please?

Harry would look at me with thoughtful, hooded eyes and say, We'll see. Meanwhile, they tested one girl after another, and I had the dubious pleasure of seeing them all in Harry's home projection room. I saw the Larry Parks test for Jolson there too, sweat streaking his blackface makeup, mouthing to Jolson's voice. Jolson himself was in the projection room as well. He scowled and squirmed when we all praised Larry's work. I had a sneaking suspicion that Jolson wanted to play Jolson.

Shortly thereafter the studio operator called me at the dance stage to say that Mr. Cohn wanted to see me. I went over to his office. He was strangely subdued, his unsmiling eyes staying on me as he clicked on the intercom and told his secretary he would be looking at film for the next ten minutes. With a flick of his hand he indicated I should follow him into the private projection room connected to his office.

The film consisted of wardrobe tests of my clothes for the picture, photographed ahead of time to be sure they looked all right. These, designed by Jean Louis, recently imported from Paris, were smashing. We watched silently, pleased. Harry never praised, only complained when he didn't like something.

We went back to his office. I waited in front of the desk while he told the intercom to hold his calls for an additional few minutes. Then he looked at me without expression, giving nothing away before he said, "I'm going to make you a very big star."

My heart threatened to stop beating. For somebody who had been struggling for six years, those words were about as thrilling as I was ever going to hear. Tears of joy filled my eyes. "Oh Harry," I gasped, "do you really mean it?"

The zinger that followed took me completely by surprise. "Because I love you," my president said.

"Oh!" I blinked. "R-really?" I stuttered, "Oh, thank you!" I said inanely, from behind the desk. A slight smile touched his lips. "Now get outta here," he said in a tender way.

I backed up, nodding my head, puppet-like. "Yes," I murmured, "Yes—sure." I turned and hurried across the room.

When my hand was on the doorknob he spoke again. "Hey!" I turned around. His eyes were still on me. "Don't," he told me, "fuck around."

I nodded again, and got out fast, thinking how there was always somebody telling me not to fuck around. That's absolutely crazy, I thought, he doesn't mean that for one second. He mentioned love to give an aura of respectability to the thing he's got in mind. The thing he just told me not to do.

Driving home, I was upset. God, I said to myself, what's the matter with you, what's the big deal? Done all the time. You want to be a top star? So give a little. Sexual favors for material favors, a fair exchange. Yeah, said a voice, it's called prostitution. So don't be so prissy. It can be called courtesan too. Think of Madame Pompadour, think of DuBarry. And Ben Franklin or someone says all cats are gray in the dark.

But dammit, the thought insisted, they're not. There's smell and touch and sound and taste. . . .

I wished I had somebody I could ask what to do.

CHAPTER 15...

"*Temptation . . . you were*

temptation. . . ."

There's an advantage in having the head guy the interested fellow. With millions of dollars riding on the production, he's not about to disturb the leading lady's beauty rest, take a chance she shows up on the set too tired to remember lines. So, Harry limited his attentions to hints and phone calls. My social life consisted only of a little Sunday afternoon tennis at friends' or the tennis club. I didn't mind. Larry Parks and I liked each other and enjoyed working together, pleased to be in this Technicolor biggie that promised to push us farther up the ladder of fame and fortune.

I loved a studio workday. Loved getting up with the sun, driving along almost traffic-free roads through still fresh sweet-smelling morning air.

Time spent in the hair and makeup departments was pleasant too, knowing that perfection was the aim of the beauty experts. Meanwhile you could go over your lines, have a cup of coffee, an egg, even snooze if you felt like it, like Charles Coburn did. Or you could watch the sights: John Barrymore sitting under the dryer, his hair in curlers. Rita Hayworth walking in, sleepy, hair tangled, superb even at seven in the morning. Rita had long-fingered, graceful hands. She waved them dramatically one morning, sitting in the makeup chair. "I don't intend to live the rest of my life on a sound stage!" she declaimed with some passion. I suppose Orson had given her food for thought.

And I loved the sound stage, where we did the filming. Loved it inside those thick, windowless, soundproofed walls that so successfully shut out the rest of the world. When the massive steel doors swung shut behind us with a soft little *boom,* it heralded the moment we could begin to create a world of our own. A make-believe world that became reality in no time at all.

A rehearsal would begin with the actors and director in the actual set—the room, the stairway—lit with only a few work lights, while the crew hovered about to place the big lights, camera, microphones and props. To powder a nose, tuck in a strand of hair. I was at home here—comfortable and safe. All these people were working to see that I looked good, sounded good, acted my best—a community project, everybody working toward the same goal. To make the best possible picture with the material at hand. No one here wished me harm.

If only the outside world had remained on the other side of the stage walls.

The only fly in my happiness ointment was having to make the damnable cloak-and-dagger calls to Harry Cohn each morning and afternoon on his private wire. Unlike Charles, who seemed to be turned on by intrigue, I was very uncomfortable with it.

Most of the time Harry wasn't alone in the office, and the conversation would be terse and brief, limited to grunts. But when nobody was with him, he did his best to keep me off balance. "That little thing of yours twitching?" he would say. Or if he had seen the dailies (the film shot the previous day), "Who thought up that hair style? (Implying I didn't look as well as I might.) "That hat hid your face." (Implying he couldn't see me at all.) Harry was never one for a compliment—you might want a raise, or find out you were a star.

Every so often he would ask, "You're not screwing around, are you?" I would answer, "When on earth would I have time?" I sometimes wondered if he had somebody following me; he seemed to know my every move, what time I left the studio, what time I got home. If I stopped to have a drink with a friend, he knew that too. His voice would inquire over my apartment phone, "Where have you been?" "To see a friend, Harry." "A man?" "Yes, Harry, *and* his wife."

And when Harry would ask, "You in bed?" I would always answer, "Just about," never that I already was, since that would bring on the question of what I did or didn't have on. I will never know if Harry was pulling a Howard Hughes, who was famous for keeping several girls stashed away at the same time, calling each of them every so often, promising to come around to see them within the hour, calling again later that hour, saying he was delayed, but would be along, et cetera, et cetera. Harry never promised to come around. But he didn't promise not to, either.

Toward the end of the picture I was beginning to feel trapped. Six months had gone by. I grew restless. So one Saturday night I took off for Palm Springs with David and Jennifer. We stayed up too late that night, and Sunday night too, playing hard at everything—tennis, swimming, games of all kinds. David Selznick was one of the big game players of all time. Sunday night I called the producer to try to get Monday off. David got on the phone too. No go. I was in the first scene to be shot Monday morning. So late Sunday night David's limo took me back to L.A., me trying to snooze in the back seat.

I felt—and looked—awful the next day. Harry was furious. When he arrived at the studio at eleven I was summoned to his office from the set. He was behind the desk, eyes blazing. "You don't care about your career," he started when I was hardly through the door, "why should I."

"Harry, I have to get out *once* in a while—"

"All the way to Palm Springs—"

"They're old friends of mine, you know that."

"Just can't keep your mind on business, can you, not through one picture."

"Harry." I walked over to his desk. "You're making a big thing out of nothing. Besides, that's not fair, you know I do my work."

"That thing of yours twitching?"

"*Harry!*" I shook my head, exasperated. "You always—"

The intercom buzzed. It always did when you were off center. I swear Harry had some arrangement with his secretary to keep his visitors off balance. "Yeah," he said to the box, then turned to me. "They need you on the set."

He was walking around his desk. He came very close. His belly touched mine. His hand reached between my legs. He rubbed. "Save that for me," he whispered. "I'm going to marry you."

I didn't move. A chill rippled along my spine. His breath tickled my face as he said softly, "Now get outta here."

I never believed that he was serious about the marriage part—he had a perfectly good patrician gentile wife who had nicely popped out the sons he wanted; divorce was expensive. But if he wanted to instill this proposed coupling with a touch of dignity and class, why then, that was very nice. Why not let him fantasize like the rest of us. Doesn't the head of the fantasizing business have a right, too?

But I finally reacted as though he had deeply insulted me.

It wasn't that I didn't like him okay, that he was *too* unattractive, or didn't smell all right. Some of it was the artist-superior-to-management bullshit I had picked up from Charles (although he himself instantly went out and married the daughter of a member of the Hollywood establishment). Some of it was the old good girl syndrome. Good girls "did it" for love. And, as Charles said, when *they* wanted to. Why not want to with Harry, but there's the rub. I would know why I was doing it—because I wanted him to make me a superstar. I mean, there's no way you can hide it from yourself. I am letting this man fuck me so that he will give me the biggest and best parts that come along. There's no way to conjure up the idea that it's love or that it's a hot sexual attraction. Nowhere to hide.

Only a couple of years ago a man asked me to dinner and while we were eating our steaks he threw a blue document in my lap. "What's that?" I said. "My will," he replied, "leaving everything to you."

I looked at it. Nobody had ever left me anything before. A couple of million dollars was in there. I stopped seeing the son of a bitch. He had loused up our friendship with his little blue document, making it so that if I said hello nicely it would probably mean I was protecting my inheritance.

In Harry's case I dashed out on a date with Sterling Hayden, home fresh from the wars, and sure to make news.

Sterling Hayden was a very tall, very serious young man, looking for direction after his traumatic bout with saving the world. He wanted to hang around my apartment that evening and read the Communist Manifesto aloud to me. It was hard to understand how anyone could become a communist if you had to plow through that. But I insisted on going dancing at the Mocambo, the "in" place, so that photographers there would photograph me with the returning hero, smiling, and Harry Cohn would see it.

Our togetherness made the *Hollywood Reporter* the next morning. With one ear cocked to the ring of a phone I was sure would come, I worked on a number with Jack Cole, on stage ten.

Almost on the nose at eleven.

I felt depressed walking across the lot. I would have liked to rush away and never come back. It was getting too tough. What a crazy bind I had gotten into. Was my career really on the line over whether I went to bed with somebody or not? I didn't believe it for one minute. Those casting couch stories were absurd Hollywood old wives' tales. Nobody ever got a job by sleeping with anybody. Or did they? What if I did it once, and it was ghastly, and I would have to do it again—and again. I would sure as hell blow it anyway, wouldn't I. A risky business, so stop flirting around with it. Just come out and tell Harry that you . . .

He hadn't gotten up but sat looking at me as I walked in, in a beam of—what, anger? Hatred? "Harry—"

The intercom buzzed. Boy, they had that figured out to perfection. "He's a prick," he said to the phone, "fuck 'im." His eyes were still on me.

When he hung up I started again. "Please. Don't do this. I'm not doing anything that everybody else . . . my God, you don't expect me to be alone all the—"

"Did you let him go all the way with you?"

"Oh God." I wanted to cry. I had set this up, and now I wanted no part of it. "I just went out to dinner, I wanted to have some fun—"

"Did you let him?"

"So what if I did!" I suddenly snapped, irritated at this stupidity. Like a bird of prey, Harry swooped: "Ha!" he cried, "so you did!"

"I didn't say that."

"But you did."

Weariness, soft as a spider's web, floated down over me. I didn't care anymore, let the chips fall, if they must. "If you say so," I sighed.

The spirit that built the Gower Street empire wasn't fooled by his female contractees with a turn-the-other-cheek manner.

"You are worse than a whore," he said with contempt, "you give it away."

"Why should I charge," said I sweetly, "for pleasure that is given me?"

He looked at me for a moment. Then he said, oh so quietly, "You'll never be a bigger star than you are right now. I'll see to that."

BOOK FOUR

CHAPTER 16...

"Love . . . your magic spell is

everywhere. . . ."

After Harry Cohn dropped me with a resounding thud, I enjoyed my new-found freedom, blissfully doing whatever I chose to do. I worked; that was always a pleasure. I had already been cast in *Johnny O'Clock,* with Dick Powell and Lee J. Cobb, before our confrontation. It was Robert Rossen's first directorial job and maybe Harry hoped he would tumble downhill and take me with him.

Free to go to parties any time, anywhere I liked, I accepted an invitation at Sir Charles Mendl's. Charles was an elderly English gentleman who chose to ignore his seventy-odd years and dash about as if he were a mere thirty. His even older wife, Elsie, decorated for the rich and made pots of money.

Their house in Beverly Hills was elegant-looking, in cool greens and whites. An enclosed terrace ran the length of the living room, beyond which was the garden, beautifully landscaped and lit at night so that it became a part of the interior. For dinner parties, tables seating six each were arranged in rows along the terrace, each with its bowl of fresh flowers, sterling silver and gleaming baccarat.

And what do you know? There was Errol Flynn seated right next to me. I hadn't seen him since the brief encounter at the beach. Handsome? More beautiful than ever, absolutely in his prime. One would have thought the auspicious moment had arrived.

But no.

My tastes appeared to have changed. It was the man seated on my right who stirred my interest. Not beautiful at all, if anything, almost ugly. Handsome eyes though, brown, well spaced. Deep pouches underneath gave them a sad look. Generous mouth, good teeth. Weird posture. The long back curved forward, a bit hunched over. A really queer nose, flattened (he told me later) by a boxer's glove. And he had a way of talking, leaning in, wrapping his melted caramel voice around you, in appealing pied-piper fashion.

I knew who John Huston was. No big trick; everybody knew who everybody else was in Hollywood. Gossip, after movies, was the biggest occupation in town. Had not his father told me, flying down from Seattle, about the son who made *The Maltese Falcon* before going off to war to make documentaries for the army? Had not these two men seated on either side of me made the front pages only the week before?

Errol and John had had a fistfight down in the bottom of David Selznick's garden. All rather hilarious, it seemed, the reports of it produced a lot of ha ha ha's. Rumor had it they had fought over Olivia de Havilland. Since neither of them had a scratch these few days later, it couldn't have been much of a scrap. Why Sir Charles whimsically chose to seat them so near to each other and with me in the middle, I'll never know. They behaved quite civilized that night, talking to me, ignoring each other. I had a fine time.

I don't remember what was said. I do remember I was keenly aware of John's presence even when talking to Errol or whoever else was at the table. After dinner was over and we drifted back into the living room—about twenty of us in all—I kept track of John.

He was easy to spot with his long lanky frame and stork's legs. Once I drifted over and joined his group. He paid no attention to me, so I didn't stay noticeably long, easing on to another group. He never once came near me.

I made a last attempt to attract his attention as I left. I made sure he was within hearing distance when I said goodnight to Sir Charles and thanked him for the evening. I wanted John to see that I was leaving, and that I was alone. I lingered over my farewell, giving him time to get away from whomever he was talking to. If he had the inclination.

I could do no more.

I walked like a snail down the path to my car. Crossed the sidewalk. Stepped off the curb. Went round to the driver's side of the car. Opened the door.

The front door of the house opened and closed. Footsteps clicked on the path. I didn't dare look around, it could have been anybody. I slid under the wheel and began to fumble with the keys.

"Evelyn!"

The caramel voice. My heart sped up. The lanky frame came around, bent down so that his head was just above mine at the window. "Uh . . ." He seemed to be pondering some momentous decision, a characteristic of his over even the smallest consideration, I was to learn. Effective, too. What he said and how he said it changed the course of my life. "Come have a nightcap with me," he said with a certain amount of urgency.

"All right. Where?" I had worked too hard for this to say no.

"Well, let's see, where would a good place be open?" He had been away in the war for four years and was turning to me, the old Hollywood hand.

"Somewhere on the Strip, maybe?" I said. "I live right off it."

"Do you now," said the mellow voice. "Then why don't I follow you and pick you up at your place? We don't need both these cars."

I pulled into my building's underground garage, came out still in evening dress, something long and green, as I remember, to find him waiting in a nondescript black coupe. His flamboyance didn't extend to vehicles.

Driving along Sunset, we discovered we were too late. L.A. bars close at two; it was almost two-thirty.

John had donned spectacles, thin little things, too small for his face. They flickered from the streetlights as he pulled over to the curb and turned to me. "How," said he so low it was almost a whisper, "would you like an adventure?"

The moment rustled with electricity. Two people, sitting in a car, such a commonplace occurrence. But I shivered with excitement. There was mystery in the way he spoke, a promise of something I had never experienced before. Is that not what adventure is? Bolitho describes it this way in *Twelve Against the Gods:* "Adventure is the vitaminizing element in histories, both individual and social. But its story is unsuitable for a Sabbath School prize book. Its adepts are rarely chaste, or merciful, or even law-abiding at all, and any moral peptonizing, or sugaring, takes out the interest, with the truth . . . and the adventurer is a truant from obligation. . . ."

Well, any obligation of mine wouldn't come around until Monday morning. This was Saturday night. Nothing ventured, nothing gained, right? I felt alive again.

"Yes," I whispered, falling under John's spell.

CHAPTER 17

"By the sea . . . by the sea . . . by the
beautiful sea. . . ."

John started driving then, silently, carefully peering out into the night. How was I to know he wasn't fond of driving, probably couldn't see worth a damn, and never drove if there was somebody else to do it? (I saw John once, some years later, sitting in a yellow Jeepster, wearing a bowler hat, reading a newspaper as a chauffeur drove him along.)

Over Benedict Canyon we went, up Beverly Glen, weaving our way over and down to Ventura Boulevard. Little was said, immediate decisions had been made, and John concentrated on getting us wherever we were going. Odd to feel at peace with a perfectly strange man, but I did.

We went through Encino, all the way to Edgar Rice Burroughs' home, Tarzana, where John turned off into a country lane. Fields, mostly, were on both sides, with an occasional house appearing in the headlights. It was a beautiful night, the stars vivid in the sky, bright spangles hanging in space. At the end of the road John turned in between a row of stables on either side of the drive.

He stopped the car and said, "Come on." He got out and I followed. He flipped a switch on the stable wall. Light flooded the area. Bridles and horse gear hung along rich-brown wooden walls. The smell of hay was everywhere. There was a great deal of loud clumping and bumping and snorting as horses' heads began to appear above the half-doors that were entrances to the stalls.

It was a lovely sight. John greeted each of them—four in all—by name, scratching their necks, petting them while they nuzzled him, their soft lips searching for some goodie he might have. The smile on his face was dear, mouth curled up at the corners like a carved Halloween pumpkin. He loved these horses. More, I was to discover later, than he ever loved people. Perhaps he's right. I know that that night, enchanted with the sight of these beautiful beasts and their owner, I forgot I had ever known an allergy.

Having distributed his affection equally among them, he turned out the light and we got back in the car to drive up to the main house. Did I know all along our destination had been John's house? It sat on a rise, the gravel drive circling up to it, crossing a bridge, whose wooden planks rumbled as the car passed over them.

The house, built on two knolls and spread across them, was of the same lovely wood as the stables. Wisconsin pine, John told me, well rubbed with linseed oil. A wisteria vine ran the entire length of the beamed front terrace, its purple blossoms dripping like sapphires. This beautiful vine would have a sad ending one year later at the big anniversary shindig we gave, when a careless bartender dumped the dregs of drinks for two hundred people on its roots.

The living room was huge, fifty feet by forty, perhaps. The wood extended inside, contrasted by white walls. The vast fireplace was built of fieldstone. Equally vast couches and chairs and a coffee table surrounded it. Books rose to the ceiling. Paintings, vases, sculpture, were everywhere. John was/is a collector.

In spite of the many *objets*, I found it a cold room that first night, rather barnlike and impersonal. There seemed to be too much indirect lighting, and it was devoid of actual life. There were no flowers. No green things growing.

We had our drink—scotch, I think—and we talked. I remember the quality more than the substance. Cool. As impersonal as the room. I believe I asked John about the paintings. And he told me he had designed the house himself, and when Frank Lloyd Wright came to visit, he told John the ceilings were too high. When John had answered, "I am tall and I like not to feel cramped," Wright had answered scornfully, "Anybody over five six is a weed!"

Dawn wasn't too far off and I was beginning to wonder how I was going to get back to my place. "But you must stay here," John said.

Oho, I said to myself, so that's it, no preliminaries, no nothing. Just taken for granted. You have another think coming, my friend. "But—" I pointed to my evening dress, "I'm not prepared to spend the night."

"There is everything you need. Come, I'll show you."

"But I have a lunch date tomorrow."

"I too must be in town by noon. We will go in together."

To make a fuss seemed a little ridiculous. I was over twenty-one, I had accepted this "adventure" without question. I couldn't cop out now; at least until I found out exactly what was in store for me.

He took me to a guest room, showed me where the toothbrush and toothpaste were, along with towels and pajamas, kissed me on the forehead and said, "Goodnight, honey." And left.

That was my first night in John Huston's house. Alone in a big double bed down the hall from him.

Drifting off to sleep I had smiled and thought, what a stylish fellow. Deep down an excitement began to stir. I was smitten, and I knew it.

He drove me in the next day, let me out in front of my building and said good-bye, still as impersonal as the night before. I was depressed. I didn't expect to see him again. I changed and went off to lunch, grateful for a crowd; it kept me from thinking.

When I returned home, I found a note under the door. "Forgot to get your phone number. Please call me at Warner Brothers tomorrow. John." I was thrilled beyond words.

But I didn't call the next day. Rossen was rewriting as we went along, handing out new pages seconds before we did almost every scene. That Monday I had a scene with Lee J. Cobb. Although he was quite helpful and worked hard with me on it, he then tried to steal it from me by chewing on a cigar and noisily spitting out pieces of it over my lines.

It kept me busy. But being busy isn't why I didn't call John. I was so eager I went the other way. I was stunned by my own feelings and thought if I followed them I might make a fool of myself. He was so *cool.* This was a much sought-after man, hadn't I seen the coy behavior of the other women at the party the other night?

I didn't know what to do. When in doubt, don't, right?

Late Tuesday afternoon, I succumbed. "Darling!" that lush voice cried with enthusiasm, "How nice of you to call! Will you have dinner with me tonight?"

How good we all were with the beginnings. How beautifully we played the courtship parts, the romancing business—we all had so much practice.

Why did I like that particular set of physical arrangement, and not Harry's? Why a busted nose, ridiculous toothpick legs and knobby knees, a curved back that made the belly jut forward? It is not a description of manly beauty. But in fact, those Greek statues turn me off. They were made for other men, I believe. In any event, I wanted John as much as I didn't want Harry Cohn.

We had a splendid dinner at Chasen's of deviled beef bones and a bottle of Chateau Neuf du Pape. I don't believe we even touched. But we both knew what was coming. What's the point of playing games when you've made up your mind? As Charles had told me, that's all you have to do, make up your own mind.

John's personality remained consistent. His lovemaking was sure, with authority, and cool as always. And it was fun. Isn't this an amusing thing we're doing! was the tone of the action.

And then he fell asleep. Out, cold, a log. I didn't want a man coming out of my apartment in the morning—my upbringing again,

Phoenix out of the ashes. "What will the neighbors think?" I shook, hit, shoved until I got him awake enough to dress and be on his way. Very uncool.

He came back for more, though. Charles had taught me well. He had shown me what a man likes, and I was a good pupil.

I was working; John was writing *Treasure of the Sierra Madre* (which would win him Oscars for writing and directing, and his father one for acting), which kept us from seeing too much of each other, and spoiling a good thing too early. But weekends at his valley place were heaven for this animal freak. Besides the horses, there were assorted dogs, cats, cows, and even a goat or two. There were several outdoor paddocks for the horses to cavort in. Orange and lemon trees swept up the hill in the back of the house where a swimming pool sparkled, and a diving board sprang off the back veranda. There was Charley, the stable man, and Belle, the cook, and her husband, Zeke, who took care of the grounds, milked the cows trailed by a passel of cats, and Nancy, who kept the house spotless and believed in ghosts. (She put a cowbell and some magic herbs in our bed on our wedding night to keep away evil spirits. It worked for about three years.)

The Fourth of July came around, and I got a call from David Selznick. The holiday fell on a Monday, so it would be a long weekend, he was forming a yachting party and could I go along? Ohmyyes, I would love it, but could I bring my new boyfriend, John Huston, along? By all means, bring him, said David.

Already there when we arrived at the dock were Jennifer (Jones) and Paulette Goddard and her husband, Burgess Meredith. William Paley, president of CBS, was along, too. I was to have been his date. Figure me for going where the money isn't.

We spent a memorable four days, plying the California waters on a black sailing ship a million yards long, whose masts rose all the way to the heavens. We left Los Angeles harbor in the afternoon, sliding piratelike through still-clean waters toward Catalina Island, dressed in our brightly colored short-shorts and bare feet. Merry as could be. There was lots of laughter, lots of liquor flowing, stories told, jokes cracked. The beautiful people at sea.

This beautiful person once more forgot and drank too much, not used to it in the afternoon, and by dusk my head was spinning, not to mention my stomach. I retired to retch and lie down. Waking up in the morning feeling rotten, I decided to turn the rest of the trip into a health kick.

We anchored off Avalon, and Paulette popped in to take a swim first thing in the morning, daintily slipping into the water in a blue bathing suit, hair piled high on her head, a diamond necklace—the real McCoy—nestled around her neck. She made delicate paddling movements with her hands and feet, with as little effort as possible, never putting her head in the water.

Then it was ashore for tennis and bowling. We organized teams, everybody suddenly (or maybe always) competitive.

I won everything. At least I have always *felt* that I won everything. John, long arms and legs thin as shafts of wheat, getting all tangled up with the racket when he served. David, a shock of tousled hair already going gray, his eyes bright when you could find them behind the thick lenses, pitching in with all his energy into whatever was going on, bringing enthusiasm and excitement to all the games. He and I had a drink together in the cool of the evening. He spoke of Jennifer who was below, napping. "—of another generation," he said, "of crinoline and lace. She was born too late." Jennifer took good care of herself, exercised faithfully, got her rest, kept lots of cream on her face in the dry California sun. (It worked. She's still here, and David isn't.)

Alexander Korda, the English-Hungarian impresario, came over to talk deals with David. Orson Welles popped in too, that marvelous voice of his rolling out over the water and back again. They came one by one in a little seaplane that would skid up to us on its pontoons. They would waddle out, and with help on all sides, none of them exactly athletes, would make the shift to our decks.

Howard Hughes dropped in from some much bigger plane of his own. In his tennis shoes. I hadn't seen him since the test I made for him. I was never to see him again. He crashed the next day, the big one that almost took his life. And obviously did serious damage from which he apparently never recovered.

On the way back, we hoisted the mammoth sails. They caught the wind, billowed out, and took us, like Jennifer, into another era. Of Columbus and the Vikings. Of the Spanish Armada and Old Ironsides. And all the while John played monkey, hanging on the edge of the boat with his monkey arms and legs. A forewarning of the future, had I only known. Monkeys of one sort or another would play a prominent part in our lives.

CHAPTER 18

*"Maybe it's just for a day . . . love is
as changeable as the weather. But after all,
how little we know. . . ."*

My mother came from Atlanta to see me for the first time just after I met John. Through the years she had resisted coming to California, using one excuse after the other. The newfangled ideas I had picked up about everybody being equal had upset her. She took it as a sure sign of Hollywood corruption. "You no longer understand the Southerner," she wrote.

Until I left home she had been my sole guiding light. Accustomed to my love and utter belief in everything she told me, she balked when it came my turn to teach her a thing or two. I was surprised. She had told me that learning was the most important thing in the world. The strings, the invisible bonds that held us together had melted away by the time she arrived.

Nevertheless, her presence had its effect. It pushed me back to childhood. As if I hadn't escaped my past at all. As if I hadn't crossed the tracks, hadn't got off the streetcar and into my own car. As if I were still wearing my sister's hand-me-downs. Because I, already widowed, divorced, ran off and eloped like a teenager the week my mother arrived.

The timing was lousy, for starters. Not only were things hot and heavy between me and my new boyfriend, John Huston, I was also working every day in a film. I couldn't go anyplace without taking my mother. John didn't seem to mind. We took her along to dinner, to a preview of *The Killers;* he had done the script secretly while serving as a major in the army. My mother thought the film was okay. That was Thursday. The following Sunday I had to work too, doing retakes on the picture I had made before. Which meant I couldn't go out to John's place.

The retakes were little quickies, a close shot here, a line there. By noon it looked as if I would be finishing up early in the afternoon. I called John to tell him. "Oh splendid," he said, "when you're through, come on out. And you'd better hurry, Ava Gardner is here."

Designed to make me jealous? It worked. I was. "Oh good!" I cried, "you've got company, I'm so glad, because I'm awfully tired—"

"Now now, none of that, you just come right along—"

"And besides, my mother's here as you know, and I ought to—"

"Then you both come out," John insisted.

"I don't think so, John—"

"Evelyn!" John said sternly, "if you don't, I'll come and get you. You call me the instant you get through, honey, and I'll meet you at your place."

I didn't, though. I went straight home and turned off the phone. I wasn't going to get caught in a dumb trap like that, competing with Ava Gardner, and rushing to a man's house to do it. I went to a movie with my mother, instead. And thought a lot about what might be going on at John's.

He reached me on the set the next day. I played it very cool. I wanted this man in the worst way. I knew being in a flap wouldn't help. We made a date for dinner that night.

We went to Mike Romanoff's restaurant, a posh place in Beverly Hills owned by a self-styled Russian prince, whose crest was a hobo wearing a crown. In those days you couldn't get in the place unless you had a name or money—preferably both. The check was never small.

I had left my mother at home.

We had vodkas on the rocks, butterfly steaks a la Romanoff, with a little salad and hash browns. Yesterday wasn't mentioned. Side by side we sat, not quite touching, John's elbows on the white cloth, cigarette smoke trailing upwards. I smoked too, then; we could have suffocated in the billowing clouds.

I was so happy to be with him again, content to watch him smile, notice his tiny mannerisms, the way he tapped the ash into the ashtray, or narrowed his eyes to form a thought with just the right amount of dramatic pause, content to listen to his quiet talk, ranging from painters and painting to horses and racetracks, to movies and books. (Once John read Joyce's *Finnegan's Wake* aloud to me, where Joyce uses fourteen languages all at once. John said, "Just listen, and you'll understand. It's music.")

Warmed by drink and good food, we slumped closer together, our elbows on the table, our fingers somehow entwining. A marvelous closeness, the kind that is enjoyed after a lengthy separation. "I missed my darling so much," John whispered.

"Oh yes," I sighed, and pushed myself closer to him. "I missed you too, John."

"I don't want to be without my girl, ever again," said John in that dramatic way he had, with words like little puffs of smoke.

I don't know what possessed me. It wasn't planned; I hardly knew the man. "Then why don't we get married," I heard myself saying.

John didn't move. He remained hunched over the table. He looked at me sideways, brows slightly raised, no smile, no flicker of—anything. He just looked at me for the longest time, eyes slowly blinking. And then he said—and I don't know what possessed *him*—"Why not?"

I became totally reckless. "Tonight. Now. Las Vegas." I really didn't want to go home to Mother!

John took out another cigarette. I grabbed one too. My hands were shaking, as were my insides. Romanoff, a short man with a pencil moustache and large nose, happened to be passing the table and stopped to light our cigarettes.

John inhaled, sent more smoke upwards and said, "Do you know this girl, Mike?"

Mike smiled at me. "Indeed I do."

"Does she pass muster?"

"Dear boy. Lucky is the man who is by her side." His restaurant wasn't a success for nothing.

"Then," said John, "do you think you could charter a plane to Las Vegas for us?"

"Of course, old boy, when?"

"Now. We're going over to get married."

"I see." Totally unflappable was Mike Romanoff. I suppose in the restaurant business one gets accustomed to everything, particularly in Beverly Hills. "I'll get on the phone to Mantz immediately." Paul Mantz was a stunt man who provided planes to the studios.

Romanoff left. We just sat there silently. I felt icy cold. Committed to jump, not knowing if the parachute would open.

Romanoff returned. "All set, old boy, the plane will be ready by the time you get to the airport." I was numb. John was saying, "We'll need a ring. . . ."

Mike Romanoff, the perfect host, said, "There's one at the bottom of my pool that someone dropped there. If you can wait a few minutes, I'll send someone to fetch it."

The interior of the small plane was dark except for the lights from the panel instruments, the pilot's head silhouetted against them. Tips of the mountaintops flew by; I could just make out their dark outline against the darker night sky.

I looked over at John across from me from time to time. He was asleep, having dozed off soon after we had left the ground.

I had never been so wide awake in my life. I never expected to sleep again. That he could, at a time like this, was a little—a lot—disconcerting. Ah, I told myself, it's only play acting, anyway. It isn't real, how could it be real? What's real? So keep cool.

Las Vegas wasn't—isn't—real. Airports with slot machines? And silver dollars still the currency? They give them to you for change, and rather than be weighted down, you stick them in a machine.

We took a taxi to town, the three of us, got a license, found a justice of the peace—just follow the garish neon signs—and with the pilot as witness, bound ourselves together, and headed for a casino.

Isn't that how one spends a wedding night? The groom shooting craps while the bride looks lovingly on? John bent over the green felt with lustful enthusiasm. He shook the dice with both hands, a joyful smile on his face, a mischievous twinkle in his eye.

Around four in the morning I remembered my mother.

I called her, and explained. She was too shocked to protest, especially at that hour.

Later, with the sun of a new day rising behind us, we flew back to L.A.

After landing, we parted, he heading for Warner Brothers, I for Columbia. "Goodbye, dear," said John to the stranger with him. He kissed me on the forehead. "Have a nice day."

We hadn't figured out how to live together. Hadn't discussed it, actually. I gulped a benzedrine tablet, stuck another in my purse in case that one didn't last the day. I slipped off the wedding band and stuck it in my purse too. Perhaps I wouldn't tell the studio just yet, I thought, feeling just a little uncomfortable about the hastiness of it all in the cold light of day.

I don't know how I thought an event taking place in public restaurants and chartered planes and Las Vegas would go unnoticed.

The publicity department was waiting *en masse* in the center of the lot when I walked in. The news was on the wires already. There were lots of well well's, and hey hey!, and you sure pulled a fast one! They wanted pictures of the two of us. While I had my hair and makeup done, somebody called John. To my surprise he came over, which was nice. There was always the possibility I would never see him again. In the makeup department of Columbia Pictures the photographers gathered and took wedding photos of John and Evelyn looking loving, kissing, hugging, gazing down fondly at the now famous (or infamous) ring. It was sort of like our honeymoon. It certainly wasn't any different from the thousands of stills I've made with fellow actors, looking loving, kissing and hugging.

Then John went back to Warner Brothers, and I went on the set of *Johnny O'Clock*.

It was weird. Perhaps it was just the hyped-up, spaced-out mood the benzedrine caused, or maybe only imagination. But it seemed strange. Or strained, all around me that day. There were congratulations, but with distinct lack of enthusiasm. Dick Powell and Bob Rossen were particularly lukewarm, almost resentful, as if I had

The baby stands up.

Graduation Day.

"Goldie" Keyes in Atlanta.

First Hollywood publicity
still.

Signing a contract with Mr.
DeMille.

My first screen role, with Fredric March in *The Buccaneer*.

Doing a scene from *Waiting for Lefty* with Anthony Quinn.

Early publicity shot for *Gone With the Wind*.

Paramount's Golden Dozen of Hopefuls.
In the lineup you'll spot Veda Ann Borg,
Patricia Morison, Judith Barrett, William Holden,
Susan Hayward, yours truly, Robert Preston and Betty Field.

Barton Bainbridge, my first
husband.

With Louis Hayward in *Ladies in
Retirement.*

Clowning on the *Gone With the Wind* set.

Cheesecake.

With Peter Lorre in *The Face Behind the Mask*.

With Boris
Karloff in
Before I Hang.

Publicity still.

With Robert Montgomery in *Here Comes Mr. Jordan.*

With Larry Parks in *The Jolson Story.*

somehow double-crossed them. Larry Parks, working nearby with Rita Hayworth on *Down to Earth,* came parading by with his whole company banging drums and blowing whistles, shouting, "Traitor, traitor! Deserter of the ship!" Helen Hunt, head of hairdressing, came by for a second to tell me Rita was jealous since she herself was without a romance at the moment. (She topped me, went out and got a prince.) Nobody seemed elated by my union. Not me. Not the groom.

At the end of the day, then some forty hours without sleep, light-headed as a feather, I went on out to John's.

He was there, in cream silk pajamas. And he had a bottle of champagne on ice. "Oh John," I said, and held him close. Perhaps I even loved him then.

I put on pajamas too—his. We drank the champagne, were soon pleasantly tipsy, pleasantly tired, we ate Belle's dinner, touching each other once in a while, exhausted, finally crawling into bed, giggling at Nancy's cowbell in the bed, leaving it where it was, settled down, entwined, and promptly fell into a deep sleep.

Thus began my third marriage.

CHAPTER 19...

"Strangers in the night . . . la la la la la
. . . Strangers in the night. . . ."

The second night of my marriage, our filming switched to outdoor work, which meant reporting to the studio for hair and makeup at six of an evening and working at the Columbia ranch until the sun came up. John, still attentive, insisted on taking me to work that first night and picking me up when I was through.

Working at night on practically your honeymoon! All those jokes made the rounds. When I finished a little early, about three-thirty in the morning, and went to the phone to call John, those sitting nearby wore knowing smirks and cocked ears to hear the conversation between the newleyweds.

The receiver was picked up at the other end, and a deep voice mumbled, "Mmmm?"

I spoke softly, knowing I had awakened him from a deep sleep.

"It's me, John, I'm through work. Can you come get me now?"

There was a very long pause. Finally the milk and honey voice I knew so well said, "Uh . . . who is this?"

He was certainly right to ask. Who was I? Who the hell was this woman who had plunged so quickly, so eagerly into a close relationship? Off with the old and on with the new in nothing flat.

It was a joke, wasn't it? That's what all John's friends took it as. How they had laughed when they heard the news—Bogie, John's very good friend, and his new wife, Betty Bacall, all of them Warner Brothers comrades. Anatole Litvak and the William Wylers all laughed and laughed. Crazy John, he's done it again, always up to something screwy, oh, he's famous for his pranks, oh, isn't he a riot. Walter Huston, my new father-in-law and old friend from Seattle laughed loudest of all at his son's latest caprice. Even John's girlfriends didn't take his matrimonial step seriously and continued to call, send notes, and sometimes even flowers. I had married a very popular man.

We were feted, wined and dined by some, though. David Selznick, feeling responsible for the union, gave us a huge, star-studded party, the tent-over-the-tennis court kind, sumptuous buffet with ice sculpture, an orchestra to dance by. Then we gave ourselves one at the ranch with a hundred or more guests.

The strange thing was, at these parties John never came near me. I would go to him once in a while and he would give me a vague little smile as if he were wondering just where he had met me.

Well, it was all pretty funny. But fun, too. Never a dull moment. And John certainly paid attention to me in bed; I *knew* he liked me there. So what the hell, living at the ranch was heavenly, my very own swimming pool and orange trees. What did I care about girl hangers-on, I was in. Also, I liked his friends. I liked Betty. Bogie went around acting like Humphrey Bogart, but you got used to that after a while. There were Sam Spiegel; Jules Buck, a producer at Fox and his wife Joyce, whose friendship would last a lifetime; and Paulette Goddard, whom I adored. It was a pretty exciting life and I thought I would stick around for a while.

Then one night, quite by accident, I overheard John and Walter talking. Walter lived in New York, but when he came West he naturally stayed with his son.

As Mrs. Huston, I had moved into John's wing of the house—and his double bed. Lovely quarters they were too, windows on two entire walls, a stone fireplace, a large mirrored dressing room, a spacious shower big enough for four (we often made it two) with jets left and right, and to top it all, a bidet—my first touch of Europe.

A few weeks after we were married, I woke in the middle of the night to find John wasn't beside me. Soon wide awake, wondering where he was, I decided to go look for him.

The bedrooms were at one end of the house over one knoll and were connected to the rest of the house on the other knoll by a long and very wide passageway, in which a full-sized billiard table stood. Beyond this and to the left were sliding doors that led to the back veranda. I was passing them when I heard John say, ". . . Well, I'm in for it now."

And Walter answered, "She's a nice enough little thing."

I froze, my heart pounding in my ears. That was me they were talking about! Then there was silence. A clinking of ice in glasses. I was afraid to move, afraid they would know I was there, know I had overheard.

I was sick, wanted to sink in the earth and vanish forever. Humiliation stabbed me. John had been getting up every night to wander about the house before coming back to bed. I thought perhaps it was his custom, perhaps he had never slept too well.

But now the truth struck me; it had been nagging back there all the while. He couldn't sleep because he was disturbed. He regretted this stranger who was in his bed every night under the name of "wife."

Walter spoke again. "And Marietta?"

Marietta! Who was Marietta? I thought I knew of all the old girl-friends by then.

John answered. "I don't know what . . . I doubt if she'll . . ." His voice trailed off into contemplative silence.

I backed away, shivering, chilled to the bone, although it was a warm night.

I crept back into the double bed, pulled the sheet up to my chin and lay staring into the dark. What was I to do? I had made a grave error. Should I call it off instantly? Well, that might be all right for John, darling, talented, wild John, so very amusing. But what about me? Would I be kookie, darling Evelyn, who does such amusing things?

Somehow I didn't think so. Every instinct warned me that a woman who went in and out of marriage practically overnight would be an object of ridicule. I didn't think my studio would be the least bit amused. Certainly Harry Cohn wouldn't. The bastard might use it for all his worth against me. Yes, I had my career to think of, since I was strictly on my own. Lying there that night, I certainly felt all on my own.

Besides, it was I who had proposed. I couldn't walk out. Not just yet.

Also, I was stuck on the man. . . .

CHAPTER 20...

"And baby makes three..."

Was it the birthday party I threw John on August 5 that reminded him that time was passing and perhaps he'd better get back in shape after his long sojourn in the armed forces?

Horseback riding was a passion. He had ridden, he told me, before he walked. His mother was a passionate horsewoman, once crossing the Mississippi River on horseback on a dare (so John said), and she often propped her young son in the saddle before her, no matter how long the ride. If John can be believed, he got calluses on his backside before his feet.

When he was twenty he went south to study with the Mexican Cavalry, got a commission, and won the jumping exhibition for them at the Madison Square Garden Horse Show.

Shortly after we were married, he heard that an amateur steeplechase was to take place at the Will Rogers Polo Grounds and thought that might be a way to get the kinks out of a rusty seat. If mere riding was a passion, jumping was orgasm time.

John owned no jumpers, but someone told him of an available ex-racehorse that simply adored leaping over the log in its owner's backyard. John was delighted. The speed of a thoroughbred plus the ability to jump was exactly what he needed to win the race. The creature did indeed leap into the air and over a log. John bought him then and there, and had him delivered to the Polo Grounds.

The day of the race, we went down bright and early, John to take his new purchase over the jumps, I to watch. I wouldn't have missed it for the world. I had never seen a steeplechase.

I settled down in the grandstand while John mounted his steed and started around the field.

Clippity-clop, along they came, rider and mount. How splendid John looked on horseback—a lovely sight, an animated Currier and Ives, the two of them skimming along the turf in a rhythmic flow. Up to the first jump they came, a little barrier of clipped hedge.

All at once the tableau cracked apart. The horse twisted, stiffened his front legs and the two of them came to a jouncing, bouncing halt. The animal had never jumped over anything but his backyard log; all that funny green stuff in front of him was alarming and foreign.

Well. John backed him up and off they started once more.

This time they came up at a whizzing speed; there could be absolutely no stopping. They fairly flew over the jump like an arrow from a bow and barreled on across the field toward the next one.

From where I sat John appeared to be trying to rein in the horse. But if that were the case the horse was having no part of it. His neck was arched and his head was tossing as if he were trying to rid himself of the confining straps. The hooves clopped along at a dazzling speed.

Then they sailed past—not over—the next jump, zoomed around the third and headed straight toward the strip of curved fence at the far end of the polo grounds that separated pavement from the turf of the field.

The next thing happened in a wink, yet it sticks in my mind like a slow motion camera shot. The horse straddled the fence, one front leg and hind leg on one side, the other two on the other. Then he went down, with an eruption of white planks—horse, man, arms and legs flailing, all spewing into the air and falling earthward.

The horse got up. The man lay very still.

He's dead, I thought. This new husband that I hardly know, is dead. It will certainly solve the problem of whether I will have to leave him or not. How does a new bride act in this case? Cry? Gasp? Scream? Fling myself over him and say I must die, too?

Fade in:
Ext: Day—polo field
Long shot: Woman running across field, hair streaming.
Close shot: Woman, in panic, breathing hard.
No no, oh please, dear God, no.
Camera pulls back to full shot: Man on ground, surrounded by a few people. Woman runs in, kneels beside him.
Woman
Don't move, John! (She turns to bystanders)
Full shot: Woman
Is there a doctor here?
Camera pans to bystanders. They are silent.
Close shot: Woman
Don't move, John, I'll go find a doctor!
Camera follows as woman runs to phone. Fade out.

A cinch scene. Everybody knows the injured mustn't move.

I called my doctor, who said, "Tell him not to move." "I told him not to move," I said. "I'll send an ambulance immediately," he told me.

Keeping the panic face, but adding a note of authority, I ran back to the fallen husband.

He wasn't there. The bystanders were still bystanding, but their heads were turned toward the field.

John was back on the horse. I watched as he took the balking animal over the first jump. And the next. And the next. He took his mount around the entire course before pulling up to where we all stood riveted.

He handed the reins to somebody and came over to me. "I'm spitting blood, honey," he said calmly. "I guess we better go to town."

I canceled the ambulance and drove him to the doctor's office myself. A few ribs had been cracked. One of them scratched a lung, the result of his getting back on the horse. But if you want to be a legend in your time, those are the breaks, right?

He was miserable for some time after, and had another good excuse to pace the floor at night.

Did his fall remind him he was mortal after all? During his convalescence he said that he would like us to have a baby.

For the first time, I got excited about the prospect. My career was doomed anyway; Harry Cohn had just turned down Robert Rossen, who wanted to borrow me for his next picture, *Body and Soul,* with John Garfield.

Maybe that was what marriage was all about. If he wanted me to have his baby, didn't that mean that maybe he—cared? This transmutation in the scheme of things came about most unexpectedly one night when I was trying to set the stage for a graceful ending. As usual, John had left our bed to roam the house for what seemed like hours. When he finally came back, I, who had been wide awake the entire time, sat up. "John," I said, "this won't do, will it? I'm bothering you. Would you like me to sleep somewhere else?"

To my surprise, he said, "Darling." Then he got in bed and folded me in his arms. "I want my girl as close to me as she can get."

We started to make love. "From now on," John whispered, "don't use anything."

To hell with you, Harry! I've got a new career! With gay abandon, thrilled with my new adventure, I flung myself into this noble project. First I hied myself off to a doctor to make sure all my working parts were in order after that little trauma I had gone through a while back. "Oh yes, you're fine," he told me, "but it takes two, you know."

"Ah?"

"I must check your husband's sperm count."

"Oh! I don't know when he's able to come in, he's working—"

"It's not necessary he come in," said the doctor. "Give him this—" he handed me a vial, "—have him fill it."

"Fill it? How?"

"He merely ejaculates in the container and then you quickly bring it to me."

Merely, I told John he had said. Mere-ly e-jac-u-late. We started dancing around the room, beating a rhythm, mere-ly e-jac-u-late. Dum dum de dum dum dum. Well . . . nothing to it, you take this little tube and instead of letting go in the usual hole, you whip around and let it all hang out in . . . the container!

Laughter got us through. (Almost interfered too.) I rushed back to the doctor's office with my precious load.

The report was not as optimistic as we had anticipated. I watched the doctor peering through his microscope. He shook his head. "What?" I murmured. "Why are you shaking your head?"

"They're very sluggish. Take a look."

What do I know of sperm? There were some little things down there. They wriggled around. I looked at the doctor. "They moved."

"No, not fast enough. They should be darting quickly about. Nor are there nearly enough. There should be millions. These little fellows are going to have a hard time making it to the top."

"Oh, John is going to be very disappointed. Is there something that can be done about it?"

"Oh, absolutely," he told me. "He must have shots, three times a week, for a very long time."

"Oh dear. He's about to go to New York and after that, Mexico."

"Oh, you can give them to him," the doctor told me, "I'll show you how. . . ."

CHAPTER 21 . . .

"Show me the way to go home. . . ."

In the fall John and I took off for New York, my little suitcase packed with baby-producing vials and needles. He was to direct the Jean-Paul Sartre play, *No Exit,* in its first production in this country. All very exciting.

However.

It soon became apparent that the after and between hours were when the real drama would be taking place.

John, I soon learned, was the darling of—just how do I describe them—Truman Capote's gang. They were well-born, moneyed, intellectually and artistically inclined. They gathered artists about them in their elegant houses and apartments—writers, painters, designers, directors and actors. But only the best, mind you. You seldom saw anybody at their gatherings who wasn't a star in his field. They all knew a great deal about paintings, design, sculpture, furniture and antiques—and owned only the best examples.

We went to their parties because John, whom they adored, was invited; his little wife, of course, could come along.

One was a cocktail party at the elegant River House, an apartment filled with beautifully lit Monets, Renoirs, Pissarros—you name it. I couldn't help noticing John talking to a willowy blonde, almost as tall as he, smartly dressed, class oozing from every pore. Their conversation was terribly intense. Sparks were flying, people were whispering, sneaking looks at them and at me. Even as I watched, John took her hand, pulled her into another room and closed the door.

It was hard to ignore. "Uh . . . who is that woman with John?" I asked the man standing with me.

He was English, I think, or wanted to be. "You haven't met Marietta?" said he with poshly raised brow, "Such a darling. But then, I'm sure John's told you all about Marietta Tree."

I stood around like a lump until John reappeared and said he was ready to go. I don't know if he saw her again. I do know I put my diaphragm back in that night and skipped John's shot, unwilling to get stuck with a baby I might have to raise all alone.

Marietta, however, would have to get in line. The first person in New York John had dashed to see was one Pauline Potter, head designer at Hattie Carnegie's. (She later became Madame Phillip de Rothschild and the proprietress of all that lovely wine.) It was obvious she was a very special friend when he presented her with an eighteenth-century bedspread for which he had forked over $750. It took me aback. I mean, what kind of a friend was she? Was the gift an apology for showing up with a wife?

She had an exquisite house in the east sixties, everything in it carefully chosen and arranged. As she was herself. Another tall one (I'm five foot four), she wore exactly the same thing all the time. You can do that when you're head designer. A schlepp movie star wouldn't dare. On her long neck she wore four strings of pearls à la Ubangi, long-sleeved black top with round neck up to the pearls, full black skirt, and black, soft, low-heeled shoes of the finest leather. Custom made, of course.

She gave little sitdown affairs for six people, as carefully chosen as her objets d'art. Terribly chic table settings with conversation to match. At one such evening John encouraged us all to give our opinions of Picasso's paintings. I didn't know a fucking thing about Picasso's paintings. "Ahh," said one, "perhaps the esthetic and philosophic understanding is lost in words."

"Ahh," said somebody else, "the vitality is almost more than I can bear. . . ."

They were going around the table, one by one; they would get to me soon. I could feel myself getting hot with embarrassment. I had seen some of those distorted (to me) things of Picasso's with the eyes all crooked, the nose where the ear should be. . . .

"Evelyn?" John's voice was mellow. "And what do you think?"

"M-maybe he's pulling our leg," I blurted. "I mean, aren't those funny-looking people jokes?"

Silence fell with a thud. Someone cleared his throat. "Well, ye-es," Ms. Potter murmured, "I suppose that's one way to . . ." Her pleasure at my gaffe was ill-disguised. "Shall we have coffee?" she said, rising, leaving me to stew in my ignorance.

My inning came later.

We asked her to dinner at the Chambord on Third Avenue the following week. Just the three of us; we were going on to a gallery opening afterward.

Gallery crawling was one of John's favorite pastimes. Himself a painter manqué, he loved nothing better than to stroll the streets of New York (Paris, London, Rome) and to wander into this showing or that.

He had had a hard day. Opening night was getting close and he was working long hours. We had been to a cocktail party before picking up the Potter woman, where John had had at least three vodka and tonics.

John drank. I mean *a lot*. No alcoholic, just a person who could—and did—put a monumental amount of booze away on occasion (with accompanying monumental hangover). Something to do, he firmly believed, with his Irish background. By the time we reached the restaurant he was, as they say, feeling no pain. With another drink before dinner and a bottle of wine with, he was tilting, with the Cheshire Cat grin I was to recognize as a sign of his being pickled. He waxed sentimental. "I love my girl," he told Pauline, throwing an arm around my shoulders. "I'm just crazy about my girl here."

"How nice," murmured Pauline, as if a foul odor had wafted by.

Drunk or sober, I was glad to hear these things from John, especially in front of Pauline. "We'd best be going, John," she told him, "or else we'll be too late."

Outside, the three of us stood on the curb, John in the middle, an arm around each of us as he hailed a cab.

One stopped. He opened the door. Taking Pauline's elbow, he guided her in. And shut the door after her. "Good night, Pauline," he said.

Her puzzled face peered out. "But John!" she exclaimed, "we were going on to—"

"Good night, Pauline darling," John said firmly. "Talk to you tomorrow."

Pointy daggers in my direction let me know where the blame for this deviation was being placed. Without waiting for the cab to take off, John tucked an arm through mine and started walking down the street. "Little place down here," he said, "used to go there during the war. Like to see it again."

After three or four blocks we turned into a broken-down looking bar with the Irish name of O'Something. Sawdust crunched under our feet as we made our way to a long mahogany bar. A man or two draped on it. Others sat at tables spaced amid the sawdust. Not a woman in sight. They were a scruffy lot, leather jackets, open-necked shirts. They looked rough; they looked tough. John was in no condition to handle any of them.

We took places at the bar; I climbed on a stool, John stood alongside. He ordered a *double* vodka. Oh God, I thought, this is it, a famous Huston spree like the one that ended in the garden with Errol, or the one John told about when he "borrowed" an army car to take somebody a birthday cake.

"What'll it be, lady?" the bartender asked.

"Nothing. No, not a thing." Stay sober. You have to play nursemaid to a little boy six foot three.

John leaned against the bar, wearing his Cheshire smile, and looked around the room. "Used to come here," he said, "every time I was in town."

A man got up from one of the tables and came over to us. "Mind 'f have one more?" he said, looking straight at me.

It startled me. "Uh, I don't mind, but maybe you better ask the bartender."

"What'll it be, Mac," said the bartender, "more of the same?"

I looked at John for help, but he was looking across me at the man, seriously nodding as if giving approval for the transaction of drink to man.

The man's shoulder nudged mine. "Y'know my wife?" His breath was boozy.

"No, of course not, how could I—"

"Sweet li'l woman." His wallet was coming out. "Here. Look." He shoved the photograph at me. Mrs. Five by Five smiled toothily at me.

Bangs and blonde. Trying to look like Lana with an extra sixty pounds.

"Very pretty," I told him. John had leaned across me to take a look. "Fine woman," he said, giving his blessing.

"That's my boy there with her."

"Thought it might be," agreed John.

Tears came to the man's eyes. "They're home," he said, his voice breaking, "waitin' for me, and here I am, in a bar, drinkin' up the money."

"Tsk, tsk," said John, looking as if he approved drinking up the money too.

I said, "Why don't you go on home?"

He ignored us both, openly weeping then. "Tha's my boy. Greates' little guy you ever saw, and here I am, in a bar, drinkin' up. . . ."

So much for rough and tough. John, who had ordered another drink, began sinking lower and lower on the bar, until his face was level with mine. "John," I ventured, "why don't we just go along home?"

Using his elbows, John raised himself to his full height and sort of swiveled around to face the room. His gaze swept the place like a lighthouse beacon. Then he cocked an eyebrow at a precarious angle. "Usually," he said, "I fight my way out of these places."

It was very funny, the way he said it. I laughed. Fortunately so did he. "Help me home, Honey," he said.

Where are the cabs when you need them? The night was chill. We started walking across town, John more or less striding along. "Fresh air," he said with a show of vigor, "good for you."

"Only for the pickled," I muttered, not too unkindly. I was freezing. We were approaching Madison when John said, "I have to pee."

"So do I," I responded, "Thank God there's a cab." I stepped off the curb to hail the approaching vehicle. Behind me I heard the sound of running water. I looked around to see John unzipped, his manly disposal out, baptizing the rear of St. Patrick's Cathedral.

When we got to the hotel, John handed the driver a hundred dollar bill. "Keep the change," he said.

CHAPTER 22...

"I guess I'll have to change . . .

my . . . plan. . . ."

I recalled that Paulette Goddard was in New York at the same time, which was fortunate for me. I liked Paulette as much as I didn't like Pauline Potter. In fact I was a Paulette Goddard fan. I adored her sparkle, her infectious laughter and joie de vivre, her ability to gather such men as Charlie Chaplin, Aldous Huxley and John Steinbeck in her web and make them happy while they were there.

I copied everything she did, even her laugh. It annoyed John. He told me in no uncertain terms to stop it, that one Paulette Goddard in the world was enough. Perhaps what I should have copied was her acquisitive talent. Not only did she have plenty of diamonds and emeralds picked up from some man or other, she had also gathered in a fine collection of paintings, of the Modigliani and Renoir genre. (Generosity for her did not always operate the other way around: one Christmas I gave her some perfume; she responded by sending over a half-eaten turkey.)

We shopped. Shopped, shopped, shopped. She and Burgess Meredith had a house in the country where we often spent weekends when John had time. But no matter how busy he was, he found time to go to the racetrack, and even taught me how to read the racing form.

And there was Pauline Potter's fashion show at Hattie Carnegie's. John, Walter and I went. My father-in-law gave me an exquisite ball gown from the collection: black lace with red satin beneath. I was very pleased, not only because of the gift but also because it appeared to me that he actually considered me a legitimate member of the Huston family.

About John I wasn't so sure. Sometimes he was seemingly devoted (he would get a baby shot) and then he wouldn't show up at all, and when he did he might bring along yet another ex-girl for me to meet. (No shot.) He seemed to have an endless supply, all attractive.

Opening night, November 26, 1946, rolled around with its limousines, jewels, furs, celebrities, critics, police on horseback holding back the crowds, and jittery nerves. Then finally, afterward, the big party—at Millicent Astor's—and waiting up for the reviews. The play was an artistic if not box-office success, enough to preserve John's reputation as a big talent, and you can't have everything. (It won the New York Drama Critics Circle Award.)

The only sour note was Pauline Potter, our costume designer who had done the clothes for the play. She had requested two extra tickets two hours before curtain for Hattie Carnegie. John had got them, a superhuman task, but Pauline and her escort had been set to go with us, and now squeezing two more into the limousine was going to be impossible. Also, we had to get there early. "Call Pauline," John said, already tying his black tie, "tell her the tickets are at the box office in her name and tell her to get there on her own steam, and we'll see her later at the party."

I too was hurriedly getting into evening dress, so I merely repeated John's words, without softening, without further interpretation, ". . . your own steam, and we'll see you at the party."

I could feel the chill through the wire, heard the "I see" and the click. Bitch, I thought, he got you the bloody tickets. "She didn't like that, John," I told him.

"She understands," muttered John, already into the coming ordeal.

But I knew she was pissed off at not going with John, and it became clearer at intermission when I saw her across the lobby and waved, and she looked the other way. I thought, fuck you, Pauline, and forgot her.

I wasn't reminded of her until the following Sunday.

We were resting in our hotel after the hullabaloo, catching up on sleep, mail, the *New York Times*. A gray day at first, the sun came out in the afternoon. All at once the streets below looked festive.

"What do you say," said John, "we go for a walk."

"Terrific!" I loved walking the New York streets with John, my latest professor. He examined every window: paintings, furniture, vases, china, tapestries, and told me what they were, where they came from, and when. A splendid way to go to school—better than attending UCLA.

John was putting on a niftily tailored suit of soft brown, a silk maroon tie with a pearl stickpin yet, and was placing a derby hat on his head at a rakish angle. "John," I said, "why are you getting so dressed up for a walk?"

"This is the correct thing to wear," he told me, rather prissily, "on Sunday afternoon in New York."

I, not wanting to be found lacking in these little etiquettes, slipped into a basic black. When in doubt, I figured.

I didn't know we were headed for Pauline Potter's house until John turned down her street. "Oh John," I said, "Pauline won't be glad to see me." She hadn't called since the opening.

He rang the bell. "It's John, Honey," he announced to the speaker. I noticed he had left out my name.

She greeted us from the top of the stairs. Him, actually, she was good at that sliding-away-of-the-eyes trick. One would hardly know if one didn't know.

John, at her invitation, went to make drinks. She immediately left the room, reappearing the moment he did. You had to admire her timing. John's properly chilled martinis showed he knew his way around there. "Cheers," he said, or some such. We sat—they on the sofa, I on a chair across the room.

The smallest talk I ever heard followed (from them, not me). Critics so unfair! A good Sunday piece, though. How is Barry? Nin? Milly? Nice exhibition of Tchelitchew's, yes? "Pauline." John paused and took a sip. A master of timing setting up his drama. "Pauline, you've got this opening night business all wrong—"

She stiffened immediately as if sprayed by lacquer. "I'd rather not talk about it."

"We must, Pauline." He tilted toward her. "You've simply misunderstood—"

"I've misunderstood nothing!" She had risen. John got to his feet too. I was still seated. The talk went back and forth over my head, like a tennis match. Had they forgotten my presence?

"You asked me for two extra tickets—"

"John, really, I'd rather not—"

"You must listen to me. Evelyn did exactly as I asked her to do."

"That's hard to believe. You would never—"

"She is not to blame—"

"—never be rude, John, it is not like you—"

"Pauline! You are not hearing—"

"This—person is allowed in our houses, John, only because of you. . . ."

We had got to the nitty gritty. I was stunned. Their voices went on, John's smooth as honey, Pauline's stiff and tight. It hadn't much to do with me. Who were these—strangers, in their correct-wear-for-Sunday?

I got to my feet, unnoticed, and walked to the door. I opened it, quite calmly, descended the steps, quite calmly, and was out on the street before the flood broke. I started to run, sobs choking me. Reaching Lexington Avenue I frantically waved for a taxi.

It seemed centuries before one came along, the yellow light on top shining like the Star in the East through the rain of my tears. It stopped. I started to get in. To my consternation, John and Pauline were inside. Had they finally realized I had left? But there they were, two people I never wanted to see again as long as I lived.

I started to run. John leaped out and grabbed my wrist. It became a farce; he got back in the cab, dragging me in after him.

So the three of us were jammed in the cab's back seat, Pauline and I, with John in the middle. "I won't do it," she said, "I absolutely refuse."

"You must apologize, Pauline, it is not her fault!"

"Never!"

Nothing had changed except from room to taxi. On and on they went while I plotted escape and the lights of New York sailed past in a blur.

"Oh, all right!" Pauline snapped finally, "if you insist—I'll apologize!" Her tone would have wilted a rattlesnake in California.

John turned to me, triumphant. "There!" he exclaimed. "You have an apology. Say you accept."

"I accept," I muttered, "in exactly the spirit she has given it."

"You see!" cried Pauline, "there is no speaking to this . . . this . . ."

"Now, Pauline," John's impatience was beginning to show, "she's right, your manner is not exactly—"

"You shouldn't ask me to . . ."

I thought seriously of screaming.

When we got to the hotel, I leaped from the cab, raced upstairs and locked myself in the only safe place I could think of: the bathroom. I wanted quiet. I wanted peace. I wanted rid of them forever.

But it was not to be. The voices entered the suite, babbled on and on while my tears dried and my outrage subsided. It's a serious failing of mine, that I am never able to hold on to outrage for longer than ten minutes.

It grew quiet out there. Then there was a scratching on the door. "Evelyn . . ." Pauline. God, was I never to be rid of her? "John's left, Evelyn, please come out."

Left? What ploy was this? I opened the door. She stood there alone. "Where is John?" I asked.

"He got angry and went out because we wouldn't make up."

We wouldn't make up! Indeed. I had a great suggestion. "Then why don't you run along too, Pauline?"

She actually looked repentant. "We must make up, Evelyn. For John's sake."

She was one hundred percent right about my inferior breeding. I didn't have any class. If I had, I would have punched her in the nose right then and there. Instead I weaseled out. "Okay," I said, "for John's sake. . . ."

CHAPTER 23...

"South of the border . . .
down Mexico way . . ."

John's next picture was to be *Treasure of the Sierra Madre*, from the book of that title written by a man named B. Traven.

B. Traven was a man of mystery. Although John had corresponded with him while writing the script, he had never seen him. No one had. Since no one knew anything about him, rumor ran wild: that Traven wasn't his real name; that he was on the lam, but from the good guys or the bad wasn't clear; that he was European, but what nationality was anybody's guess.

What was known was that he was a sensitive and perceptive writer and that he lived in Mexico, presumably deep in the jungle somewhere near Acapulco. He received his mail at a post office box in that resort town.

Back from New York and with the shooting for *Treasure* scheduled for the spring, John decided to go down to Mexico to case some possible locations and to see Mr. Traven, if he could. He had written requesting a meeting, but Traven had replied that he himself wouldn't be able to make it. However, his secretary, Hal Croves, who knew as much about his work as he himself did, would be available. It was a small step nearer to the real thing, someone who actually knew the mystery man.

I wanted to go along, and Paulette Goddard agreed to join us. I had never been to Mexico (hadn't been much of anywhere, the war had got in the way) whereas Paulette was practically a native. Rumor had it she had had a fling with one of their presidents, but what did I know. She sported a mammoth gold filigreed watch that indicated *somebody* Mexican had been interested. She knew Diego Rivera, the painter. And she knew the owner of Mexico City's Plaza de Toros (bullring), which was where we headed first.

Mexico, with its vivid colors, quickened pace, new sounds, was exciting. At the Plaza, after buying bouquets of flowers (arranged in a special shape for bullfights), we went to visit the famed matador, Manolete, in his dressing room and had our pictures taken with him in his fabulous suit of lights.

I went to the *corrida* not judging or moralizing, but trying to view it through my hosts' eyes. Had not Hemingway written that the bull lives a fine free life up to the moment he enters the ring? And that he goes out in style within fifteen glorious minutes? Compare this, Hemingway wrote, to zoos, where we lock up proud beasts—lions, tigers, gorillas—in small cages and doom them to a slow and miserable death. That, he said, was cruelty. The fighting bull has a perfect life—and death.

He hadn't prepared me for the rivers of blood that poured from the bull's shoulder after he had been pierced repeatedly by banderillas and pics. And though he wrote that the horses were a necessary part of the spectacle, I hadn't expected the sadness of these pitiful nags, who seemed to know they were expendable.

Fortunately, Manolete's greatness made me look past the gore to his style: his arching arrogant back, his incredibly graceful cape, as he taunted his two-thousand-pound adversary to get him if he could. (One did, the following year.)

Paulette threw her bouquet to him when he made his triumphant walk around the ring. She made me save mine for the other matador. I knew what she was up to; she wanted him to dedicate the next bull to her. He didn't. And when we saw him later in a restaurant, he passed our table without looking in our direction. Even Paulette couldn't win them all.

Afterwards, the three of us took a small plane to Acapulco. As we touched down on the dirt landing strip along the ocean's edge, a tire blew, spinning the plane about and just missing dumping us into the sea—a near-grim reminder of that afternoon's flirtation with death.

The man who presented himself at the hotel was small, no taller than I, with pale, pale hair that blended with his pale skin. His eyes were blue and small, his nose large. "Hal Croves, I am," he said vigorously in excellent English. "Señor Traven has asked me to come to you." The accent was hard to define.

He and John went off to have their story meeting, and Paulette and I went off to frolic. We swam, soaked up sun, saw part of a jai-alai game, and later, because John was still busy, had dinner together on the starlit roof of our hotel. We watched Lana Turner dancing with Tyrone Power, in the first throes of a love affair. We were jealous; we only had each other.

The next day John insisted on going fishing. "That's what Acapulco is all about, honey, all the rest is nonsense." He insisted that Hal Croves come along, saying they could talk as well on a boat as in a hotel room. Paulette would have no part of it. So the three of us climbed aboard the fishing charter, I in white shorts, John in old army khakis, and Croves in a proper suit and tie. Fishing evidently was not his bag, nor were boats. He declined the offer of a rod, so John and I each took one and settled aft with our lines following in the wake of the boat.

John, it seems, had been searching for marlin all his life, without any success, not even a nibble.

Hours went by. The hot sun bore down. Croves kept in the shade, but his fair skin turned bright pink anyhow. He and John talked spasmodically. John wasn't really interested; his eyes were skimming the dip and shift of the waters behind him.

No fish appeared. Hour after hour. I had handed my rod over to the captain so that I could stretch, but John hadn't budged. Finally in the late afternoon he felt the need to straighten out the kinks and asked Croves to hold his line for just a moment. "Oh no no," said Croves, "I have never done anything like that."

"Nothing to it, Hal," John's resonant voice insisted, "do you good." He placed the rod in Croves' hands, rose, and guided the smaller man to the fishing chair he had just quitted.

John started to walk down the deck.

At that instant, a marlin struck.

The biggest, goddamnedest fish anybody had ever seen. A veritable Moby Dick of marlins. It leaped from the water, shot straight upward near on to a mile, on the end of John's/Croves' line.

Croves, aghast, let go. Of everything. Of rod, of line, of fish. Swish! In a flash everything vanished, was gone gone gone. Everything.

John turned white beneath the day's accumulation of sun. His hands gripped the back of the chair, the knuckles vivid white. I thought poor Croves was going to faint. "Oh, John, I am so sorry, oh! Now look here, John, I told you, I never—Oh I am so sorry. . . ."

John's control was superb, I mean, he didn't throttle the man, or anything. "It's all right, Hal, it's quite all right, it wasn't your fault, not in the least. . . ." John's eyes raised up and looked out over the sea. He shook his head. "But oh," he said softly, "what a big son of a bitch that was." Then he turned to reassure the yelping captain that he would be reimbursed for his lost equipment.

We caught two sailfish on the way back, one each. But it wasn't the same.

At the dock when a photographer rushed up to take a picture of us and our catch, John invited Croves to stand with us. "No no," he hastily backed away, "it is only the tourist that makes the pictures."

We thought he was being reticent because he had made such a fiasco of the marlin. We were headed back to the hotel before John remembered how the man had signed the ship's log: H. Croves. With just the initial for the first name. Exactly the way B. Traven always signed his name.

Soon afterward, we returned to Hollywood. Then in April, when filming was to commence, John and I flew south again, this time accompanied by Humphrey Bogart who was in the picture, his wife Betty, and my father-in-law Walter, also in the cast.

The location site chosen was a spa named San José de Perua, just west of Mexico City in the state of Michoacán. It had a hotel large enough for cast and crew, and the surrounding terrain, beautiful and rugged, was ideal gold-seeking territory, which the script required. The tiny village of Jungapeo, which could be used as a movie set, was nearby.

The hotel rambled carelessly around a hill, the rooms large and airy. It sported bowling alleys, swimming pool, and private baths where one could enjoy the mineral waters the spa was famous for. (John and I tried them one Sunday, sitting naked together on the steps in a little tiled cubicle, the water up to our chins while bubbles slowly formed over our bodies and we grew quite warm. I don't know if it improved our health, but it was quite a turn-on.)

While the men worked all day, Betty and I would hang around the set, sunbathe near the swimming pool, or succumb to the great all-American pastime of shopping. After dinner the four of us—Bogarts and Hustons—repaired to the bowling lanes to live it up with a game or two. Every so often Bogie would utter the only two Spanish words he thought worth learning, "Dos Equis," a Mexican beer. His hair was falling out in chunks, although it would grow back later. (I think he was getting hormone shots too.) His head looked like a mangy dog's, but he never wore a hat to cover it up the way another actor might have. It's as if he were saying, this is who I am, like it or not. It was very winning.

Betty, too, had the same straightforwardness—the yin to his yang. I liked her. I liked her looks and ways and I envied Bogie's devotion to her. She seemed even then to have a clearer idea of what she wanted than I did. (As the years proved.) She called John "The Monster," as did all his friends, with affection, to be sure. But still, it should have been a clue.

There were other famous guests staying at the hotel: Paulette's friend, Diego Rivera, sat outside every day with his easel and canvas and paints vibrant and hot in little pots rather than tubes. There was Maria Felix, the most famous of all Mexican movie stars outside of Cantínflas. She was very beautiful, with long black hair and enormous black eyes. She behaved early Theda Bara, sweeping into a room looking neither right nor left, a retinue trailing her, which included a tiny composer of a husband, Augustin Lara. Bogie, our own movie-star-in-residence, was amused by her attitude and persuaded us to play a little joke on her.

Practical jokes were part and parcel of the Huston–Bogart circle. Sometimes witty, more often plain foolish, they were designed to relieve the tension of work and keep pomposity at a minimum. To take yourself too seriously was a sign of weakness, a grave flaw that was sure to bring Bogie's—or John's—quick mockery upon your head. Ms. Felix's overblown stance asked for it.

At dinnertime, Bogie gathered together Betty, Tim Holt, Walter Huston, John and me and had us line up at her table to ask for her autograph. She never acknowledged anybody's presence and merely scribbled irritably on the pieces of paper we stuck under her nose, without looking up. Until Bogie came along. He pushed the paper at her so forcefully he knocked her elbow off the table. "Scuse me, ma'am," he said in unmistakable Bogartese, "real sorry about that, ma'am."

She stalked out in a fury, and left town. One can assume we've been on her shitlist ever since, her pomposity intact.

Bogie got his comeuppance in a scene in the picture in which he has to reach under a rock—for hidden gold—and is told by the other actor that a gila monster just crawled there. John had put a mousetrap where Bogie had to reach. Bogie, thinking gila monster, jumped twelve feet when the mousetrap snapped on his finger.

This, then, was the ambiance Hal Croves walked into. Only of course it was B. Traven himself. He gave himself away in countless ways, saying "I" when it should have been "he," using phrases similar to those he used in his letters to John. But for reasons known only to himself, he preferred to play out his mystery man role, even to the tune of taking the job as technical adviser at $150 a week as Croves, when he could have had the $1,000 offered Traven.

Apparently he thought he could maintain his privacy as Croves and still have the pleasure of seeing his baby come to life in a film. And perhaps he could have if he hadn't suffered from the same unforgivable flaw as Maria: He took himself super-seriously.

John admired Traven's works tremendously but became most intolerant when Traven began showing up in the dining room every night —and here's the crime—with lifts in his heels, trying to bring up his height to maybe five feet six. It seems he had fallen for the very tall and very buxom blonde wife of one of the Mexican assistants, and he came to the lower part of her ample bosom. He was, unfortunately, a little ridiculous.

John pounced with glee. First he had the crew pointing cameras at the little man, which made him jump like a startled deer. Of course they took endless photos when he didn't know, adding further reason to keep him the figure of fun. And John, really evil, would ask him, in front of the entire company, all sorts of silly, outrageous questions on how to handle the filming, advice on various scenes, etc. The observers would snicker behind their hands when Croves/Traven tried in all earnestness to answer.

He must have caught on that he was being made a fool of, because a few years later, after John and I had separated, Croves looked me up at the Beverly Hills Hotel where I was staying. He wanted to talk about what a terrible man John was. I suppose he thought since we were apart that I would agree. Instead I tried to explain John to him. "Oh, he can be rough," I told him, "but he's just trying to cut us all down to size. The thing is not to let him get your goat. Give it back to him in kind. John's the first to laugh if he's the butt of the joke."

Croves/Traven didn't care for my explanation. I never heard from him again.

After awhile Bogie began to nag John because the shooting was taking longer than scheduled. Bogie wanted it finished in time to race his boat, *The Santana,* in the annual Fourth of July sprint to Honolulu.

John took it good-naturedly, smiling enigmatically and not answering. He wasn't about to rush his first picture after a four-year absence in the war. After several of his Dos XX Bogie would push his case harder. "Out to make a fuckin' masterpiece, right, John?" he would say. And John would smile agreeably. "Jesus," Bogie would mutter, "you're turning this into a goddamn marathon." John would smile.

As time got shorter, so did Bogie's patience. He even lost a necessary quality around John—humor. "For crissake, John," he growled one night, "just how much longer is this miserable picture going to take?"

Still smiling agreeably, John reached across the table, took Bogie's nose between two fingers, and twisted. Hard. Tears came to Bogie's eyes, but he didn't flinch, didn't try to pull away.

He never brought up the subject of delay again. The boat race went without him.

My turn came when I bought a bright Mexican print skirt of coarsely woven cotton with a separate top that was—well, brief. Not much more than a glorified bra, its deep round neckline plunged to the edge of my bosom, and its lower boundary left the midriff quite bare. Of course nothing could be worn under it. Very Carmen. All I needed were castanets.

The trouble was that when I leaned forward, my breasts bounced into view. John wasn't pleased. "For God's sake, take that thing off," he muttered, "I don't want to see it on you again."

But I loved the outfit. I would just remember not to lean forward.

A couple of nights later I put it on again. I was waiting in our room, all dressed up for dinner, when John came home from work.

He didn't say hello, didn't smile. He didn't even frown. All he did was reach out, take hold of the brief top, and rip it in two. "Put on something, honey," he said, "and let's go to dinner."

I was the first one to leave the fun and games. Columbia actually sent me a script I couldn't turn down. Another with Glenn Ford, a comedy called *The Mating of Millie*. The night before I left, John brought home a large bundle of grass—two pounds of pure Acapulco Gold that he had picked up in the village where he had been shooting. He claimed it was the town crop, that all two hundred villagers had been turned on all day.

We didn't know exactly what to do with it. None of us had had any experience with the funny weed, and if you were found with it they shut you up and threw away the key.

Nevertheless, some of us gathered in our room. You never know if you don't try. Only I got chicken. I said I had better watch, that somebody had to play nursemaid if needed.

A visiting writer friend, Charley Grayson, John, and my father-in-law, Walter, plunged in. They proceeded to empty the tobacco out of three cigarettes and stuff them with this new green stuff. One for each of them, that's how much they knew.

For the next five minutes they sat silently, puffing away furiously, all their concentration on the intake of smoke, at twice the speed with which they would smoke an ordinary cigarette.

After awhile Walter looked at Charley. "I don't—feel anything yet," he said solemnly, "do you?"

Charley shook his head. "Not a thing."

John, finished with the first cigarette, made himself another and started furiously pulling in smoke to the bottom of his lungs and jetting it out again.

Walter tilted toward Charley. "Anything yet?"

Charley, puzzled, shook his head. "Nope." He tilted toward Walter. At this angle the two men were slanting toward each other in a sort of tent shape, peering into each other's eyes, suspended there. Then Walter laughed. And Charley laughed. They stopped for a moment and then burst into laughter again.

Then I caught on, not so much because they were laughing foolishly but because they were frozen in this funny tilt and couldn't seem to move out of it.

John, meanwhile, paid no attention, a veritable smokestack in the corner. All at once he stood up. He froze there, suspended. He took one stiff step and froze again, like those long-legged birds who wade in water looking for fish. "How much time has passed?" he asked.

"What do you mean?" I said. "From what to what?"

His head swung to me. With effort he focused and froze again. "From . . . ." He never finished. He had turned to stone.

I got up, concerned. "Are you all right, John?"

"No," he said, turning the color of the grass.

"Maybe you should sit down," I said, "if you don't feel well."

"How . . . much time has passed—since you—spoke?" His eyes seemed to be trying to anchor to mine.

"No time, John, I just spoke."

"Days . . . like . . . days. . . ."

Walter and Charley thought it was the funniest thing they had ever heard. They laughed and laughed, while John turned greener and greener.

Alarmed, I ran for the company doctor. I told him what had happened, which made him laugh too. He gave John something to balance things out, and John went to bed and slept like a piece of granite. I stuck two pounds of illicit weed (minus four cigarettes worth) in a bag of mine, forgot it was there, and unwittingly smuggled it into the States. If an industrious official had opened my bags, would he have believed the truth? In any event, I quickly destroyed the stuff. John's experience had scared me off.

CHAPTER 24 . . .

"I guess I'll have to change my plan . . ."

Back from Mexico, I rattled around in the house and was pampered by the help for a few days. Then enchanting Walter Huston finished his acting chores and joined me. We had two pleasant weeks together, just the two of us. He was good company after my long day's work, amusing, concerned, peaceful. And one night he gave me the best acting lesson I ever had.

We were listening to an album he had made with some other stars, a patriotic effort in which each of them performed a poem, song or a piece from a play. Walter was best. "Why," I asked him, "is yours better than the others?"

He knew it was a serious question, not a silly compliment, and took a good hour to answer it seriously. He played the record over and over to demonstrate his point. He would play his section, then the others. "This voice," he explained (it was Bing Crosby, I think), "comes to a period before the period is there."

"What exactly do you mean, Walter?"

"A period comes only at the end of a sentence, does it not?" He leaned forward. "A period is indicated by dropping the voice, and mustn't be done in the middle of the phrase, the way this fellow has." He paused. "It is with the voice that we actors indicate the punctuation of a sentence and since the period comes only at the end, we must be careful not to let our voice infer that we have completed what we are saying before we are ready to relinquish the attention of our audience. There are commas, colons, semicolons, dashes, and even question marks, all to be observed—with a lilt, with a sustained inflection. . . ." He demonstrated as he talked, keeping me dangling in midair, hanging onto his every word.

It was a grand moment.

John phoned in the middle of it.

How happy I was. I felt loved. Wonderful Walter giving so generously of his time, his vast store of knowledge. And John, my husband, calling me. He had even written to say he had missed me. Finally, slowly, I was beginning to feel as if I might be married after all. "We've finished shooting," John was telling me. He and the rest of the company would be returning to Warner Brothers to finish the picture.

"You're coming home, then?" I cried happily.

"Not for a couple of days. I'm—arranging a surprise for you."

"A surprise?" I cried, "Oh, I love surprises!" I hung up, feeling how good life was.

"Evelyn," Walter's voice called behind me. I turned, beaming. "Yes?"

He patted the cushion on the sofa beside him. "Come sit down. I think I'd just better tell you what the surprise is. You remember the boy, Pablo, the one around the set all the time?"

"Sure. Of course I do."

Pablo was a young Indian boy who had attached himself to the company. He was very attractive, about twelve or so, with an alive, smiling face, bright black eyes, intelligence shining through. And he had made himself useful, fetching Cokes or chairs when needed, cleverly anticipating needs. When it was learned that he was an orphan, sleeping in doorways, surviving as best he could, he became a sort of mascot. John put him on the payroll; he in turn hired other kids to work for him. Pablo was most resourceful and John was quite taken with him. Just how much I was about to learn from Walter.

"John is arranging to adopt him. That is what this delay is about."

"I see."

I stared at Walter. He looked back at me, making no further comment. I can only guess at his reasons for telling me of the "surprise." He probably figured a wife ought to have something to say about adopting a child.

My heart sank with a thud, then rose in outrage. What a lunatic move! I wasn't even ready for a baby, much less a practically grown boy. He might have asked me how *I* felt, he might have considered me—

The thought was cut off by a sharp and sudden stab of guilt. How could I even consider *not* giving this boy a home, this poor orphan, going hungry and cold, scrounging in doorways, all alone. John is so kind and I am a selfish monster. I scraped a smile together and exclaimed, "Oh Walter! How wonderful! How very exciting!"

But I didn't feel very married any more. . . .

I met John at the plane and tried to show sufficient surprise at the kid holding onto his hand. Pablo was a slight youngster, under five feet, with straight black hair and olive skin; mournful big eyes looked out from under a Mexican sombrero ten times his size, evidently a purchase of John's. He was hobbling painfully, wearing shoes for the first time in his life. He probably thought blisters were part of the package.

And he looked absolutely dazed. No wonder. He had never been outside his native village of Jungapeo in his entire life. He spoke no English, and now he had got in one of those big things that fly like a bird and come all the way to Gringoland, with these strange people who spoke strange words, not one of which he understood.

John's Spanish was nonexistent, mine was limited in those days to how-are-you, how-much, where-is, good day-good afternoon. Not much to keep a conversation going. We all smiled at each other a great deal on the ride to the ranch.

I did understand when he said *café con leche* when I asked if he would like something *beber*, pleased that we were communicating, pleased that he drank *some* milk, even if it was only a drop in coffee. He was small for twelve, so we knew he must be lying when he told us he was sixteen. A dentist and a doctor could tell us his exact age, we decided. In any event, the boy should be checked out thoroughly, to ascertain his state of health.

There was much to do to get Pablo, our little primitive, ready to join our "civilized" American way of life, including what a toilet was for. And once he got the hang of *that,* how to flush it. Then there were clothes to buy, appointments to be made. And who was delegated to the job?

Right.

Pablo's very first English word was "mo-ther." He followed me about like a docile puppy. Even when the dentist poked about, he patiently endured, watching me with baleful eyes. I held his hand and said, *"Será mejor."* The dentist put his age at thirteen. So did the doctor. "You are *trece,"* I told him. *"Muy bien,* mo-ther," he answered, grinning.

There is no doubt that Pablo had never seen a woman treated as I was, as a leading lady is, on a movie set: catered to, followed by a retinue, pampered and petted like a queen. I can only guess at what he thought. I do know he was happy to do anything I asked of him without question.

Gradually I picked up a little more Spanish and he began to learn English (more important) during his days spent on my set at Columbia or John's at Warner Brothers. One day Pablo and I ran into Orson Welles on the lot. After I introduced them Orson asked Pablo, *"Tiene soledad?",* then asked me if that was how you said, are you homesick. But Pablo, with a broad smile, answered Orson, *"Sí, sí."*

We found a school in Ojai Valley that would be able to cope with the language difficulty, and also with where he was scholastically—if anywhere. He would live there, coming home for weekends—and it wasn't one minute too soon.

An odd (or maybe not so odd) development had come to pass in this John-made, mother-son relationship. Clinging to me as if I were his anchor in an unfathomable sea, Pablo always sat as near to me as possible, even on the same chair, if he could. The first time he touched my breasts I thought it was an accident. But when it was repeated again and again, I realized he knew what he was doing. At every opportunity he would snuggle close and flick my nipples with his finger, grinning at me all the while.

Since my Freudian awareness was coming into being, I didn't knock his hand away, thinking it best not to scar him anymore than we and life had already done. Instead I would pretend I wanted something on the other side of the room. Or endure it as if it weren't happening. It was a relief when the school term started. I wasn't up to thirteen(?)-year-old Mexican boys who called me mother while twiddling with my boobs.

I wondered if John—we—really did him any good. It sounds advantageous when you talk about it. You find a kid at the tender age of thirteen scuffling to keep life and limb together, no home to go to. You take him in hand, you feed and clothe him, fix his teeth, give him an education. Sounds really okay. Except everything has been mentioned but love.

Some years later I was renting Anatole Litvak's beach house at Malibu and Pablo came to see me. He was bigger—not too much— eighteen (?) years old and able to speak a heavily accented English. I had been in Europe and out of touch, so he was telling me about himself: He had enrolled in agricultural college and drove a jeep to school. "I've got a girl, too," he said, and then added, "she's a Mex, like me."

My heart constricted. His choice of word, the tone that went with it, so clearly implied that minorities must stick together.

Is that what John and I had given Pablo? The privilege of knowing prejudice?

CHAPTER 25...

> "My country . . . 'tis of thee . . .
> sweet land of li—berty . . ."

My presence and Pablo's in John's life hadn't made much change in the way John conducted himself. He continued to live like a bachelor, which included the company of females any time he felt like it.

And yet I hung around. Tensed up, on edge, like a horse in the starting gate, I was poised to run. But I didn't. Why? My unconscious prevented me, I suppose. But also, I was stuck on the guy. I mean I had a big crush on my husband. And anyway, most of the time our life was exhilarating.

By the time our first anniversary rolled around, our household had grown considerably. Besides a "son," the Burgess Merediths had given us a burro after the completion of *Treasure;* from a pair of big pigs a litter of small ones came forth and they had the run of the place, their curly-cue tails at full mast. Cats increased and multiplied. Somebody gave us a goat, somebody else a white shepherd dog to add to the assortment already present. A couple of thoroughbred brood mares were purchased and properly knocked up—John was determined to get into the horse racing business—and we had to find proper living quarters for the expectant mothers.

We purchased another ranch further up the valley with stables on the grounds and not much else. Combining our names, we called it Keyston Ranch. I must confess: Left on my own I would never have owned a racing horse or any other kind of horse. But a healthy portion of my money went for horse feed all the same. I was to learn that a slow racehorse eats just as much as a fast racehorse. John tried to teach both Pablo and me to ride, jockey style, nose buried in the horse's neck. We were both disappointments: I sneezed my head off and Pablo fell off.

For actually making it through a whole year we gave ourselves a bang-up anniversary party. It was the best goddamn party I ever went to. We gave it in partnership with two other couples, both the men movie directors like John, the Lewis Milestones (All Quiet on the Western Front) having their tenth and the Jean Negulescos (Three Coins in the Fountain) having their first, also. We invited about two hundred guests, a star-writer-director-producer-mogul-studded cast, as usual.

Festivities began at ten o'clock in the evening, and there was a continuing buffet during the night, with rotating dishes from each couple: The Negulescos did a Roumanian dish of sauerkraut cured in champagne and caraway seeds called varza cu carne; the Milestones furnished ham with all the fixings. And the Huston cook whipped up a Mexican spread. Bars were set up on the front and back terraces, which was how the poor wisteria vine got done in.

My contribution was a dance band. Freddie Karger, the pianist, under contract to Columbia, had rehearsed The Jolson Story numbers with me. I asked him to get a group together for our party. It was such a smash success that night that he formed a permanent band and has been playing gatherings ever since (besides marrying and divorcing Jane Wyman). Freddie's music turned everybody on so, they danced and cavorted non-stop. The party caught fire, I mean, red hot. Somewhere along the line performers began performing spontaneously, for the sheer joy of doing what they did best: Judy Garland, Danny Kaye, Oscar Levant, and Frank Sinatra.

You can't have a rounded Hollywood party unless somebody dives in the pool in full evening dress. We had that. We also had an altercation of two women, one the wife, the other the girlfriend, squabbling over the husband—all three of them stars. The girlfriend reached in and pulled the falsies out of the wife's dress. And some people fell in love and some broke up, or did both, and nobody went home until daylight. Some didn't even leave then, so we served them eggs and bacon and lots of coffee and finally sent them on their way sober (hopefully) in the light of dawn.

Our town, at play. Reminiscent of Isherwood's *Berlin Stories,* of Sally Bowles and her friends carousing as the heavy beat of Nazi boots marching grows louder and louder in the background.

The House Un-American Activities Committee had been rumbling along in Washington for some time, looking for Reds, seeing them everywhere they turned, as if they on the Committee alone had the ultimate Word about who was a good American and who wasn't. If you didn't agree, you were mighty suspect. Their cause, they felt, was noble and people weren't enough aware of their valiant work. So how do you correct that? You get yourselves mixed up with movie personalities. You invite them to Washington to appear before you, or you go to Hollywood where half the press of the world hangs out. Soon you'll make headlines and have instant stardom. Richard Nixon was on that committee, and look what happened to him.

The month after our August shindig, HUAC turned its unseemly eyes west and began searching diligently for signs of communist monkey-business in such films as *Thirty Seconds Over Tokyo, Kitty Foyle, Best Years of Our Lives, Forever Amber, Meet Nero Wolfe,* and *Murder My Sweet.* They subpoenaed people right and left (no pun intended).

The heads of the studios, instead of closing ranks and protecting their own people—who had earned them millions of dollars—fell all over themselves declaring what good Americans *they* were. They all quickly agreed to purge their studios of anybody even suspected of having leftist leanings. It was all thoroughly illegal, but to say so in those days was to get labeled commie yourself (other names came into being, such as "pinko," "fellow traveler," and "pre-fascist"—meaning you had seen the light too early about the coming Nazi tide).

It was witch-hunt time.

HUAC succeeded in winning over the American public. For some lunatic reason, this country went hog-wild over anticommunism (like the hula hoop and skateboard).

When the investigation of the motion picture industry first began, John was very courageous. (He became less so later when the watchdogs of patriotism got to him, threatening him, too, with oblivion.) But that September, innocence still prevailing, he decided to do something about fighting back. He joined forces with Philip Dunne, the writer, William Wyler, the director, and Alexander Knox, the actor. Together they created the Committee for the First Amendment. Its purpose, in effect, was to remind the little band of ambitious congressmen that there was a First Amendment that guaranteed certain freedoms—speech, religion—which they, with their irresponsible poking around, were placing in serious jeopardy.

I was with John all the way. In short order more than five hundred people joined us, among whom were Humphrey Bogart and Betty Bacall, Gene Kelly and Betsy Blair, Danny Kaye, Katharine Hepburn, Burt Lancaster, Eddie Robinson, Jane Wyatt, Sterling Hayden, Paul Henreid, Charles Boyer, Ira Gershwin, Richard Conte, June Havoc, John Garfield, Gregory Peck, Henry Fonda, Kirk Douglas, Van Heflin, Eddie Cantor, Billy Wilder, Paulette Goddard, Burgess Meredith, Myrna Loy, Joseph Cotten, Fredric March, Melvyn Douglas, and Lucille Ball, among others. And then there were Thomas Mann and Albert Einstein, Norman Corwin and Leonard Bernstein and Helen Keller and Rabbi Stephen Wise. And on and on. Not exactly a motley bunch. And the membership kept growing.

Some of us chartered a plane, a biggie, and with much fanfare, flew off to Washington to complain to our congressman in person about these Un-American Activities Committee's shenanigans.

Innocent babes.

We faced a hostile, sophisticated, worldly press who made us look like stupid children interfering with grownup problems. When we entered the House hearing room, which looked like a movie set with its cameras, bright lights and star performers, the chairman, J. Parnell Thomas, switched the scheduled witness and brought on Hollywood writer John Howard Lawson, whom the Committee claimed was a bona fide, card-carrying member of the Communist Party. The purpose was to make us appear as Party members too, since we were clearly sympathetic toward Mr. Lawson. He was what the Committee called a "hostile witness," meaning somebody who took a strong stand against them and refused to answer their questions. Mr. Lawson was indeed hostile; these people were attacking everything he believed in and were taking away his livelihood.

When Lawson started to read his prepared speech, Mr. Thomas, not liking its contents, crashed his gavel downward, blasting through the microphone as if the Washington Monument itself were crashing to the ground. That thundering gavel blocking out freedom of speech was meant for us. For you and me.

Our First Amendment Committee was soon listed as a Communist Front Organization (whatever that meant), and the juggernaut rolled on, sending the likes of Dalton Trumbo, Academy Award winner, and Ring Lardner, Jr., to jail for not answering HUAC's illegal questions. And Larry Parks, my friend and co-worker from *The Jolson Story,* was finished off forever.

It was a sorry time in our history. It didn't matter that Mr. J. Parnell Thomas went to jail himself for defrauding his government, nor that the HUAC member who made it to the Oval Office was forced to resign some twenty-five years later. Lives, careers, and families had been destroyed. And it left a permanent scar on all of us —whether we know it or not.

CHAPTER 26...

"Jingle bells . . . jingle bells . . .
jingle all the way. . . ."

We closed our eyes like the rest of America and got on with our lives. Besides, Christmas was coming. Christmas was Bogie's birthday, and the Bogarts were throwing their annual Christmas Eve bash. Work at the studios came to a grinding halt very early in the afternoon and from then on it was drinking and kissing time.

Our plan for the day was this: John and I would attend our respective studio's gatherings to wish everyone a Merry One. Then I would go home to dress for the evening, and wrap presents. None of this store-packaged and store-sent. It wasn't the true Christmas spirit unless you personally wrapped each gift and delivered it in person. I would then meet John at Charley Grayson's house where he would be going for a drink after he left the studio. From there he would deliver presents to our friends before proceeding to the Bogarts. My plan entirely. But John had said, "Why not?" amusedly.

I wrapped the things beautifully, with the finest paper and ribbons. Then I got into one of Pauline Potter's little basic black numbers, my hair positively gorgeous, having had it done earlier at the studio. I pinned on a ruby here and there, donned my mink coat, piled the festive-looking array of packages in the car, and went to pick up my husband.

It was instantly apparent that we were in different gears. He was already well on the way to pinning one on, and I was cold sober. I was on a serious mission, in no mood for this clowning.

Besides Charley and John there were two girls—God knows I was used to that—strangers to me, and all four of them high. They were dancing, not together but in a row like a chorus line, and John had unzipped his fly and poked his finger through the opening, with this absurd grin on his face, looking for all the world like the proud possessor of the world's smallest penis. A glass brimming with booze was in the other hand.

I was not amused. "John!" I had to shout over the music. "Come along, you promised you'd go with me to deliver these presents."

"Anything you say, honey," he answered, dancing with that finger sticking out of his pants, wiggling in time to the music.

"Well, come on then." I started toward the door.

"S-so long, John, see you," Charley managed.

"Yeah," echoed one of the girls, "see you."

John followed me dutifully out to my car, the finger still hanging out of his pants, the drink in the other hand. His playmates had gathered at the door to wave him off.

My irritation blossomed to full anger. He was drunk too early, his attitude wasn't right, he was raining on my parade. "Oh for God's sake, John," I snapped, "stay here. I'll do it without you!"

"Okay, honey," he said, as dutifully as before, turned and went back in the house, his finger still sticking out of his pants.

I could have killed him. But only to the bottom of the hill. I had to start concentrating on streets and house numbers.

The rest of the afternoon I with my gaily wrapped packages combed Beverly Hills and vicinity.

What a bust. Nobody was home—all obviously at studio parties or dancing around somewhere with fingers sticking through their flies. I handed out gifts to the butlers, gardeners, maids upstairs and down, whoever was holding the fort while employers frolicked. They all looked at me as if I were some sort of lunatic. After a while I was inclined to agree.

It started to rain and dusk was falling early as I wound my way up Summit Ridge Drive toward the Selznicks. David and Jennifer lived at the top of a very curvy road. I deposited my gift into the hands of their major domo, and started back down the mountain.

It was hard to see through the blinding rain, which had begun to come down in earnest. The winding road, which dropped off into a deep ravine on my right, looked slick and dangerous.

Suddenly I came to a curve that swung to the left. Nothing but that sheer drop to the canyon bottom was ahead of me. I pressed my foot on the brake to slow down for the curve. Nothing happened. I pressed my foot all the way to the floorboard. No resistance at all.

The rest happened in a split second. I grabbed the hand brake, at the same time pulling the steering wheel to the left so that the car would sideswipe the rising side of the mountain and hopefully come to a halt.

There was an awful grinding sound of metal against rock, and a sharp wrench as the front wheels were yanked sideways as they jammed into the hill and the car jerked to a standstill.

I held onto the wheel of the now stilled car, shaking like a leaf. For some time I sat immobile, bewildered by my plight. Darkness was total by then, the only sound that of rain hitting the roof of the car. I couldn't see a light, nor a house—no sign of civilization. I might have been on another planet.

I finally realized I had to do something; it might be hours before anybody came along, and nobody knew where I was. At the Bogart party, a generally happy, drunk, noisy affair, no one would even notice I hadn't shown up. There was nothing for it but to get out and start walking until I found a house.

The second I stepped outside I was drenched. The fresh hairdo turned into soppy strings, the mink coat a drowned rat.

I walked and walked—down—I wasn't going to try it back up— and finally, *finally* way up above me, through trees and jutting rocks, I glimpsed a light.

I had a devil of a time finding the house since it seemed to be sitting on the top of a steep cliff. I began to circle the hill, stumbling in the dark, winding down and around, and finally coming across some steps. Steps that went up, and up, and up. . . . There must have been sixty or so.

But all things, even steps, come to an end, and there before me loomed a large house. And there, through the open door, was a huge roaring fire.

And there, seated on a couch alongside the roaring fire, having tea on a tray, was Katharine Hepburn.

I was never so glad to see anybody in my whole life. I imagine she was a little startled to see this bedraggled apparition appear on foot from nowhere in such an isolated spot.

I had never met her. I quickly explained who I was, what had happened. She was immediately efficient, sympathetic, and absolutely dear. She got me out of my dripping coat, sat me near the fire to dry my hair and feet, gave me some tea. Then she arranged for her car to drive me to the Bogart party. And she gave me a raincoat so I wouldn't get soaked any further.

It was a lovely moment. Only one thing disturbs me: I never gave the raincoat back. I had every intention of doing so, but I never did. It hung in my closet for years. "That's Katharine Hepburn's coat," I would say to people, "I must get it back to her."

I enjoyed saying "that's Katharine Hepburn's coat," and so I postponed. . . .

I don't know what happened to it. Moving around the way I have, things get misplaced. Even husbands. When I remember Katharine Hepburn's coat, I feel a pang of guilty conscience.

I was right. Nobody had noticed my absence at the Bogart party. John was on the floor playing with the Bogarts' boxer dog, tweaking his balls, to be exact. I've never known why.

CHAPTER 27 . . .

"Oh, Johnny—oh, Johnny . . ."

The main reason I stayed on (aside from an unwavering physical attraction between us) was because just when I despaired, John would invariably do something incredibly dear.

When he set his mind to something, time was no object. When he was on your side his patience was infinite, his thoughtfulness as thorough as his thoughtlessness could be at other times. (Actually his thoughtlessness toward me would be because his thoughtfulness was directed elsewhere at that moment.)

That Christmas Day after the Bogart party was overcast and chilly. We built a crackling fire, gathered around the tree with Pablo to exchange presents and toast the occasion with champagne; the servants were there too, having their glass and collecting their gifts. Then Pablo, whose social life was progressing nicely, had a party to go to. After he had been picked up John and I settled down by the fire to nurse our hangovers.

It was nice. It was lazy. We felt close. We had made love in the car the night before, in our own garage, rather than wait for the bed that was no more than a house-length away. I would invariably believe, during these moments of closeness, with just the two of us warmly together, that the future would be different; that we would be loving, with tender togetherness the way marriage was meant to be.

John was quietly sketching. He seldom sat doing nothing; he drew —faces, figures, torsos. If he didn't have a pad, on anything. A painter manqué, he had decided somewhere along the line that writing for movies was an easier way to make a living.

One of the small dogs, Jerry, dashed into the room, leaped on the couch and into John's lap, his tail wagging furiously. John chuckled and stopped drawing to scratch the furry head. "You know what, John," I said dreamily, "I think I would like to have a Kerry Blue puppy." I had read that Kerry Blue dogs were strictly one-person dogs. It was understandable why I might want one.

John cocked his head to one side and looked at me. "Would you now," he said softly. He reached over and put one large arm around me. "Then we'll go and get you one, honey, this very instant."

He laid down his sketchpad, set Jerry on the floor, got up and went to the study. Puzzled, I trailed after. He was looking through the yellow pages. Suddenly excitement was in the air. A new adventure. "John, you mean. . . .?"

With his finger on a number, he picked up the phone.

It wasn't easy. It appeared that the only available Kerry Blue puppy in all of southern California was in a kennel out in Rosemead, a place out past Pasadena, past South Pasadena, past Alhambra. Past everywhere if you're in Tarzana. Nevertheless, armed with a map, we set out on our journey in late afternoon.

Neither of us had ever been to Rosemead, so we would have to carefully consult street signs as we went along. Unfortunately the rains started to come down again in thundering sheets soon after we left.

Although these downpours occur every year during the rainy season, the cities in southern California remain steadfastly unprepared. Streets turn into rivers, low areas into lakes. Soon we were creeping along flooded streets, unable to go more than three miles an hour, unable to see the street signs through the walls of water, but too near our goal to turn back.

It was nearing midnight when we finally arrived at the kennel and picked up a little black ball of fur. Imagine her shock, being snatched from her warm mother and siblings to be carted off by strangers into this cold and soggy night. She promptly demonstrated her appreciation of this questionable act of kindness by throwing up all over the car and me.

She was a dear creature, though. We named her Jennifer, and she turned out to be nothing like the Kerry Blues I had read about. This one loved everybody who came in sight.

And a lot of people did. When anyone felt like dropping by the ranch, he or she was welcomed. I remember one Sunday when Ronald

Reagan and his wife at the time, Jane Wyman, dropped by unexpectedly. Although it was noon, we weren't all that wide awake, having been up all hours the night before. The Bogarts, Ida Lupino and Collier Young had been to dinner, and instead of going home at a decent hour the "boys" had begun to play football in the living room with a Chinese vase (would you believe, a $1,000 item?), and Collier dropped it. It fragmented nicely. Bogie, in bare feet, stepped into the debris, cutting his feet on the sharp pieces. Betty, scolding all the while, had to pick them out with tweezers. It took time. Then they all left.

We hadn't really recovered when the Reagans showed. Bloody Marys seemed to be in order. That tomato juice can certainly fool you. In no time the sun shone brighter, the jokes were hilarious, our guests were our dearest friends in the whole world.

Somewhere along the line we got hungry, and after someone's positively brilliant suggestion that we go down to Olvera Street for tacos and enchiladas, the four of us piled in a car and took off for the Mexican Quarter. It was a colorful place—sarape-, huarache- and basket-filled—with mariachi music dinning in your ear. The tacos and chili and refried beans were delicious. John and Jane were drinking beer, but Ronnie and I had had enough, if indeed he had much of anything at all. I remember what he said when we got back in the car —mainly because he became such a hotshot politician.

Jane and John, giggling and clearly anything but sober, were told to get in the back seat. "Evelyn and I will sit up front," said the future governor of California. "We'll be the policemen, and I'll drive."

A sober-minded, responsible citizen, even then. A nice Democrat, then. I wonder where he went wrong.

John played vigorously between pictures (and perhaps worked that way too; I wouldn't know), as if some heated energy had the frailer body in its grip. A delicate child, the condition seemed to have offended him deeply and he was bent on exorcising it even if it meant killing himself in the process.

His earlier pictures all have people overcoming monumental odds to attain some goal. His movie characters are pushed by greed, unscrupulously willing to do anything—rob, kill, suffer untold hardships— to gain riches of some sort. I don't know what pushes John. His movie people always get their riches, and then lose them in the end, caught in the clutches of the same greed. Does he feel that he, too, will have to pay a price some day?

CHAPTER 28 . . .

"Ain't we got fun. . . ."

After completing *Treasure of the Sierra Madre* and making various trips here and there—to the racetracks, to Palm Springs, to New York again—John \and his camp follower went off to the Florida Keys to prepare the script for his next picture, *Key Largo*. Bogie, Betty, Eddie Robinson, Lionel Barrymore and Claire Trevor would be in this one. And Claire was to win an Academy Award for her performance in it.

John hated to write alone; *Treasure* is one of the few times he did. For the new one, Richard Brooks was his collaborator. Brooks' wife, Harriet, who preceded Jean Simmons, came along too.

It was midsummer and sticky hot. The Keys were deserted. The sensible natives had fled to cooler climes. Key Largo sported one small hotel at the time, and it was closed tight. The owner, we were told, was down in Key West. We found him at the end of that lovely narrow ribbon of a road that connects the Keys. He said he would be most pleased to come and open his hotel for us.

We found the place oddly proportioned. With no more than six guest rooms, the lobby—if it could be called that—was vast. And empty, except for a few tables in one corner.

The days and nights were like steam baths, with no air conditioning, and little gnats everywhere, tiny enough to slip through screens. The two writers were getting the atmosphere they had come for, right enough, except that that same atmosphere was making work almost impossible.

They made a valiant effort in the beginning, going at it each day while their wives had all the fun swimming, sunning, reading and keeping cool. A cook and a waitress were brought in, and the owner stayed on to see that things ran smoothly. He was usually around when we took our meals, acting the genial host, chatting with his visitors from Hollywood.

One evening after dinner, my nose deep in a book, I didn't hear the beginning of a discussion between him and John about the Immaculate Conception—as unlikely a subject as I could imagine. I tuned in to hear John say, "No no, it's actually not Mary and Joseph who didn't indulge, but rather her parents who didn't."

The owner frowned and shook his head. "Mmm. I—don't believe you've got that right, John."

John leaned forward, mischief dancing in his eyes. "I'll bet you a hundred dollars I'm right!"

Did I detect a gleam in the owner's eye? "You're on," he said quietly. He picked up the phone. "The Monsignor of Miami is a friend of mine. I'll ask him who's right, okay?"

We all gathered around, caught up in the contest, as he spoke on the phone, nodded and hung up. "You win, John," he said, smiling.

We chortled as he handed over the hundred dollars to John. Little did we know that the last laugh would be his. For he had learned that John was a gambling man, and we learned what the big empty lobby was for.

The next day a huge van rolled up, and out came crap tables, roulette, blackjack, chemin de fer, the works. The place was a gambling joint.

Well.

The work came to an end. John began to gamble all night and sleep all day. And whenever he was at the crap table, the waitress was at his elbow with a ready drink on the house every time his glass was empty. Richard, who wasn't a gambler, got in the act for want of something to do. It made his wife very nervous and bored me to tears. It's not my idea of a bundle of laughs either, watching somebody rolling dice and thousands of dollars disappearing in rapid succession. The number of lost dollars kept climbing as the liquor supply diminished. "Come on, Harriet," I said, "let's get out of here."

We took a plane over to Nassau. I don't think our mates ever noticed our departure. We stayed close to a week before winging back. For a gift, knowing John's penchant for animals, I bought a baby capuchin monkey to take back to him.

As we got out of the limousine that had met us, and started across the lawn in front of the hotel, I held the monkey in my arms so John could see her. He came rushing across to greet me, his arms outstretched, crying, "Darling!"

But when he spied the monkey, his attention swerved and zoomed in like a closeup lens. Gingerly and with loving care, he scooped her up. He began crooning monkey talk, and I, laughingly, had to bring up the rear on the way to our room.

He had lost ten thousand, Richard around eight. It was time to leave. They had their atmosphere, they had best go someplace else and transfer it into words.

Before flying back home I bought a basket, lined it with a baby blanket, placed the small monkey named Dodie inside, and carried it on board the plane as if it were my bag. I slipped Dodie pieces of apple and carrot along the way and she made such a mess in the bottom of the basket that I decided to tidy her up when we were changing planes in New York.

When the ladies' room was empty I let her out for a bit of exercise while I brushed off her blanket. At that precise moment—the picture of it hangs in my head like a framed painting—the fattest woman I have ever seen opened the door to come in. Dodie, on the counter, stretched up on her hind legs to her full height—all of twelve inches—and baring her teeth as monkeys do when frightened, let out a blood-curdling shriek.

The fat lady then shrieked in an almost identical sound, rolled backward and out the door. I quickly grabbed Dodie, shoved her back in the basket and scurried to the other side of the terminal.

One wonders what the lady told her husband when she got home.

Back in Tarzana we had a large cage built for Dodie, painted it red and placed it in a prominent spot in the billiard room. She was soon incorporated into our lives, sassy with the dogs, entertaining the guests, causing monumental havoc far beyond her size if let out and not watched, once peeing on the head of a man interviewing me. And once she got drunk on the dregs of four martinis when nobody was looking, lounging about afterwards like early Theda Bara on leopard skins, so funny it was tempting to ply her with more liquor.

Her crowning achievement, however, was sneakily dealt to Sam Spiegel, future multi-Academy and Irving Thalberg Award winner. He and John were forming a partnership to be known as Horizon Pictures (known affectionately between themselves as Shit Creek Productions) as soon as John finished *Key Largo,* his last picture for Warners.

One evening John and I and Joyce and Jules Buck—who would act as secretary-treasurer to the fledgling company—were sitting around talking things over, drinking, waiting dinner for Sam who was late. We had let Dodie out of her cage, and she was playing about on top of the coffee table when Sam's car arrived. He leaped out, letting the door slam behind him.

The startled Dodie whirled, peed into the bowl of nuts on the table, and leaped over to nestle safely on John's arm. "Sorry I'm late," Sam said, crossing the room. "God, I'm famished." Before we could speak, he scooped up a fistful of nuts and popped them into his mouth.

Stunned into silence, we all sat wordlessly watching him chomp away.

Having heard his arrival, Nancy, the maid, had come to announce dinner. "Is that ape," glared Sam, pointing at twelve-inch Dodie, "ever allowed in the kitchen?"

"Oh sure, Mr. Spiegel," answered Nancy, "she's in there all the time."

"In that case," said Sam disgustedly, "I think I'll just stick to these nuts."

CHAPTER 29...

"I got the horse right here,

his name is . . ."

It wasn't all monkey pee and giggles, unfortunately. Could it have been, I wondered, had I been older and wiser and more able to cope with John's—irregularities?

Well, Christ, he was hardly behaving how I had been led to believe Prince Charming would (and should). His rambunctiousness often taxed even his closest of friends. Even Bogie. Once at their house, high as a kite, John decided for no apparent reason except mischief to slip his hand under Betty's skirt, crying out, "I'm going up the Amazon!"

Said Bogie, "Oh no you're not!" and leaped upon him (although he came only to John's shoulder).

Everybody joined in the ensuing altercation, either plowing in or pulling out and off. Jules Buck and I pushed John out the front door. Walking away from him and toward the car, I caught a too tardy glimpse of him coming at me from behind, in a flying tackle. He caught me full blast around the ankles and together in a jumble we slid about fifteen feet across wet grass. My pale blue dress sported a green seat that never did come out.

Some of us sometimes tried to emulate his loose ways. For example, Paulette Goddard, never much of a drinker, had far too much brandy out at the ranch one night and decided to drive, alone, back to her apartment in Hollywood—and she couldn't drive too well when she was sober. She left the car out in the street all night, the keys in it, her emerald bracelet lying on the seat.

I tried some mischief too, of another sort. All that lipstick in telltale places, the winning body tilt and Pied Piper charm turned on females at parties; he played around anytime he felt like it. Well, screw it, I wasn't going to sit around home moaning and feeling sorry for myself. There was only one way to go.

I took a lover. If you can call a one-night stand that. I felt far too conscience-stricken to continue. I felt no joy in my straying act, though I pretended to myself I did. I had every reason to—my partner was darling, a marvelous sense of humor, a delightful story-teller, delicious as French pastry. But then, everybody knows that about David Niven—single then, and ripe for plucking. But I didn't know how to get out of the bind I was in. I was still hung up on John, still hung up. . . .

Later I made a picture with David. It was *Enchantment* for Sam Goldwyn; the studio had actually loaned me to him—to justify the salary I was getting, I suspect. Sam had tried to borrow me before without success. He professed to be one of my greatest fans, booming out every time he saw me anyplace, "Ahhh! My favorite actress!"

David was under contract to him. So was Teresa Wright, also in the picture. It covered a wide time span, ranging from David as a very young man to a very old one. All my sequences with him were in his aged period (I played the niece of his former young love), and I saw him only in the old makeup, gray hair, gray mustache, wrinkled, a little stooped.

Farley Granger played my paramour. One day as we stood giggling about something between takes, David, who was standing nearby, spoke up rather querulously, "You two are ignoring me as if I really were old and can't understand your youthful chatter." It was true. I couldn't remember the other David at all.

The picture flopped. Sam stopped calling me his favorite actress. He had to blame somebody, and he owned all the other players. That was bad luck, the Goldwyn picture not working.

And it certainly wasn't good luck being allergic to horses. The allergy interfered with decisions I made, kept me confused about what I should do. Or not do.

Watching the horses running around a track from boxes in jockey clubs didn't bother me. We had a couple of them out on the track doing their thing once in a while, so when John was working and I wasn't, I became a horse follower. Hollywood Park, Santa Anita, up to San Francisco if one of them was running there. I became quite familiar with the ways of the thoroughbred, with enclosures, jockeys, stables and their colors (ours were green and white), and could ably and precisely read *The Racing Form,* my picture once appearing on its cover.

John owned half a horse (Virginia Bruce owned the other half), a filly named Lady Bruce who actually won a few races for a while there. Her first time out, John sent me to the track with a thousand dollars in my hot little hand—borrowed from Tola Litvak for the occasion—with instructions to check with our trainer, Tony, before placing a bet and find out from him if our filly had a chance. "If she does," John had told me, "then throw it all on the nose. If not, well, just make a token bet, say, of a hundred across the board, honey. We can't let her run without betting a little something."

Tony was a nice fellow who limped (probably kicked by a horse). He shook his head at my question, the straw in his mouth swinging with it. "Don't think so," he told me, "she's gonna run against colts.

Gonna be too tough a race for her." He spat on the ground for emphasis.

Armed with word practically from the horse's mouth I went to the grandstand and placed a hundred bet across. Then I went out to watch the race.

Lady Bruce shot out of the starting gate like a jack-in-the-box. A good six furlongs ahead of the rest of the pack, she never faltered once all the way to the finish line. I got sicker . . . and sicker . . . and sicker the faster she ran. A chill settled over me when the final odds flashed on: 20 to 1.

But I had followed John's orders, hadn't I? The trainer had said no, and anyway, I thought hopefully, we had won quite a bit, even at a hundred across.

On the set, John had heard the thrilling news of his horse's win. He was ecstatic when I phoned. He had multiplied a thousand times twenty and had planned how to spend and/or bet it, as he did most of the money that came through his hands.

"B-b-but, John," I interrupted, "don't you remember you told me to do what Tony told me, and he said that she couldn't . . ."

"You mean . . ." the melty caramel crystallized, ". . . you didn't bet it all?"

"I bet the hundred across like you—"

"You . . . didn't . . . bet . . . it . . . all?"

"John! You told me—"

I was talking to an empty phone.

That night he didn't come home at all.

Lesson for the day: If you want to win brownie points with gamblers, better to lose big than to win with a chickenshit bet.

There is something to be said for gamblers, I mused. They can be generous. They can fling money or things money buys at *you* as well as at the gambling machines.

Our second Christmas, when John was working and wouldn't have time to shop, I got more alarmed as the big day drew nearer. I might not go traipsing about delivering presents, but I wanted some under the tree in my own house. "Oh John, please," I begged, "*something* to put under the tree from you, if it's only a bunch of violets."

Joyce and Jules Buck were spending the holidays with us. They brought some things, I had put packages under the tree for everybody and it looked most festive. The household gathered that morning, Pablo home for the holidays, Nancy trooped in with her cowbell, along with Belle the cook, Zeke the yarn man, Charley the horse man. Champagne was passed around, presents began to be opened.

I came across a tiny package with my name on it—from John. "Oh John!" I cried happily, "you did get me something after all!"

Inside was a gold key. Really gold! I was thrilled. It was certainly better than a bunch of violets. "How perfectly adorable!" I exclaimed, and got up to kiss him, really touched. He was so busy, yet he had found the time to do this.

His eyes twinkled at me. "It's outside," he said.

I was puzzled. "Outside? What's outside?"

His grin was mischievous. "Take a look."

I walked to the door. Outside in the bright sunshine stood the prettiest car I had ever seen before or since. A yellow, red leather upholstered, convertible Cadillac. A miracle had been wrought. So soon after the war they were impossible to come by. But John had managed. "See if the key fits, Honey," he said.

Dazed, I walked to the car, got in, put the key in the ignition, and turned. The gas gauge shot up to "full."

"Oh my God," I cried, "look at that. Gas, too!" and burst into tears.

CHAPTER 30...

"My time . . . is your time . . ."

John's first picture with Sam Spiegel under the Horizon banner was a story about a pre-Castro revolution attempt, to be called *We Were Strangers,* with John Garfield, Jennifer Jones and Gilbert Roland. And lo, they came to my studio, Columbia, to make it.

The writer Peter Viertel (now married to Deborah Kerr) would do the screenplay on this one. On April 30, 1948, he and his then wife, Gige, boarded a plane for Havana with John and me, and we didn't have to hold the pilot at gunpoint to do it.

We immediately fell in love with the place. What was there not to like—the weather was soft and creamy, and they handed you frozen daiquiris right there at the airport. The Nacional was an old, elegant hotel with enormous, high-ceilinged rooms and big French doors opening onto balconies, beyond which sparkled the waters of the famous Morro Bay. The castle itself was outlined against the sky across the way.

As if all that wasn't enough, Cuba had Ernest Hemingway too. Papa himself. And Peter Viertel knew him! In no time at all after our arrival, the four of us climbed into a hired limousine and were driving through bustling streets, on out to the countryside past palm trees and lush foliage, to the tiny village of San Francisco where Papa and his wife, Mary, lived.

I knew I had made a serious error in judgment the moment we got there. To meet the great man I had foolishly changed into a chartreuse, clinging, silk jersey dress. Very movie star, à la Paulette Goddard. Mary had on some nondescript dungarees, and Papa wore a pair of tattered, faded shorts and a shirt with a rip in it a nine-year-old child could have fallen through. The house too had a careless, almost sloppy, look—books, manuscripts and paintings were strewn about on tables, the floor, on chairs, as if they had been left wherever they happened to land. And I could have sworn, that night, that the stream of expletives—beginning with "cocksucker"—that flowed from Hemingway's mouth were aimed at my gaudy chartreuse jersey.

Papa's speech, I was to learn, was rampant with four-, five-, six- and whatever-letter, juicy Anglo-Saxon words and phrases. (Not that any of the scatological references were new to me. The color and variety of the Hungarian language's counterparts far exceed anything our Puritan culture has dreamed up.)

He didn't work in the house, the writing was done in a tower apart, approached by an outside circular staircase. A very special inner sanctum where all Cuba spread out before him. Their place harbored some twenty-odd cats, all locked up in the garage at night, for what reason I shall never know.

Hemingway invited us to join him and Mary on his boat the next day. May Day in Havana, he told us, was not the safest place to be. Demonstrations of a violent nature could easily take place. Revolution was a constant possibility before they finally got around to it.

Bright and early next morning, we hied ourselves down to the harbor and piled on board Ernest Hemingway's forty-foot craft, *The Pilar*, named after the character in *For Whom the Bell Tolls*.

It was another perfect day with brilliant sunshine and a smooth sea. Papa—everybody was soon calling him that—wore the same tattered shirt and shorts. He kept them on for the entire two days we were on the boat. I was impressed. However, not a complete fool, I had got out a pair of shorts, wet them, rolled them up in a ball until they were wrinkled, and I was ready for come what may.

The entire venture was pure Hemingway, as if he, we, the setting and the happenings themselves, had all stepped out of the pages of his books. To begin with, the wheel was on top of the boat so that Papa could navigate and case the waters for fish at the same time. He would permit no one to spell him but stayed there the entire day in the broiling Caribbean sun, a sturdy bearded figure in charge, plying his craft through the Cuban waters he knew so well. We did take turns going upside to talk to him.

And Hemingway was a talker. He talked of the fish we could expect (which never showed), he talked of Paris, of New York. I ought to have collected a few Hemingway gems as I lounged happily in his august presence. But all I remember is when he spoke of Dorothy Parker. "Dorothy," he said he told her, "I wouldn't fuck you with a ten-foot pole."

There was fragrant freshly baked bread, Morro crab, and plenty of rum. Mary, tousled and boyish with her close-cut crop of hair, cleaned her toenails with a long knife and cut the bread with it afterwards. She said "divina" a great deal, as if it were a new Spanish word she was practicing. I used it later on Pablo, but he thought it was a new English word, having never heard it in his former Michoacàn circles.

We pulled into an exquisite little cove for the night, just big enough for the boat, the shoreline a jagged line of rock and cacti. The water was still as glass. We ate and drank and Papa talked of people and animals and books and hunting, while the water swished gently against the hull. (In *The Green Hills of Africa,* Hemingway wrote of rest periods as loving things.)

We stayed on in the cove the next day, sunning and reading. It was around noon that the iguana was sighted sunning itself on one of the boulders onshore. "Look-a there," Papa said quietly, "want to try your luck, John?" He unhooked one of the rifles lashed against the cabin and handed it to John. John lifted the gun to his shoulder; the blast of it filled the peaceful day and a quick jerk of the animal's head indicated the bullet had found its mark. The beast fell backward out of sight.

With a whoop and a holler, John, the big game hunter, leaped off the boat with Peter after him and the two went splashing ashore to retrieve John's kill. Their excited voices reached us across the water. "There's blood! He's hit!"

But "he" was missing. We watched from the boat while the two men scurried about, peering behind rocks, in crevices and bushes, looking for John's nearly bagged game.

No iguana. It was his terrain and he knew how to hide from these dangerous aliens. Finally bored with their lack of success, and overheated, John and Peter splashed back to the boat.

It was then that Hemingway acted out in full detail the classic

Hemingway legend. "The animal's been wounded," said Papa, "and must be found."

He picked up a rifle and, holding it above his head, slipped overboard and paddled his feet slowly until he found solid ground. He then walked ashore, holding the rifle clear of the water.

Peter and John, like chastised children, followed after him. Hemingway went to the rock where the iguana was last seen, where the spot of his blood remained. From there he began to walk in circles, with the rock as center. Wider and wider.

The children remained with him a while, but soon growing weary of the game, returned to the boat and the shade. Papa stayed on. He went back to the spot of blood and started over. He drove in little stakes so that he would know where he had been. Round and round he went, peering under every crevice, behind every rock, beneath every growing thing.

For two hours Ernest Hemingway stayed out there in the sizzling midday Cuban sun, bent over, searching for a wounded iguana although it was not he who had done the wounding.

He found it too. Quite dead. He brought it back to the boat in one hand, the rifle in the other, the same way he had gone ashore. The hunter's code was fulfilled.

Then he steered us back to Havana.

John decided to go out that evening. I mean, like *that,* no "would you mind" or by-your-leave. He just went out into the Cuban night and took Peter with him. Peter had the decency to shrug sheepishly. Gige and I were left in a strange country to shift for ourselves as best we bloody well could.

I suppose he went gambling. He usually did. And lost. He usually did that too. I know for sure he went to a whorehouse. His and Peter's big joke the next day was how one of the girls smoked a cigarette with her sweet little cunt, and when John offered her a cigarette later, she said, "No thank you, I don't smoke."

In Havana, I was thus reminded rather sharply that life with John was never going to be the marital bliss I had envisioned for my future.

CHAPTER 31...

"Give a man a horse he can ride. . . ."

When another birthday of John's rolled around I decided to give him a saddle horse he had expressed a desire for. The day fell on Sunday, so he would be home when the horse was delivered—surprise! surprise!—like my car had been.

The night before, we were to go to a big party Sonja Henie was throwing—another tent-over-the-tennis-court variety, several hundred of the pretty people, orchestra, buffet.

On the way to it I, singlehandedly, brought our marriage to the very brink of its inevitable end. My behavior was unconscionable. Resentment of John's Havana prowl (and others before it)? Out-of-control fury about Pauline Potter's bedspread gift eons ago?

We were dressed to the teeth, John in black tie, I in gold lamé. Sonja lived in a big modern house in Bel Air off Sunset Boulevard. It's tricky to find houses in there; Sunset is curvy and the street signs are often hidden behind lush foliage. John was driving my car—the yellow, red-leather upholstered, convertible Cadillac he had given me—peering into the night, trying to find the street we should turn off on.

It didn't occur to me that he hadn't seen the very large car parked on the right dead ahead of us, until it was too late. The sound of crunching metal filled the night. We weren't going fast, and weren't hurt, but the front of my darling car was crushed in like an accordion.

I was struck with blinding rage. He had destroyed this precious object, this hopeful symbol that maybe-he-did-care-for-me-in-spite-of-everything. "What . . . have . . . you . . . done!" I hissed. "My car! Oh my God, you have ruined my car! You crazy . . . *lunatic.* . . ." The words wouldn't stop spewing out, they had a life of their own. "Why didn't you *look?* Oh, it's too stupid. . . ."

Perhaps initially John had been in shock. But now he took my arm and twisted. "Shut—up!" he snapped with the impact of a striking cobra.

I was shocked into silence. I certainly *would* shut up and never speak to him again.

Someone headed for the party came along just then and picked us up, murmuring sympathetically about our mishap. But the minute we arrived John and I went separate ways as if a knife had sliced us apart. I quickly gulped down a glass of champagne. Then another. And another. Soon I was feeling quite marvelous.

I had a fine time. I danced; I chatted; I drank more champagne.

The more I drank the more I decided, to hell with him. He can do what he likes and with whom, I couldn't care less. There was exquisite freedom in the thought, and I drank more champagne to hold on to it.

Bob Neal, a splendid young man from Texas with plenty of money and playboy instincts to go with it, was there, and late in the evening we wound up laughing, chatting, drinking more champagne together. I suppose it was around three when John finally walked over. He caught me in the middle of a laugh, and I stopped immediately, all at once guilty that I was enjoying myself without him. But my sudden clamming up made it look as if I were hiding something.

Without a word, he turned away. I watched him walk through the living room and out the front door. Was he leaving? I bid Bob a hasty goodnight and went after him. I reached the front entrance in time to see him step into somebody's car and disappear down the drive.

So there I was, at three o'clock in the morning in the middle of Bel Air, a good thirty miles from where I lived, without a car, and the party was breaking up. High on champagne too, only now without the joy.

I didn't dare ask Bob Neal for a ride—whoever he was with was pissed off at me too. I asked perfect strangers if they were going through Beverly Hills and could they drop me off at Sam Spiegel's. I certainly wasn't going to the ranch, I fumed silently, even if I had a car. Never. That son of a bitch could drop dead for all I cared.

A freewheeling, generous man, Sam was, spending money even when he didn't have it. He had escaped Hitler's clutches by the skin of his teeth, and one had the impression he felt he was on borrowed time.

Since no one answered the door, I had to throw gravel on his window to get him to wake up. He wasn't surprised. I don't know what could have surprised Sam. He let me in, eyes at half-mast, explained that the bedrooms were full, led me to the living room couch and went back to bed.

Drink, as always, wrought its usual disaster on me. After two fitful hours I was wide awake again, heart racing, head throbbing, limbs paralyzed. Lying there on Sam Spiegel's couch in the sober dawn light, still in gold lamé, trying to figure out how to die as quickly as possible, I remembered it was John's birthday, and the horse that was to be delivered.

God. What would I do? As the light seeped in, I tried to remember what I had been so angry about. After all, John hadn't *meant* to wreck the car, had he? He had given it to me, for God's sake. With super-human effort I struggled to my feet. I had better get on out to the ranch and finish what I had started.

I took one of Sam's cars and drove swiftly to Tarzana.

It was my turn to be surprised. John wasn't home—hadn't been all night. I was feeling too miserable to figure out where he could have stayed.

I showered, got into slacks, drank a gallon of orange juice, took an entire bottle of aspirin, and sat down in the living room to wait for something to happen.

About eleven John showed up, still in black tie. If this keeps up, I thought, we'll change the dressing habits of the world. He didn't speak but went on past me down the hall to the bedroom. I didn't care. I didn't feel like talking anyhow. I went down to the barn to wait for the horse. A friend of ours, Arthur Fellows, had promised to bring him.

They showed up promptly at noon, Arthur's car pulling a horse van. It was a pretty horse, I thought, a chestnut, and Arthur had tied colored ribbons in its mane to give it a festive birthday air. He and Charley, the stable man, led it up to the front door of the house. In fact, they even opened the door and encouraged the animal to put its head inside the living room. I sent Nancy to get John, figuring he wouldn't come if I called him.

He certainly *acted* surprised and pleased, for Arthur's and Charley's benefit, if not mine. Certainly not mine; I knew I had spoiled the occasion with my antics of the night before. He went outside and fondled his new pet, even saddled up and went for a ride.

I hung around. I couldn't think of anything else to do. When he and Arthur came back, they sat around the living room talking, smoking, drinking. I did too. (Except drink. I'd never drink again.) I thought Arthur would think it queer if I disappeared and I didn't want to spoil his fun as he had been so helpful.

Then some other people came along, the Viertels, I think, Tola Litvak and Eddie Robinson, to celebrate John's birthday. Through it all, John managed not to speak to me without letting the others know. He had taken Pauline Potter lessons back in New York. When they left he headed for the bedroom again, still without a word.

We were finished. I knew it, and I knew it was my fault. I followed him to say so. "John, look, it's silly not to speak to me—here I am under your nose. I mean, right now I am. But you needn't worry, tomorrow I'll pack. What I mean is, you don't have to avoid me, I'll sleep in a guestroom tonight, out of your way. I realize it's over between us and . . . I'm sorry."

Something I said must have gotten to him. Or the way I said it. His eyes softened. He put his arms around me. "You don't have to do that, honey," he said gently, "come to bed."

Unfortunately he had been petting, fondling, riding a horse.

I sneezed all night.

CHAPTER 32...

*"I went to the animal fair . . . the birds
and the beasts were there. . . ."*

At last my conscience found a legit excuse to leave John's bed and board. Jealousy? Feeling unloved and unnecessary? That my prince visited hooker establishments under my nose, acting altogether like a single person most of the time? Nonsense. Nothing so mundane as any of that. I had a real justification. I had my looks to worry about.

The bugaboo of every leading lady film actress is the business of guarding her looks. Boy has to want girl visually or the picture goes out the window. She must arrive on the set looking her best, well rested and mind uncluttered with extraneous problems. So it was with utter righteousness, feeling gloriously justified (I mean, I really believed it), that I said to John, "Look, I think I'd better move into town, John, away from the horses, to make this picture. All this sneezing is making my eyes red and puffy."

"That's an awful lot of baggage for four weeks, honey," John said, looking at the mountain of it at the door.

"I'll need it," I said. I believed that too. I had taken everything I owned, when all I needed while working were a few pairs of slacks and some shirts.

I took a place at the Shoreham Apartments up above Sunset Boulevard overlooking Hollywood, where Paulette and Burgess Meredith had theirs. Mitchell Leisen, a director at Paramount, owned them and had decorated each of them like lush jewels. The one I took had thick green carpet, green velvet drapes, tufted shocking pink beds strewn with piles of colored pillows, white satin chairs, fluffy white bear throw rugs and miles of antique mirror along the walls. Perfect for one single woman.

It wasn't to be, quite yet.

John had gone back to Cuba shortly after I left, to shoot some exterior stuff. He called me from Havana when he was to return and asked me to pick him up at the airport. He too had a pile of luggage. "Let's see the apartment, honey," he said.

"You'll like it, I think."

"Not too bad," he said, beginning to remove his tie.

He stayed for more than a year.

We worked on adjoining stages at Columbia, him with his revolution, me with my hearing aid (for my role as a deaf woman). Which is how I happened to run into him one day when I was leaving my set for lunch. He was with the largest female I have ever seen. Fully as tall as he—six foot three (more or less)—and mammoth in all other directions too. The knockers were the size of the Goodyear blimp, each of them. I suppose John wanted to investigate all that expanse of flesh—and maybe he did—but not at lunch he didn't. I saw to that.

"Why hello, John, fancy seeing you here," I called out gaily. "Going to lunch? What a coincidence, so am I. Let's go together!" I've never had such a fine time feeling unwelcome.

He was up to his onstage pranks too. In a scene where Jennifer Jones and John Garfield were supposed to be digging a tunnel through a graveyard, John put a fake arm where Jennifer was digging. Her scream was real.

She got even though, but good.

At the end of their picture, John and Sam threw a big party for cast and crew. I was late getting there, tied up with my own picture, and things were well underway when I arrived. Music was blasting, people yelling above the din, that loose sound that goes with drinking.

I looked for John in the shifting, dancing crowd. Sam came up to kiss me hello. "Where's John?" I asked him.

"You have a surprise," he answered, gesturing across the room.

"Oh my God," I exclaimed.

"Exactly," said Sam.

"Where did that come from?"

"A little gift from Jennifer."

John had a chimpanzee draped around his neck.

Well, it *was* funny. They looked like a pair of far-out lovers, John and his chimp, she (what else) with her arms around his neck, he with his arms around her waist(?). And she was not to be dislodged. Brought from her relatively quiet home at the animal farm to this wild, babylonic place for her first introduction to the outside world, she wasn't about to let go of the first solid object she had glommed onto—John. And so they stayed, the two of them entwined, during the whole affair.

But when the party was over and the guy from the animal farm came over to collect her, she wouldn't have it. Those hairy arms around John's neck couldn't be budged.

John, as usual—at a party, at a late hour—was tilting to the wind, that everything's-right-with-the-world smile on his face. "Well," said he to me, "I guess she'll just have to go along home with us, honey."

Home. He meant my apartment. I couldn't very well tell him to take his monkey and go to the ranch this late at night, in his uncertain condition, but even so. . . . "John, you can't keep this animal. Where would we put her?"

The animal farm man began to pry her fingers loose, but she let out a shriek and burrowed in like a suction cup.

John stroked her back. "It's all right," he said to the animal man, "we'll just have to keep her with us, won't we. We don't want to upset her now, do we. Come along, honey." I wasn't sure which of us he was speaking to, the chimp or me.

We trailed him out to the parking lot, the animal man and I. John saw my yellow Cadillac, back in shape, and got in, monkey intact. The animal man said, "I've got her cage in the truck. I'd better follow you and bring it to you, you're going to need it."

John and his companion sat quietly at my side as I drove home, those big, sad chimp eyes rolling in my direction from time to time.

The animal man brought the cage into the living room, a box-shaped contraption about six feet by four, with bars on the front. It looked very peculiar sitting on a plush green rug, reflected by an antique mirror. John sat on the floor in front of it, the animal man opened the door, and together they eased the chimp inside. John scratched her head through the bars. "She'll be just fine," he said to the man, and stood up to shake his hand. "Uh—yeah," the man said. "Good luck," he said to me with a shrug, and left.

The chimpanzee sat looking up at John. She *was* appealing with those solemn eyes, I had to admit, even if she did smell a little gamy. Those eyes rolled from John to her own hands gripping the bars, then back to John. I could have sworn I saw the wheels of her brain whirling as she put two and two together and the bars parted like so much spaghetti. Miss Chimp stepped onto the plush green rug. From there it was one leap to John's neck. Right back where she started from.

"My God!" I cried. "What are we going to do?"

John laughed, and yawned. "It's too late to think about it now. Let's go to bed, we'll figure it out tomorrow."

"John!" I was horrified. "We can't—just leave this chimpanzee loose in here—"

"Ah, she'll be all right." He scratched her head.

"My God, John, there's no telling what she might do. Chimps are very active, you know that—"

But John was already headed for the bedroom, his friend snuggled on his shoulder, his eyes drooping, the drink taking over, not long for this wide-awake world I resided in. I followed to watch while he managed to get out of part of his clothing, sort of slipping things past the chimp, who was not about to let go of her chosen place ever again.

Half-clad, John lay down on the bed, 'midst quilted shocking pink and a bank of multicolored pillows, his monkey snuggling beside him.

He closed his eyes instantly. The chimp watched me with mournful mien.

I wasn't about to sleep with an ape.

I called Paulette in her upstairs apartment. It was around three o'clock again, the hour I seemed to be calling on my friends a lot in those days. She said, "Certainly, come up," convinced John and I had had an argument. She didn't believe there was a chimpanzee in my bedroom for one second. I wasn't sure I believed it either.

It was true, though. The next morning the stench seeping under the bedroom door, that I had had the presence of mind to close, assured me it was no dream.

My entrance disturbed neither of them. John and his latest conquest were stretched out side by side, dead to the world.

There was evidence, however, that one of them hadn't remained in a dormant condition the entire night. The room was a shambles! Every drawer had been pulled open and every article in them ripped out and flung helter-skelter. Lingerie, hose, jewelry, handkerchiefs, shirts, sweaters and scarves were strewn about the room like so much confetti. And that wasn't all. The chimp had added her own special, personal touch to—everything. But everything.

Chimp shit was everywhere.

Not only had she left her mark on each and every article of clothing, she had made handsome deposits on pink bedspread, white satin chairs, fluffy throw rugs—not to mention the wall-to-wall green plush. Not to mention *in* the drawers themselves.

And that wasn't all.

In what was probably a fit of sheer monkey exuberance, she had swung on the green velvet drapes in grand Cheeta style. They were ripped from their rods and left to sag limply at half-mast. Every lamp was knocked over, its shade crushed and the gaily colored pillows scattered everywhere like punctured balloons.

The odor inside the room was overpowering.

Rage, like an atomic blast, welled up. *"John!"* I shrieked. Only the chimp woke up, looking at me with a jaundiced eye, shrinking from my intrusion to press closer to John. I strode to the bed, fully intent on murder. I would have ripped him apart had I been able, snatched off a leg or an arm if I could have got hold of one. "Wake *up!*" I snarled. "Will you . . . just . . . *see* what this . . . creature has *done!*" I hammered on his head with my fists, the only part of him above the covers. The chimp shrieked and hid *her* head with her hairy arms.

Finally John came to. It wasn't easy. He was miles down there somewhere. He raised his head with great effort, obviously in pain, and looked about like a turtle peeking out of its shell, groaned, sat up and swung his stork legs over the side of the bed. From there his eyes traveled slowly around the room. "You see?" I hissed, looming over him, "You see what you have accomplished here? You *see?*"

All at once John began to laugh. It began at the bottom of his chest, bubbled to the top and flooded over. Ho ho ho ho ho ho ho ho ho! He couldn't stop. The more he saw, the more he laughed.

Well, it was funny! I suddenly saw how absurd the whole thing was. A fancy boudoir covered with monkey droppings. I began to laugh too. We couldn't stop. If one of us managed to contain our laughter the other failed, and it would start all over again. We cried; our sides hurt. Then the chimp climbed on John's lap, the hairy arms hugging tight. That really broke me up. She looked so baleful in the middle of all the laughter.

Finally we pulled ourselves together. "What are you going to do with her, John?" I said. "God knows she can't stay here."

"Let me shower and clear my head, honey, then I'll figure it out. Here, hold her while I get myself together." With that, he set the chimpanzee on the floor, placed one of her hairy little hands in mine, and went into the bathroom, closing the door behind him.

The monkey watched him go, started to follow, but I held on tight. "Don't worry," I told her, "he'll be back."

She looked around at me. She looked down at the hand that was holding her hand. Two and two got together again. Her big teeth descended and caught the skin on the back of my hand. Two and two got together in my head too. I let go with a very loud shriek.

She raced to the bathroom on all fours, stood up, tried the knob, found that nothing budged, and *she* started to shriek. Loud enough to be heard all the way to New York.

I opened the bathroom door, but fast. This chimp had my number.

John was in the shower with the water streaming down. The chimp moved right in and began imitating her beloved, rubbing here, scrubbing there. When he gave her the piece of soap, I left.

When John was dressed, and the chimp dried, I gave them both breakfast. "John," I said firmly, "this creature goes with you. She cannot stay in this apartment one second longer."

I watched them go, tall, lanky John, dressed in suit, tie and hat, stooping over to hold a short, hairy ape's hand beside him.

Then I picked up the phone to call Mitch Leisen, the owner of the apartment. "First let me tell you, Mitch," I began, "whatever the cost of redoing the apartment is, I'll pay. Now. You'll never believe what happened. . . ."

CHAPTER 33...

> *"It was just . . . one of those things*
> *. . . just one of those crazy flings. . . ."*

Both Harry Cohn and I seemed bent on the destruction of my career. He in his way, I in mine. After he put me in a picture in which I played a deaf social worker (*Mr. Soft Touch*), he followed it with one in which I had smallpox (*The Killer That Stalked New York*). Was it a subtle scheme to set up a defective image to turn off my following?

My tactic was to drop everything and follow where the man in my life led. . . .

In January John's Cuba picture was finished and in need of being tried out in front of an audience. The author-critic James Agee was in town and wanted a story on John. John wanted a vacation to clear his head. It was decided to put them together: go up to Idaho for the deer season and come back by way of San Francisco for the sneak preview there of *We Were Strangers*. Agee agreed to join us. Gilbert Roland, who was in the picture, decided to come along for the hell of it, I, to keep in good standing with the camp follower union.

I bought a chic hunting wardrobe: fleece-lined jackets and boots, red caps, long underwear and heavy socks. What did I know of hunting? John wanted to go, I'd go. I was told the deer were overpopulating in Idaho, and starving to death. We would be doing them a favor by shooting them. Nobody asked the deer.

The four of us drove in two cars, tandem style, out of the California orange groves into the heavy snows of the Salmon River mountains. Leaving our cars at a tiny place called Tree Creek, we were flown into the interior in a one-engine job, soaring through gorges, between the mountains, their peaks rising above us on all sides, so close it seemed we could reach out and touch them. Roland, who never flew if he could help it, sat the entire time with his head down, eyes closed, crossing himself. His message must have got through; we made it—with a sideslip to miss the mountain on the right, a cut in speed to avoid plowing into the one in front, and well-applied brakes when we touched earth once more.

The hunting lodge nestled in a miniature valley in the heart of giant masses of earth and rock. There was a central room where the food and the heat were—the *only* heat. Our cabins were the same sub-zero temperature as outside. So was the toilet. I gave up going.

The next morning John handed me a thirty-thirty rifle. I know it was that because he told me it was. He took me to the front of the lodge where some targets were set up, showed me how to load the thing, cock it, aim, and pull the trigger. Then he had me lie on the ground (cold!), raise up on my elbows, brace the gun, and proceed with what he had just explained, preferably pointing in the direction of one of the targets.

I hit a bull's-eye. "That's good enough, honey," John said. "You'll get a deer."

I beamed. I do enjoy being star pupil.

Off we went on horseback, the only means of travel in that perpendicular, snowbound terrain. Fortunately my allergy was held in abeyance by the cold. We rode single file: the guide, me, John, Agee, and Gilbert Roland, weaving our way back and forth along the steep slopes.

All at once there was a young buck in our path, two spanking new horns sprouting from his head. He was so young and inexperienced in the ways of man that he just stood looking at us with big brown Bambi eyes. John turned to me and whispered, "That one's yours, honey. Go ahead, take him."

"M-me?" I stared at the baby buck, who stared right back. "I c-can't d-do it. I-can't-do-it!" I cried. The men all laughed, and at that sound the innocent deer fled.

The weather was crisp, clear, and exhilarating. I noted John's eagerness, felt his excitement, and decided I must put my queasiness about killing in abeyance; starving to death *was* worse than getting quickly shot. And, I told myself, you eat meat; don't be such a bloody hypocrite.

We sighted plenty of deer. John got his the first day, leaping from his horse with lightning speed, flinging himself to the ground and doing all the things he had told me to do. Bang. Bang. One deer that wouldn't starve.

The last day it snowed. My feet, heavy-socked and fleece-booted, were dangling icicles down the horse's side. I hadn't bagged my deer, and John, his quota filled, came along with the guide, just to keep me company.

We'd been all day without a sighting, about to call it quits, when the guide suddenly stopped his horse and motioned us to do likewise. "Let's get off," he whispered.

Snow crunched under boots and hooves, reverberating against the mountains like exploding firecrackers. Congealed puffs of air from our lungs came in quicker spurts.

At the edge of the ledge the guide halted, and without looking around, beckoned us to join him. The mountainside dropped downward at nearly a ninety-degree angle. About two hundred yards below us was a herd of deer standing in profile, heads raised, listening to the clumsy racket we humans were making. Six does. Two bucks. "There he is," John whispered. "Take him this time."

After my first day's failure I had rehearsed in my mind exactly what I must do. Like a scene in a movie. And now here it was.

Like an automaton, reflexes taking over, I slipped out the thirty-thirty, sat too abruptly on a boulder—my legs had given way—and raised one knee. It was quivering like a feather in the wind. On this uncertain rest, I placed my equally jittery elbow, and sighted a buck along the barrel.

The herd had long fled, but one six-pointed buck remained, waiting for me to get into position, as if our meeting had been preordained. The blast sounded like a bomb as it hit the sides of the mountains and bounced back.

The animal fell. That beautiful creature collapsed and rolled down the steep incline, quickly disappearing behind clumps of bushes that stuck jaggedly out of the mountainside.

"By God, you did it!" cried John. "I'm proud of you!" He helped me to my feet (a good thing, I couldn't have done it alone), and gave me a big hug. Then he gave me the old zippo-bang Papa Hemingway philosophy we had all learned that hot May Day back in Cuba. "Now honey, you're going to have to go on down there and be sure your game is dead. Can't leave it lying there wounded, you know."

The guide said, "We'll come round the other way with the horses."

The slope was too steep for our animals. But I made it, slipping and sliding, digging in, grabbing hold of brush and rock. The two men and two horses, plus a pack mule to carry game, had vanished. I was alone in this vast wilderness, in sub-zero weather.

There are moments in our lives that transcend all others. What if they never came back? I hadn't the faintest notion what direction the camp was in, or how far. How helpless we have become since civilization blunted our survival instincts.

But they did come back. My deer—quite dead—was slit open by the guide, its entrails removed, and the carcass hung over the mule. Reduced to meat. The heads of both our deers were taxidermied and sent on to be hung in our Keyston ranch, to haunt me until the place was sold, and them with it. . . .

John later said that that hunting trip was the best part of our life together. Go figure that. So what was the cue I missed for the binding together of the marriage bonds, if that deer kill was the best part of the bonding? It was inevitable that someone would come along who wouldn't miss any cues. . . .

To abandon a man's house, one he loves, particularly a man not bound by standard conventions, is asking for it.

So I got it.

It is the female who is the predatory half of our species. She has fewer scruples, fewer qualms—I'll change that to *no* qualms—about setting her cap for a man who is already involved—like married—to another woman. And she learns young.

Ricky Soma was only eighteen when we came across her at one of the Selznick gatherings. Actually John had met her before at her father's New York restaurant, Tony's, when she was nine and a budding ballerina. Is there something appealing about a girl-child growing up to a fuckable age under your nose? Probably. Particularly if the girl-child has no hesitancy in using her new-found wiles. And the wife has cleared the way. A wife who never comes near your house —or your horses.

It wasn't long before Ricky was showing up regularly at the ranch. I was warned. "You better get out there," somebody or other would say. "That girl's really moving in on John." Did I pay any heed? No. I believed it to be a losing proposition. If it wasn't this time, it would be the next.

It wasn't long before she moved in altogether, and the split between Evelyn and John was finally complete. According to tradition, Walter Winchell's announcement of it on his Sunday night broadcast made it a *fait accompli.* However, John at least called me to ask if it were really true.

My soon-to-be ex-father-in-law came to see me. "What happened?" he asked quietly, deep concern shining from his eyes.

I tried to explain. "He has somebody now, but that's not . . . the real reason, not where the end began. It was . . . what bothered me most was never knowing where we—where I was. I felt off balance too much of the time. . . ." I stopped. It was too lame an explanation, too lopsided a version.

But Walter had nodded, listening carefully. "I'm sorry. And I understand. John has always been a bit of a free soul. I'll tell you something, for what its worth. When he married the first time, he was twenty and broke, and I gave him five hundred dollars to set up housekeeping. That was a lot of money then. He spent the entire amount on a chandelier.

"I haven't worried about him too much since then. Perhaps you had better do the same. . . ."

BOOK FIVE

CHAPTER 34...

" . . . the best things in life . . .

are . . . free. . . ."

It was a year of madness. A frantic, erratic montage of ups and downs, ins and outs, searching, searching. Only I didn't know for what. Another picture helped postpone decision; I was loaned to Dick Powell for a flick he was producing and starring in called *Mrs. Mike.* I played a Boston girl around the turn of the century who marries a Mountie, goes north with him and suffers various hardships—including the inevitable baby in the wilderness with the crazy lady in attendance. Louella said I would win the Academy Award. Wrong.

John still came around, we made out on occasion. Somehow in the shift I had come to play the role of the mistress and Ricky the wife. And her turn to wonder where he was.

A new restaurant opened, and "the gang" was there: the Wilders, the Wylers, Sam Spiegel, and John with Ricky. I was with . . . God knows who. And John began to flirt with some blonde. At some point in the evening I looked around and saw her sitting on John's lap. I went over, took a fistful of the blonde stuff, turned her head around and said, "Listen, you, I'm his wife, and that's his mistress over there, and you are one too many." And I pulled her up off his lap by her hair.

It made the papers. Everybody thought it hilarious, except Ricky.

Everything I did made the papers. Things I did, people I saw, places I went, all were newsworthy. A week or so after the split, I was off to the bullfights at Tijuana with Amigo (Gilbert Roland) and friends. Who should be at the Plaza de Toros but John and a redhead (I don't know where Ricky was), and in another spot, Bob Neal, the rich kid from Sonja Henie's party. It all looked like a quick replay.

A festive day: Amigo had a bull dedicated to him, and we returned to Caesar's Bar. So did John and his redhead, and Bob Neal and the pilot of his plane—all at separate tables, of course. But not for long. I was soon in a happy conversation with Bob. Only this time I had no husband I had to pay attention to, so when Bob suggested I fly back to Los Angeles with him, I thought it a hell of an idea.

Bob had a one-engine plane big enough for four passengers, and we took off in that thing without any light on the field from the bumpy Tijuana airport. I'm sure the pilot was as full of tequila as we were. It's nice we didn't get killed. I took up with Bob for awhile. He had a gray Cadillac with a telephone in it, and I liked the whole setup so much he gave it to me, with my initials in bright red on the side. John didn't like it at all. He said it was vulgar. I suppose he thought I shouldn't replace the one he had given to me. And do you know, I gave the car back to Bob. Plus the five fur coats he sent over one day. What John said still had an effect on me.

We flew all the way to Mexico in Bob's tiny plane to see Paulette, who was working down there. Commercial planes were not flying out of Mazatlán at the time. We soon found out why. Thunderheads were everywhere—those gray mushroom-shaped clouds that can tear a little plane to pieces. We flew between them until there wasn't any more space and had to make a forced landing near Tepic, in the state of Nayarit, in a cow pasture, in pouring rain.

I loved Paulette in Mexico, the background suited her, and she, it. Bob went off to Houston—I suppose that's where the money was—and Paulette and I went about a bit. To a cocktail party for Diego Rivera. He was in the midst of some scandal with Maria Felix, the snobbish actress who had been down at San José de Perua. Or so the papers blared every day. He had painted something they didn't like, like a statement in the picture that there is no God, and the press was up in arms. I learned more Spanish than ever before on that trip, reading about Diego. They said he had been Maria's lover, that she particularly liked something Diego could do without his teeth. And in the bathtub too. It does stir up the imagination.

Back in L.A., Charlie Feldman, agent, producer, good friend, gave a big party. He took over the whole Crescendo nightclub on the Strip for the occasion. I went with Farley Granger. Seated next to me was Kirk Douglas. I was instantly struck. That shock of hair, that dimple, that jaw. I had just seen *The Champion*, and I knew he knew his craft. If you must be an actor, at least be a good one, I thought. He was with Rhonda Fleming, but I couldn't have cared less. Have I not explained that women have no qualms about somebody else's man? Being around John Huston for three years had taught me the sweet art of survival.

I turned on every ounce of charm I could. Subtly, of course. I let it out, and pulled it in. Chatted with others. Moved about. It's how I happened to be at the bar when big John Wayne dropped in. He never got further in the room, we stood there talking for about an hour—I probably told him I was a Communist. I mean, how else can you get the Duke's attention? Then he left. I have never seen him again, anywhere. We don't travel in the same political paths.

And John Huston was there. He-e-ey! I remember you! An old husband, right?

He had some news for me. Ricky was pregnant. I guess she would show me a thing or two about sperm. "Are you sure it's yours, John?" I asked.

And then he said something that made me realize I hadn't understood him the whole three passing years. "It doesn't matter," he said.

A light bulb went off in my head. I hadn't been paying attention at all. He wanted progeny any way he could get them. It was he who had brought back Pablo. Wasn't it backwards? Isn't it the woman who is supposed to have the driving force towards children?

I went home that night with one more what's-wrong-with-me item to tuck away in the guilty bag. (Later Paulette had her little joke. She said my shots had gotten John ready for the next wife.)

But I soon ceased dwelling on what John had told me. Hardly my problem, right? I was working, I was busy moving into a larger apartment, now that I was single! I had wound up with the best of the pre-Columbian figures and paintings we had, and Mitch Leisen was decorating an apartment for me around these objets d'art. John could hardly ask for them back after telling me about his enceinte girl friend.

And there were parties, and more work, and trips and tennis and exercise classes. Oh, I was busy.

And there was Kirk Douglas, in and out—in more ways than one. Our—uh—whatever it was—lasted no more than four months, but in that short time Kirk was responsible, directly or indirectly, for two very important decisions in my life: I went to a psychoanalyst, and I broke my contract with Columbia.

Kirk, just parted from his wife, with two small sons to worry about, already knowing that success wasn't synonymous with happiness, was looking for it on the analyst's couch. I somehow became an extension of his treatment. He would come to my apartment, sometimes before his doctor's appointment, sometimes after. He would quote me to the doctor, and then he would come back to say the doctor had agreed with me, quoting the doctor to me, and I would comment on that. I should have received an assistant's fee, I spent so many hours at it. "A ragpicker's son!" Kirk would cry, pacing my living room (or bedroom), "facing the world, cock in hand!"

Kirk deplored as much as I did what the House Un-American Activities Committee was doing, and said when he was nominated for an Oscar for *The Champion*, that if he won, he would use the opportunity to tell how he felt. Somebody must have talked him out of it. Just as well; otherwise he wouldn't be the millionaire he is today.

I envied him his doctor to talk to. I even envied him having me to talk to. Who would I talk to if I wanted to talk? Paulette? Her marriage to Burgess had come apart, they had taken her out of a picture at Fox, Gable hadn't given her the Rolls Royce. No, she had *tsouris* of her own. Joyce Buck? She had Jules and a new baby to think about. Anyway, what did I want to talk about? What was the matter? A third marriage gone astray? Big deal. So what. What could a doctor tell me.

I did tell John I didn't seem to want to do anything but play tennis when I wasn't working. "Well then, honey," he answered, "you just keep playing tennis until you know what you want to do."

Harry Cohn was back in the act. The minute John was out of the picture and I was back in the columns, Harry was back at his old tricks. The phone calls began again at eleven of a morning, not even a hello. "You don't miss anybody in town, do you?"

Hell-bent on some demolition course I snapped, "I try not to, Harry!"

It was 1951, and I was in another picture, *The Killer That Stalked New York*, a diamond thief returning from foreign parts, bringing the smallpox I had contracted—plus the diamonds—to the entire city of New York. Harry knew where to find me. He didn't mind stopping the picture to have these little bouts.

"Yeah," he said, then, "that's what they tell me—"

"They' don't tell you one damn thing—"

"You lay down for this bum, Douglas, too, didn't you?"

He was standing behind his desk, I in the middle of the room. Now I walked over, furious. "With that gorgeous body of his," I spat, "wouldn't I be a fool not to?"

"A prick like that—"

"Oh, for God's sake, Harry, get off my back!" I cried.

"*On* your back is your favorite position."

"There are other positions."

That gave him pause. The eyes flickered. "You go down on him?"

I smiled. "What a foolish question. I go down on everybody."

He couldn't resist. "A big cock?"

"Just about the right size."

"I suppose you let him go down on you?"

"Let him! Why on earth would I want to stop him!"

Disgust—pretended or real—curled his lip.

I suddenly hated myself. I cried, "Why do you make me say these things, Harry? Please don't do this to me!"

The eyebrows went up. "I'm not the one doing anything to you," the president of the company said.

It finally came to a head the day Kirk dropped by the studio unannounced. On that particular day I had a taxing scene: the confrontation with my double-crossing husband after having spread my smallpox over the city, staggering about with it myself. It took all my energy and concentration.

The morning went quite well, and we broke for lunch. Columbia didn't have a commissary on the lot; we players had to go out. To my surprise Kirk was sitting in the outer waiting room. "Kirk!" I cried, "what are you doing here?"

"I dropped by to see you." He laughed. "But they wouldn't let me in." Kirk could afford to laugh. He was the hottest star in town. "I got a lot of offers sitting here, though."

"Oh God, that's crazy. I'm sorry." I tucked my arm through his. "Come on, we'll have some lunch and you can come back with me—if you're not afraid of catching smallpox."

"From you, what a way to go."

We had our greasy spoon fare and returned to the studio. As we started in the officer at the desk stopped us. "Mr. Douglas can't come in," he said to me, "and Mr. Cohn wants to see you in his office right away."

I was shocked. This was the place I worked, the studio I had been under contract to for ten years. "Well! I don't know if I'll go in, either—"

"No, no," Kirk said, "I didn't come around to get you in trouble."

"It's going to be very big trouble if I can't have my friends—"

"Please," said Kirk, "it's all right. You go on in, I have an appointment soon, anyway." He kissed me on the cheek and was gone.

I was livid. I stormed into Harry's office, hissing like an angry dragon. "What is this, a jail?" I yelled. "Nobody can come in here unless you give—"

"Can't wait, can you, got to get a quick fuck in between takes—"

"How can you *think* of such a thing!" I screamed, beside myself. "I work damned hard, and you know it."

"There'll be no screwing around on my sets—"

"A friend wants to come and visit me and you—"

"A bum."

"—keep him off the lot, one of the biggest talents around, and you—"

"The biggest prick, you mean, which is what you want—"

"*You don't know what I want!*" I screamed at him. "I won't . . . I'm not a . . . slave, I can't—" I started crying. I didn't know what I was saying. I ran from the office and went to my dressing room. I knew they were waiting for me on the set. The scene was set up, with only a few more closeups to make. There was nothing for them to do but wait for me, and I didn't care. I hadn't caused this delay, the president had. I couldn't work like this, I was terribly distraught.

I called my agent. "I can't go on this way," I sobbed, "I can't do my work, something has to be done!"

He held my hand, calmed me down—all part of an agent's job—and got me back on the set and able to finish the picture. He didn't want the studio to have anything on me. Because he had a plan. We would sue Harry and the studio for undue stress, or whatever legal issue was suitable.

The studio quickly agreed to settle out of court. Harry, having gone through a similar suit with Charles Vidor, didn't want to go through another with a female. Although I would have to pay Columbia twenty percent of my earnings for the length of the contract, it was worth it to be able to make any deals I wanted, immediately, without going through a lengthy court trial.

Well, isn't it great to be free. That is, if you have something in mind for the future, some plan. Me, all I was doing was getting out, divorcing everything and everybody. In one day I signed a paper so John could get his divorce, and I made the new arrangement with Columbia. In one fell swoop I lost a husband and the protection of a major studio.

Some victory, right? My agent and I congratulated ourselves. The world, he said in effect, is your oyster.

He didn't reckon on sabotage from me. . . .

CHAPTER 35

"South America . . . take it away. . . ."

Luck was on my side, even if I wasn't. Sam Spiegel wanted me to do a film for Horizon Pictures with Van Heflin. *The Prowler* turned out to be the best picture I ever made. Joseph Losey directed with loving care an almost perfect script by that fine screenwriter, Dalton Trumbo—a fact I didn't know until twenty years later, because Dalton was blacklisted at the time, and out of sight. Sam had had to credit another name on the screen or the picture couldn't have been released. It was like that. Joseph McCarthy, taking over the ever-popular red-baiting role from HUAC, was starring on TV in his popular series of the period, calling everybody Communist who didn't agree with him, and people were suddenly disappearing from the scene. It was Joe Losey's last picture in Hollywood. He found himself on tainted lists and had to go elsewhere to work. I hated it all. My foundations were crumbling. The people I admired and respected most were no longer around.

Then Walter died, in the middle of my picture. Just . . . up . . . and . . . It was like you're reaching for a solid object, and you find empty space instead.

I rattled around, the bobbing apple in the barrel, going out with this one, with that one. John still came around from time to time. Kirk checked in, for the night, not so much to see if he still wanted me as much as to find out if I still wanted him. They burdened me with their insecurities, and I pretended I was strong.

One night at a party where a black singer performed terrifically, I, in my exuberance, asked him over to my apartment for a drink. We had a fine time. He had a special affinity for my pre-Columbian pieces, as if they were soul brothers. That pleased me. I liked how he talked about the way he coped with his color; how he sounded, how he thought. And. One thing led to another. And—the southern girl did what she had to do to make sure the shackles of prejudice were shaken off forever.

I don't know what I expected. Superstud? That has got to be the black man's burden, carrying that myth around. Actually a damper was put on integration early in the proceedings. My partner must have been wearing a hairpiece, because in the midst of the melée, the soft wooly stuff gave way under my clutching hand. He gracefully excused himself to go to the bathroom. I gracefully pretended I didn't know why. But the thrill was gone.

That was that—he was off to other parts—except for one little thing. Mother Nature capriciously decided to play a wee joke on me. My period didn't come round the following month. I had become very careless in the past three years.

It was a bit of a predicament. It could have been any of three, including John. Without knowing who, exactly, or even what color, I had only one option. All I needed was money, and that I had.

But one thing I did know. This shapeless, aimless existence I was leading couldn't go on. It was time to stop postponing seeing a shrink.

The moment I picked up the phone to make the appointment, I felt foolish and self-indulgent. The doctor would surely tell me what any number of people had told me. "What in the world have you got to worry about? Beauty, talent, career, money flowing in. Run along home, little girl, and count your blessings."

Another man behind a desk, behind spectacles as well. I told him my story: ". . . from Atlanta . . . out to get in pictures . . . got in . . . did this, that . . . met these men. . . ." Blah blah blah. Such a boring tale, I felt embarrassed to have come.

But when he gave me another appointment, my heart leaped with pleasure, and I went out elated. I had passed the test! I had been accepted!

I was in the car driving home before the other thought struck. Was I . . . really in trouble? Was I really a crazy, mixed-up kid?

There was comfort, knowing the doctor was there. Now I had it made. My agent-daddy made a deal with Universal for two pictures at $80,000 each, and he would keep arranging deals for more and more; meantime I had this nice doctor-daddy sitting in his office ready to straighten out the rest of me.

With all these wise grownups nursing my life along, I reverted to childhood. I took up with Sidney Chaplin, Charlie's number two son, and we began to play. It's *all* we did. Tennis and cards, cards and tennis, movies, parties, back to tennis—doubles, singles, at the club, up at Charlie's house. Charlie too played with us once in a while, a little white-haired man zipping around the court faster than any of us.

There was a small flirt with the theater, and Charlie-daddy was going to direct Sidney and me in *Othello,* but Universal called and I had to do this junk movie called *Smuggler's Island* with Jeff Chandler, in a recreated Macao on the back lot surrounded by an ocean six feet deep.

Going to the analyst didn't offer the relief I had anticipated, nor the joy I thought to have talking about myself to a paid listener. On the contrary. The way he asked the simplest questions, was like . . . an attack, as if he were . . . after me. How do you feel about your mother? Brother? Sisters? "Well, how should I feel, I love them, no? Doesn't everybody?"

It was alarming how he poked, prodded. Still a child under this layer of sophistication? Looking for love? Approval? The allergy to the horses all connected with that? It's a cry for help! Bring me your dreams, the nosy man told me, they represent your unconscious, they will tell us something.

Not on your life, Doc. I'm no fool; I stopped dreaming. He wasn't going to catch me.

My second Universal picture was with Jeff Chandler, too, *The Iron Man.* A fight story, all that slugging and grunting business. Jeff had hair on his chest and his back and it was shaved off for the boxer-short scenes. He itched all the time, poor fellow. (Poor fellow, indeed. They killed him a few years later in a Culver City hospital with an overdose of the wrong medicine.)

And then my escape route opened up.

I was invited to a film festival in Uruguay, a place called Punta del Este. "You must not go," my analyst said, "we've only just begun."

"Not go?" I cried, "not grab such a marvelous opportunity—"

"You are running away from me."

"I am not!" I cried guiltily. "How can you say such a thing!"

"There will be other opportunities."

"There may never be another to go to South America!"

What glorious relief to get on the southbound plane and out of the sound of his probing voice. I would be back. Was he crazy, thinking I was running away? What nonsense.

Joan Fontaine was along. Lizabeth Scott, Joseph Cotten, Patricia Neal. June Haver, sitting next to me, read a religious book all the way down, and flipped when she saw the mammoth figure of Christ standing on the mountain above Rio de Janeiro. She dropped to her knees then and there. (She had reason to give thanks. We had dumped a few thousand gallons of gasoline in the ocean earlier and were limping in on three motors.) The half-mile-high Christ statue was an impressive sight, arms spread out in blessing, clouds gathered around the head to resemble a halo.

Below, in earthly fashion, we were whisked off to a party where we met the Guinle brothers. And who were the Guinle brothers? Rich is who they were, and in Brazil, that is very rich indeed. They flew down to the festival in their own plane, and the younger, Carlos, was my escort the whole cavorting time—dancing the rumba, cha-cha-cha, mambo, parties, lunches, cocktails, dancing the samba, cha-cha-cha, mambo, seeing movies, playing tennis, dancing the rumba. . . .

And when it was over in Uruguay, I flew back to Rio with the Guinles, without a visa. If you are rich, you can do anything (even not pay income tax). "Don't speak," they told me, "and the police will think you are one of us."

For two illegal months I remained in Rio, with its mosaic sidewalks and shining waters, at the Copacabana Palace Hotel as Carlos's guest, playing some more—tennis, swimming, boating, dancing the rumba, cha-cha-cha, the mambo.

Reality finally caught up in the form of retakes, and I had to step back through the looking glass.

I wasn't happy with what I encountered.

Dutifully I returned to my doctor. Once more there were the pulled drapes in the middle of the day, the worn couch, watchful eyes, big ears to catch each nuance, the big box of Kleenex within easy reach in case I burst into tears. I loathed that box of Kleenex, sitting there, daring me to break down.

He neither welcomed me back nor commented on my absence. Such a cool way of dealing with hot emotion. Charm, teasing, a joke—nothing had an effect on his placid manner. "I had a perfectly marvelous time!" I announced, perhaps a little too brightly.

"Tell me about it." Me the butterfly on the pin, he the biologist.

"Rio is beautiful, mountains and water and green, green. And there's this statue—"

"And your friend . . .?"

"What about him?"

"Will you see him again?"

"Well, no. God. They don't all have to last forever!"

"So far, none of yours has lasted at all."

Why, I thought angrily on the way home, should I be subjected to that shit. At fifty dollars a throw, too. Too tough, the hell with it. Besides, I told myself, I had a perfectly legitimate reason for leaving again. I had to work, didn't I? I had to follow where that led, didn't I? I had been offered a picture to be shot in Mexico, but the truth was, I didn't read the script before accepting. Having got rid of my original roots, three husbands and one studio, one lousy doctor was a cinch. For good measure, I gave up my apartment too.

CHAPTER 36

> *"Here I go again . . . I hear that*
> *trumpet blow again . . ."*

In Mexico City I looked up Cantínflas (Mario Moreno, number one Mexican attraction of the Spanish-speaking world), whom I had met at the Uruguay film festival. More than movie star, he is a national treasure, because he is a matador too. He actually clowns in the ring with those lethal weapons, the fighting bulls. We had no mutual spoken language, but it's surprising what can be done without. My film was being directed by some cold-assed Englishman with whom I had no communication at all in spite of our similar mother tongues.

The last day of shooting, on a beach at Acapulco, I met a handsome Czech woman who lived nearby on a mountaintop overlooking the sea. She asked me to lunch; I stayed six months. Why should I return to Hollywood? The infamous Washington Committee had chased all the good guys away. I certainly wouldn't go back for a shrink. I could learn more moving about the world.

I ignored scripts sent me, and took up water skiing as if I were training for the Olympics. I was out there morning and afternoon, sometimes even at night. I turned the color of mahogany. I braided my wet hair in bright strands of Mexican wool and wore Mexican print dresses, sans shoes. For the entire six months I never had a pair on my feet. Between water runs I would lie on the beach and study Spanish. With a little perseverance I not only would get rid of me but my own language too.

Parties were nightly, the ones we gave, the ones somebody else gave. Dolores Del Rio had a house nearby, as did Teddy Stoeffer, who took Hedy Lamarr to wife for a while, Jacques Gelman, Cantínflas's partner, and his wife, Natasha—all part of the gang.

There was nightly jai-alai too, and I met one of the players, a Spaniard from Madrid, who looked the way a Spaniard is supposed to, dark curly hair and black flashing eyes, slim muscular body, hard from his athlete's life; one of the most handsome men I have ever seen. Our affair was Erica Jong's zipless fuck, reality suspended, hanging there in never-never land. We went to Spanish (not Mexican) theater, restaurants, dancing; bullfights with him took on a special meaning. There was water skiing by moonlight, that warm Acapulco water on naked skin on a cool night being heaven itself. We found private beaches for our swims, private coves for lovemaking afterwards. And with all that hard leanness, he played the piano with an extraordinarily delicate touch—like the kind of lover he was. It was all very beautiful. I really did slip into another world for awhile.

But then he and his team moved on to . . . wherever jai-alai players go.

So I took another lover.

And another. It was not—never—the same, I couldn't recreate the ambiance, the adventure was over, gone. I began to suspect my Acapulco bubble was not as burst-proof as I had thought. The climax of lunacy was reached the night I went off with the last one after a lot of tequila to look for somebody to marry us. Fortunately it was too late and the official outside the government building turned us away.

I often woke up in a sweat over that near miss. Out of the reach of my doctor, my dreams had gone berserk, having returned in Technicolor spectaculars.

Sam Spiegel came to the rescue. The cable read: COME TO LONDON FOR OPENING OF "THE PROWLER."

There was little doubt it was time to move on.

London in December of 1951 was an unrelieved dismal gray; the use of coal hadn't been banned yet, and those thick pea soupers of Jack the Ripper days still hung over the city. English faces were pale and wan from lack of sun. I looked freakish with my dark skin and sun-streaked blonde hair—hobbling everywhere with huge blisters from the reintroduction to shoes.

The city still suffered from the war, ragged edges of bomb damage were everywhere. Rationing remained, stamps were necessary for everything, there were no decent clothes in the stores nor food in restaurants. But the English took it in their stride, there was hustle and bustle and *life* in the streets that was immediately invigorating. It is probably a romantic notion of mine, but I thought they were happier then than when they got so chic and miniskirted later.

I know I loved London instantly. Even the grayness of it. The oldness and the solidness of it. The ritzy accent that I began to ape the moment I stepped off the plane. Perhaps this was the place to settle down forever.

Many of my buddies had crossed the ocean too. John was there, so was Kirk. My old friend Kathryn Buchman (now Mrs. Pandro Berman). The Jules Bucks had settled down to make pictures in Paris, merely a channel away. The Peter Viertels, Paulette and the Irwin Shaws. Everybody had shifted to Europe.

Sam had a flat in Grosvenor Square, leased from a maharajah, a handsome place filled with antique mirrors and big beds. (But no heat; there was no heat in all of London.) Sam went off somewhere and I took it over. Soon it was the gathering place for the American "waifs" in town, "misplaced" via Joe McCarthy or the IRS. When New Year's Eve came round, it seemed only sensible to gather in Sam's flat to celebrate, whether he was there or not, his parties for that event having been famous.

That night I had the chance to see, from a detached vantage point, John's negligence as a husband and even a lover.

We had filled ourselves with champagne—about eight of us altogether, among whom was John—and were preparing to leave for Les Ambassadeurs to bring in the year, when I heard John on the phone. "Forget the call, operator," I heard him say.

"What was that, John?" I asked.

"Oh, just somebody I had a date with," he answered.

"John," I said firmly, "this is New Year's Eve. You can't not keep a date on New Year's Eve."

He sighed. "Oh, all right." He picked up the phone again. Perhaps if a few more people had done that for me, we might have made it two days longer.

She joined us at the club, a sad-eyed actress, to whom John paid not the slightest attention. By this time, he and Ricky had *two* children. I don't know where they were.

The sad eyes grew more so as the evening progressed. Midnight had come and gone when the woman grabbed my arm. "Look!" she said, pushing her hand at me, "John gave me that ring!"

The design was that of a snake. Did she think it was an engagement ring? "It's very nice," I murmured. Had he not mentioned to her he was married and the father of two? I realized he was missing from the table. "Excuse me," I said to her, and went to find him. He was sitting in the lobby, in his coat and hat. "Are you leaving, John?" I asked.

He nodded. "I'm tired."

"What about your friend in there?"

He shrugged, not too interested.

I went back to tell her he was leaving. "You'd better hurry if you want to catch up." I didn't want those sad eyes to deal with when she found out he was gone.

She called me the next day to tell me she had just left John, and how wonderful it had been, how wonderful he was. To thank me for sending her after him.

She was the first of a series of Huston women who would come around to cry on my shoulder. I never knew exactly what they wanted from me. I was having a hard enough time figuring out what I wanted.

I instantly fell in love with Paris as I had with London. Perhaps *this* was the place to stay forever! Their suffering was over. Their restaurants were—well, French, delicious, rich and abundant. John was there too, and we gallery-hopped, went to the races, we drank Beaujolais de l'année. I don't know where Ricky and the kids were. John said that even French dogs were different from English dogs. "French ones strut and show off," he said, pointing at a French poodle. "English dogs are somber, very serious." The poodle then proceeded to get up on a restaurant chair and sit, upright, for close to an hour. I never saw an English dog sitting at table in a London restaurant. Perhaps John knew whereof he spoke.

Then fate stepped in to furnish the missing ingredient in my life. Romance.

I ran into him walking down the Champs Elysées my first week in Paris. He was Argentinian, a diplomat I had met sometime before in New York. Dark, an athletic build, and he moved well. He was somewhat bald, but you can't have everything. His accent was charming. Meeting him like that, by chance, surely had glass slipper overtones.

We dined, we danced, we roamed the city, and in the excitement and glow that was Paris, fell in love—or pretended that we did.

When he had to leave for Buenos Aires for diplomatic business he suggested, to seal our new-found togetherness, that we become engaged. Well, why not, I thought, I had never been engaged; perhaps this was the path to take, follow society's yesterday rules, do things properly in the crinoline and old lace manner. I had visions of myself as mistress of vast stretches of pampas, seas of cattle nursed by silver-saddled gauchos all looking like Yul Brynner. I also saw this enormous rock on my hand, fifty carats at least, enough to make Paulette green with envy.

He left without even giving me a cigar band. A mere oversight, I decided, he would send along one of his family's ancient and valued heirlooms.

I told John I was engaged to this fellow down in Argentina, and that is where I would be living. "Good God," he said, "you'll be in the middle of a revolution, that place is going to explode any minute."

"Good," I answered, "I would like to be a part of history instead of reading about it second-hand all the time."

"How long have you known this fellow?"

"Two weeks."

"Good Lord. You can't marry somebody you've only known for two weeks."

"John. We were married after three weeks."

"But," answered my ex-husband, "we were lucky."

Back in London I ran into an English producer in Curzon Street whom I had met at the Uruguay film festival the year before. He asked me if I would like to go down again, this time with the English contingent. Frisky fate was still pushing. Buenos Aires was a mere hop and skip across La Plata River from Uruguay. I could go see for myself just who and what I was engaged to.

It was a perfect stranger who met me at the plane, who seemed uneasy in his home town. Or was I the uneasy one? It was like the actor's nightmare: I didn't know why I was there, what was expected of me. I never saw the pampas. Nor a ring—of any size. Perhaps he thought I was the rich movie star. I saw one more hotel, and more restaurants, tango-flavored accents replacing French or British ones.

I learned the first day that I wouldn't live in Argentina for anything in the world. The men are crazy as loons. They stared unabashedly, even turned and followed you down the street, pinching your ass without hesitation, as if you were a cow for sale. Their machismo seemed to be in deadly peril every moment so that they were constantly driven to prove to themselves it was still intact. This quality, blended with anarchy, resulted in an inglorious display of ugliness the day we went to the races.

My friend and I, along with some friends of his, were in the jockey club directly behind the finish line. The judges' stand, a circular edifice, all glass, was just below us. It was an average day at the races, win a little, lose a little—the same in any language—until the third race. That one was a photo finish between number three and number five. Holders of those ticket numbers waited in excited expectation.

The signal flashed on. Number five had won. All the fives cheered lustily.

Then another signal flashed on. Inquiry. It seemed that number five had jostled number three out of position. Holders of number three scurried around retrieving their discarded tickets. When the announcement flashed on that the threes had indeed won, their exuberant cries rent the air, mixed with groans from ex-winners number five.

The excitement over, we had turned back to our racing forms when we became aware of a ruckus along the fence that divided the jockey club from the grandstand. Twenty-five or thirty men had gathered at the fence and were shaking their fists at the judges, shouting something. More men joined them. There might have been a hundred or more, and the shouts grew louder. I assumed this irate mob were all disappointed number five ticket holders.

Suddenly the guard at the entrance was shoved aside, and a stream of yelling, chanting men poured into the jockey club area, smashing whatever was in their path. Benches were upturned, chairs flung crashing against stone, potted plants knocked helter-skelter. With a roar they rushed the judges' cubicle, the sound of breaking glass splitting our ears as they yanked the officials out onto the lawn and began to beat them up. Spurting blood turned the green grass red.

I thought the revolution had come—the worker against the establishment—and stepped discreetly behind a pillar. My friend-fiancé and *his* friends, I noticed, had stepped behind one, too.

Police charged up on horseback, took one look, wheeled and galloped away. The law, I thought, was on the side of the number five ticket holders. I knew that revolutions started in unexpected ways. But no; they had gone for reinforcements and guns. Back they came, with pistols firing straight into the battling mob, plunging their horses into the thick of things. Loud shots, puffs of smoke, and human shrieks filled the air. The brave woman-pinchers turned to flee like frightened termites.

When the horses came out for the next race the damn fools threw pillows and beer bottles at the transgressive jockey but of course hit the bigger object, the horse. The poor creature naturally went berserk and had to retire from the race.

What with events like that and those interminable tangos—there was actually a law that they must be played half the time—I soon flipped out. In the middle of dinner a few nights later I told him, "I can't go through with it, I really can't. . . ."

He immediately understood; my reactions hadn't been exactly subtle.

My plane didn't leave for two days, which made for a very clumsy exit. He would come around to the hotel, looking gloomy. I was terribly sorry about the whole thing. So I decided we ought to consummate this . . . nothing. Up to then we had been following the time-honored rules—no wedding, no hanky-panky. I guess I wanted to turn the nothing into something, so it shouldn't have been a total waste of time, perhaps. So there, in my hotel room, we clashed in a reasonable facsimile of the sex act. A futile gesture, and empty for us both. He got up, punched his fist through the door, and left. The end.

At least there was something to be said for *one* Argentine man. The fist could have been aimed at me. . . .

CHAPTER 37

"Somewhere . . . a voice is calling . . ."

Back in Paris, I got a French car, a French license plate, a French driver's license, and dived right in, paying little heed to Thoreau who put it quite plainly: "It is not enough to be busy. The question is, what are we busy about?"

I would never go back to crummy Hollywood—Paris was by then Hollywood-sur-Seine anyway; everybody I liked was here, would be here, or would be passing through. John was presently making *Moulin Rouge* here. It might be thirty years too late for F. Scott Fitzgerald's Tender Nights, but there was still caviar and vodka at the Russian places, sad songs played on the balalaika by misplaced dukes. There was Monseigneur's and its army of violinists playing gypsy soul music in your ear and drinking champagne from the edges of their instruments without spilling a drop. There was Dom Perignon at Maxim's, white wine and oysters at Brasserie Lipp. And walks through winding streets, glorious works of art, and sidewalk cafés and talk.

It was some of the café talk that won me the entire pre-Columbian collection that John and I had accumulated when we were together. I had wound up with the half of it that had been moved into my Hollywood apartment—now in storage—and he had the rest. This night a group of us—the Peter Viertels, the Irwin Shaws, Tola Litvak, John, and Bob Capa, the photographer *extraordinaire* of the Spanish Civil War and subsequent conflicts (getting himself killed the following year photographing the Vietnamese War), and I—were sitting around *schmoozing* one night at Alexandre's, a place at the corner of Avenue George Cinq and the Champs Elysées. It had become more or less a gathering place for "the clan." Quite late, when a few drinks had been drunk, and talk had come around to some new piece of sculpture John had acquired, he turned to me, leaning in cozily in that posture I knew so well, and turned on the melted caramel sound. "Honey . . ." It was thoughtful, overflowing with meaning (Uh-oh, I thought, watch out), "I've always thought it a pity that that collection of ours should be separated—" His eyes narrowed to send out darts to pinpoint me under his spell. "Don't you?"

"Oh yes," I said, "I certainly do agree." I smiled. "So send yours back to me."

He was not amused. His eyes began a slow blinking, the mannerism that preceded some devious plot. He shifted away from me and toward the others, to get their full attention. "I have a splendid idea on the way to settle this," he announced.

"Oh yeah?" somebody murmured. "What's that, John?"

He was positively triumphant. "We'll toss for them!"

Everybody laughed. They all knew of John's gambling. "Don't listen to him, Evelyn," Peter said.

"I wouldn't dream of it," I laughed. "I have all the best pieces as it is."

Our lightness rolled off John's shoulders. He was not having it. "No no." He wagged his head solemnly. "It's the only possible way to settle it."

"Oh come off it, John," they all urged, "forget it. Let her be." They could see I didn't want to toss, I knew I would lose. And I liked those pieces.

"This must be decided, one way or the other. Now." John's dogged insistence ceased to be fun. I could feel the discomfort around the table. "Oh for Christ sake, John," I said wearily "go ahead and toss."

He made a fine ceremony out of it. He got out a coin. (A twenty franc piece.) He jiggled it. He moved it back and forth between his fingers, as if warming it up. "Heads or tails, honey?" he asked.

I shrugged. "Heads."

The whole table sat watching, silent, as John flipped his coin into the air, caught it as it fell, and slapped it on the back of his hand.

He held it there, in dramatic pause, looking at me. I waited, the table waited. Triumphantly he removed his hand to reveal the fateful coin.

It was heads.

After all, you can't lose them all.

Work came along too. John Berry, one of the blacklisted directors, was living in Paris making French films. He came around with not too bad a script—written by a blacklisted writer—rich American girl comes to Paris, takes up with French gigolo. That story. But what the hell. And we would do it in two versions, French and English. What better way to improve my burgeoning grasp of the French language: *C'est Arrivé à Paris!*

A picture in London came along quick on the heels of that one, with old friend Robert Parrish as director, script by Eric Ambler, with Joel McCrea the solid American interest. The plot was so complicated I still don't understand it. I found myself commuting between the two cities, always *schlepping* to London large chunks of beef, chocolate and eggs for English friends who were still on war rations.

I was even presented to the Queen during one of my London stays. Gene Kelly next to Keyes in the line-up. Vivien Leigh too. The first time I had seen her since GWTW. She still treated me like the bit player I had once been. She curtsied to her Queen. I tried, got my heel caught in the hem of my dress and remained in a bent position for the rest of the ceremony. Charlie Chaplin was in the C spot in line. I was invited down to Rome for his grand opening there of *Limelight*. And grand it was, the entire Italian government showed.

It was Christmas, so I drifted off to Venice. The Venetians had gone somewhere else. There was not a single Christmas decoration, the streets almost empty, with an occasional figure scurrying along muffled against the icy wind coming off the canals. Harry's Bar was warm and cheerful. One could have expected Papa to be sitting at a table near the bar.

At midnight, as church bells heralded the arrival of Christ's birthday, all alone in my Danieli Hotel room I watched a full moon rising over the dome of San Giorgio across the way, its light spilling across the Canal Grande in a silver stream, revealing one single enclosed gondola passing silently by.

I shivered. Was this to be my future? Watching cold moons in strange hotel rooms, alone?

Back in Paris I received an invitation to go to Morocco. Artists from several countries were being asked to help celebrate the opening of a casino. Well, why not. Who knew what might be around the corner.

Casablanca. Glaring sun, soft dust, and white white buildings. But no Bogie. Only a woman holding on to a donkey with one hand and pulling her veil aside with the other to vomit.

Marrakesh. Crackling hot, desert dry with lots of camels about—and their dung—a buzzing, spreading marketplace filled with many wondrous gifts (for a price), and rows of blind beggars, flies crawling over their dead eyes. But still no Bogie. Not even a fabulously rich, oil-well-glutted sheik dying to add me to his harem.

David Selznick and Jennifer Jones were there, however, relics from old films and past weddings. The world, it would appear, had shrunk to the size of Hollywood. I was beginning to understand that it didn't seem to matter where I went anymore. It was all going to be the same. And one thing for certain remained diabolically unchanged. I took *me* with me every step of the way.

Back to Paris. Back to Rome. Up to London. Even over to Klosters for skiing. And I don't ski. The train ride there was spectacular though. If it wasn't the Orient Express, it should have been—all thin whistles, clackety-clack and lots of steam. But no Bogie. No young man to glimpse me across the way sipping Soave Bolla and knowing when the right one comes along.

Going off to Palermo, though, was the final straw.

On the Via Veneto in Rome I ran into Charlie Feldman, who said, "Hey! We're flying to Sicily tomorrow for a soccer game. Why don't you come along?" I accepted. Who knew—maybe what I was looking for was in Sicily. Charlie's ex-wife Jean, who sometimes acted as his wife, was along.

At take-off time the next morning I felt lousy. My head ached, my abdomen was uneasy. I had been up far too late—until four. But I couldn't not go. It might be very well the moment for the wondrous thing to come along, and I would miss it.

We flew in a large private plane belonging to the Agnellis, the car manufacturers. It was their soccer team playing too. Two Agnelli brothers were on board, but my head ached so, I never did get them straight.

Fortunately, en route, Charlie and Jean opted for a day at an Agnelli castle somewhere on the water instead of going to the game. I said, me too. I didn't think I could sit in the hot sun for a whole afternoon.

One of the brothers drove us to the castle in racing driver style, at ninety kilometers an hour, through village and town, never braking once, while geese, dogs, children, old folk and cripples, carts and donkeys skittered out of the way as best they could. To the manor born, right? You don't have to be rich to be a shit, but it certainly helps.

The castle *was* lovely, big and rambling, of stone and tile—what I could see of it through my splitting headache and insides. I really felt crummy. I found a bedroom, lay down, dozed off and stayed that way until it grew chilly later in the day. Rising, I found out why I was feeling so rotten; my period had arrived unexpectedly four days early, and I didn't have a damn thing to take care of it.

Stuffing in a wad of Kleenex, and hoping for the best, I went to look for Charlie and Jean. They were outside pacing, looking worried. The car that was to take us back was long overdue. And try to phone from some isolated castle in Sicily to the outside world.

Finally, as the sun slipped dangerously near the edge, a car arrived. No sport, this driver, he took his own sweet time. And when we got to the spot where we'd last seen the plane, it wasn't there. The bastards had taken off without us.

So there we were, outside of Palermo, without our passports— Charlie had said not to bother bringing them for the day. But Charlie Feldman wasn't super-producer for nothing. He had the car take us to a hotel, got on the phone to somebody (the Mafia?) who arranged for us to stay overnight without our passports.

By then I was getting desperate. "Charlie," I said, "I've got to get to a drugstore."

"Right," agreed Charlie. "We need toothbrushes, paste—my God, I didn't even bring a comb."

The girl at the *farmacia* didn't speak a word of English, of course. I tried Kotex. Tampax, per favore, Modesta? I tried cursing too. Nothing worked. Charlie came over. "What's the trouble?" he asked. By then I didn't care who knew the fix I was in. "How the hell do you say 'sanitary napkin' in Italian, Charlie?"

He shrugged. "Would I know? Why don't you go back of the counter and show her," he suggested brightly.

It worked. The years spent playing charades had not gone for naught.

That night another full moon rose outside my window. Spilling its light over water. That it was warm, the air soft, didn't matter much. It was still one more hotel, one more country.

What I was looking for wasn't in Sicily. Who could have guessed it was waiting in the backyard of my own home town, Hollywood?

BOOK SIX

CHAPTER 38...

"We did it before . . . and we can do it again. . . ."

I was excited about going back. The script they sent me eventually became *99 River St.* United Artists, who had released *The Prowler* as well as the English film *Shoot First,* would release this film as well. I had been away almost two years. What, I wondered, would it be like, how would I feel?

I wasn't prepared for the razzle-dazzle that was my country. Grown accustomed, without being aware of it, to the low-lit European cities —even the cars used parking lights for night driving—I was bowled over at the sight of our incredible electrical display. It was my good fortune to fly west over the continent just as America was turning her evening lights on. I sat entranced at the wondrous burst of man-made illumination. Breathtaking. And discovered that I felt pride in being an American, a citizen of such a big, rich and shining nation. (No nasty term like "energy shortage" was being bandied about to spoil my burst of chauvinist joy.)

The Beverly Hills Hotel is not just *any* hotel. Pink and green like a candy stick, it is a home away from home. "Welcome home, Miss Keyes," said the doorman. "Nice to see you again, Miss Keyes," said the bell captain. The higher priced a hotel is, the friendlier the greeting, one soon learns.

After a good night's sleep, I went over to the studio to meet my producer, Edward Small. He was, too. If laid on end on his desk, the desk would have won by three lengths. He wasn't alone. Another man sitting on the couch had risen as I entered. "Meet Mike Todd," Eddie said.

I vaguely knew who Mike Todd was, a producer of shows in New York. I had seen one of them, *Star and Garter,* with Gypsy Rose Lee doing her strip act right there on Broadway, in pre-*Hair* times. A promoter, I believe they called him. Whatever that meant.

I didn't like the way he looked at all. He had on yesterday's pin-striped gangster suit. Shoes with perforated toes. And if that wasn't bad enough, he had long, slicked-down, patent-leather style hair that even George Raft had stopped affecting years before. And a perfectly monstrous cigar in his mouth.

Pushy, too. "Where you been all my life," he said, coming up very close to me, almost touching. I backed away.

Really.

I could have backed all the way to the edge of the earth for all the good it would have done. What Mike Todd wanted, Mike Todd usually got. Or made one hell of a run at it.

The phone calls started, the visits to the set where I was working. Wherever I was, there was Mike. He embarrassed me with his possessive hugging, touching. "You're my girl," he would say. "No, I am not," I would answer emphatically. I was headed back to Paris the minute this picture was finished.

He would always bring a present too, any silly little thing. Like the see-through bag covered with enormous rhinestones and the card reading, "Happy Arbor Day to the love of my life—Your Mike."

He came around later to follow it up. His arms were tight around me when he said, "Let's have dinner tonight and celebrate a tree."

I squirmed away. "I can't go out with hair like that," I answered facetiously, gesturing at his head.

"Then we'll change it," he responded airily, and left.

He was at the stage door when I finished work. "We got a date with a barber," he said, taking my arm.

"What?" I had forgotten our earlier conversation.

"You'll supervise. That way you'll get what you want."

I laughed. He *was* amusing. His eyes danced. He did have a flair. But the eternal cigar. . . .

The barber played along as if women coming in to his male sanctum sanctorum to direct his hair-cutting procedure was a daily occurrence. Beneath the pomade Mike had luxuriant hair. As the scissors did their stuff, he began to look like a new man. Even a few years fell off. Hey, I decided, not half bad . . . and I'm here for the next three months. . . .

He watched me during the whole operation, head tilted, lips pressed together, amusement threatening to get the upper hand any second. I kept a straight face. I thought it was darling how he was going along with the whole thing without thinking twice. Here was a man so sure of his identity that changing a few outward odds and ends didn't matter in the least. It was very winning.

We were having fun, the game was highly enjoyable. But somewhere along the line a subtle shift occurred, and it became . . . something else. It became the preliminary bout, the fencing between male and female (and probably other combinations as well) that takes place before the main event. As everybody knows, anticipation is the best part of the game.

He had taken off his shirt when he sat down in the barber's chair, revealing a hairy back. I'm not fond of rampant body hair. The chest is bad enough, but the back! As long as I was at it, I thought, I might as well get exactly what I want. "Shave all that off," I said to the barber, pointing.

He blinked at me, and looked at Mike.

"You heard the lady," Mike Todd said.

When the barber had finished, brushed him off, and he had dressed, Mike took a long look at himself in the mirror. "Mm," said he, "the Keyes cut."

"We're not through," I said. "Those have to go too." I pointed to his feet.

His eyebrows flew up. "My shoes?"

"Old hat."

"Let's go."

Before we were through, Mike had a new wardrobe from top to bottom. Loafers, gray slacks, Italian knit shirts that could be worn in or out without a tie. They became his stock-in-trade, especially for traveling, which he did the major part of his life.

Yes, I changed the way Mike Todd looked, for better or worse.

The man underneath was something else. . . .

I was working long hours, with early risings and early to beds, even doing night work for a couple of days; no way I could fit romance into my tough schedule in the middle of the week. So we made a date for the following Saturday to—as Mike said—"do it."

In the meantime he visited the set at steady intervals. We lunched, he scarcely touched me anymore—"scairt," he said, he might blow the whole deal. Sometimes he even left his cigar outside. Two of the days he flew to New York and back. The phone calls were several times a day from there, too. (I was to learn Mike Todd always had a phone in one hand or the other, and sometimes both.) He was busy getting together a new film technique to be called Todd-AO, a combination of his chutzpah and a scientist at American Optical: a new wide lens camera, to replace the recently introduced Cinerama which took three cameras to accomplish what Mike's gadget could with one. His enthusiasm, the excitement he engendered about it, about "us" and our future, even about where to have a dinner, was catching. He soon had me believing his was the greatest invention since the wheel.

The build-up to our coming affair was handled in the same high-powered, keyed-up intensity. Nobody ever "had love" before. We had the "right chemistry," how could we go wrong. Since he stayed at Joe Schenck's house when he came out, and my single room would never do when history was about to be made, he got a suite at the Beverly Hills Hotel for the occasion.

The sex act is a neatly worked-out ritual for every living thing of this earthly kingdom, whether feathered, furred, scaled, multi-legged or chlorophylled. Whether it's whinny, thump, whir, clack or twitter, each of them knows exactly what to do, how and when, without nervousness, without pressure, and void of self-consciousness.

Man is the exception. He and he alone among the myriad of species must shed his/her furs and/or feathers before this particular form of togetherness can be accomplished. It does make for awkwardness. It also makes for uncertainty since we don't know what we're getting into (so to speak) beforehand. All the goodies are hidden, kept a mystery until the very last minute, past the point of no return. When the "what you see is what you get" moment arrives, and you don't want to play, what do you do?

Owners of thoroughbreds follow a kinky custom (things get that way when man tampers). They use what is known as a "tease" pony to get the mare ready for the stallion. This nondescript breed nibbles, licks—whatever horses do to turn on—the lady through a fence, never getting closer, so that when the mighty stallion arrives, all he has to do is "do it." (The pony has never been asked how he feels.)

Lacking a pony, Mike and I turned to navy grogs at Trader Vic's to blur our nervousness. Two of those, and one can—if not climb Mount Everest—most certainly go up the elevator to the third floor of the Beverly Hills Hotel.

Personally I prefer to have the first time over with; lovemaking starts afterward. (Mike, I was to learn, turned himself on in the middle present goings-on by talking about the next time.) The usual cellophaned fruit basket was in the suite, compliments of the management, a bottle of iced Dom Perignon, compliments of Mike. Otherwise not a trace of life in the joint.

But listen, neither of us was exactly a fumbling virgin, we had been there before, and we . . . managed. . . .

Here . . . you don't want to keep holding on to that . . . let's just . . . get rid of . . . mmmm . . . I've been . . . wanting to . . . do this . . .

Christ, like . . . silk . . . unbeliev . . . able . . . you smell like . . . too
much . . . mmm . . . this is in the way, let's . . . just . . . slide it out of
. . . oh God . . . they're . . . beautiful like I knew they . . . I can't . . .
here, let me . . . a hook is caught . . . I'll . . . there . . . yes . . . oh hey
. . . oh God, that's . . . good . . . so good . . . don't stop . . . oh I love
. . . that . . . touch me . . . see what you're . . . doing to me . . . there
. . . yes . . . *there* . . . oh Christ, I can't wait, next time we'll . . . I'll . . .
you'll let me . . . Oh . . . My . . . God! You're so . . . oh that's . . . nice
. . . very nice . . . ye-a-a-ah . . . ooooh, oh yes . . . yes . . . yes . . . yes
. . . oh . . . oh . . . oooooooooooooh!

CHAPTER 39 . . .

"That old . . . black magic . . . has me
in . . . its spell. . . ."

I kept thinking I was going right back to Paris when my picture
was finished. It was my home now, my apartment, clothes, car, all
were there. This Mike Todd was most entertaining during my Hollywood stay, but nothing more than that. Who could take him for a
steady diet?

Perpetual motion itself, he thought nothing of flying to New York
and back to L.A. several times a week, or to Europe for the day—
London, Rome, Milan, Zurich—and back again. Dashing to Palm
Springs for a day's "rest." Chicago for lunch. Deals whizzed in all
directions, ideas for new ones popping like buds in spring. He seldom
held fewer than two telephone conversations at once, with the third,
fourth, fifth to infinity waiting in the wings. Gregarious, he liked
people around him wherever he went. He enjoyed food too, and good
restaurants. He gave fine parties, buzzing around, tending his guests
himself. And between it all had a steady gin rummy game going in all
cities and also found time to lose his money in Las Vegas or Cannes or
wherever a racetrack or crap and baccarat table could be found.

He talked of marriage immediately. "I got love," he would say,
"what else can I do." Though I admired his whirling dervish ways
and jumping *joie de vivre*, he wasn't really the "artist" type I was

inclined toward, the creator of things rather than the hirer. And that eternal cigar. The atrocious grammar. "Anyways," he would say. The repetition of certain phrases. "Walk around money." "He's around forty-ninth street" (somebody's age). "I wouldn't tip a waiter that" (too little money). "Prepartée" (prepared stuff made to sound like repartée). "Rootin' interest" (a piece of the action). "Calling from the police station" (really in trouble). "The weather is so changeable I don't know what to hock." "S.I.B."—these letters over the phone meant, stay in bed, I'll join you there.

After hearing these same phrases over and over, in a matter of weeks they began to grate like steel wool pulled across flesh. I knew I would be happy to leave for Paris the moment I was able to. And then he would do something so very thoughtful, and utterly charming. Or tell an amusing joke or story I hadn't heard before. Then I would begin to wonder what I actually ought to do.

Certain worries had a way of nagging at me back there somewhere. Another birthday had come and gone. Time was rushing by with the speed of light. Forty, at one time unthinkable, was beginning to be a distinct possibility. Unless I chose to die in the next few years, there was nowhere else to go.

But if dying is out, I would tell myself, you had better do some serious planning. Is it wise to go back to a place where you have to get a work permit every time something comes along? Do you propose to go through life running from one man to another? Here's a hell of a guy crazy about you, wanting to marry you, do every goddamn thing for you, a man in the midst of things, about to revolutionize the entire motion picture industry—that's what he says, and maybe he will. Why do you hesitate? Because you don't like some odds and ends about him? What, you're so perfect, you don't have any little foibles he might be putting up with? Ha. Learn a little patience, little friend, and maybe others will have a little for you.

Instead of flipping back to Paris I signed for another film to be made in Hawaii in August. When summer stock was suggested, I went for that, too—I would be busy for the summer instead of getting sucked into Mike's whirling pool.

And wasn't it fun to meet Oscar Hammerstein! And Dick Rodgers! Noël Coward! S. J. Perelman! John Ringling North! The genius at American Optical who was inventing the lens! I had to ask myself, what did the likes of them, supereducated, supertalented, worldly-wise sophisticates, see in this man who appeared to be not much more than one step removed from carnie spieler, whose garbled grammar and cocky manner hinted at street-urchin background? That he amused them wasn't enough. That he wouldn't take no for an answer wasn't all of it either.

Soon I began to see that Mike knew very well what he was about. It was true he hadn't had much formal education, that what he knew came from the streets. He was keenly aware of the lack. But he wasn't going to hide it. Instead, somewhere along the way he decided he wasn't going to imitate his scholarly peers, become a second-rate copy of *them*. He would become a first-rate *him*. If he couldn't say it right, then he would exaggerate the wrong, and make it work for him. The language would come to him, not he to it.

He made it into a fine camouflage behind which he could hide. Play a bit of the mug, a bit of the clown, the vulgarian, from whom no one would expect a pearl of wisdom to flow, or any grasp of cultural knowledge, so that when it did it was a pleasant surprise and all the more impressive.

Life was a game, to be played with zest and exuberance, with a firm grasp onto Peter Pan's coattails. That every day *was* the first day of his life was true for Michael Todd.

But none of that was the real reason I got caught in his web. For a daddy-prone person like me, Mike the planner, the organizer, the doer, was made to order. It was too easy to let this dynamo make all the arrangements; he was doing it anyway: where to go, when, how, tickets, reservations, cars. In no time at all he had taken the place of the studio I had relied on, and was missing terribly. Big Daddy had returned.

We flew east together. Still prop plane days, the trip was an overnight voyage. You boarded the plane at midnight, crawled into a berth, and woke up in another city. We sat up for a while in the half-light, smoking, drinking champagne, nuzzling and making plans. He would be at all my opening nights. (I was doing Sally Bowles in *I Am a Camera*.) He would visit me between all his other trips as I traipsed about New York State and Pennsylvania. " . . . Once you have found her . . . ne-ver . . . let her go. . . . " he sang, not quite on key.

And we indulged in everybody's favorite pastime, gossip. Who was doing what, and to whom. Mike mentioned the name of a widely-known actress, and told me it was rumored she was having an affair with—and he mentioned a black performer.

It was the *way* he told me that touched a nerve, as if he were telling me something outrageously juicy. As a reformed alcoholic shies away from liquor, a converted bigot bristles at the *hint* of racist overtones. Somebody's ethnic toes being trod on? I must instantly rush to the rescue.

Mike had formerly made all the right liberal sounds. But was he a closet bigot? So I said, rather too sharply, "What's wrong with that?"

"What's wrong!" Mike sputtered indignantly, "Would *you* have to do with . . . with a—"

"I have," I answered, with all the righteousness of an archangel.

Mike shook his head. "Bite your tongue. You have not."

"I most certainly have," I snapped, "and what the hell difference does it make whether I have or not? You surely know it doesn't rub off."

He stared at me. Even in the low-keyed plane light, I could see he had paled. "You really mean it, don't you," he whispered.

"Of course I mean it!" I answered with irritation. "What's the big deal—"

He leaped out of his seat as if he had caught on fire, went charging down the aisle and disappeared into the toilet.

Damned hypocrite, I thought. He had told me horrendous stories of his suffering from anti-Semitism as a kid. The world had recently lived through Hitler. How could Mike *dare* to harbor "anti" feelings toward any other group of people!

He came back and sat beside me, looking as though he were in great pain. He just looked at me. Just sat there and looked at me.

I shook my head. "Mike," I started to say, "for heaven's sake, why are you—"

"Why did you have to tell me?" It was a pitiful plea.

"Why shouldn't I tell you? Why are you carrying on so—"

"Why did you have to tell me?" he repeated faintly, looking at me, sitting without moving. The picture of a broken man.

I was getting angry. "Jesus Christ, Mike!" I snapped, and launched into a long and heated lecture about prejudice, how, as long as it existed in any form there was no hope for peace, that he, a Jew, ought to know that, etc.

I might as well have been talking to a deaf-mute. He remained perfectly still without shifting his gaze from me. Tears started to trickle down his cheeks.

Oh God. What had I done? Hurt him is what. What good had it done? We all have our prejudices and hitting somebody over the head doesn't change him. One must be led gently, shown patiently, the way I had been.

I reached over to put my arms around the weeping Mike, and he recoiled from me. Recoiled!

It was my turn to stare. Rejection! Daddy had done it again. Gone off and left me to wait on the porch. That's that, I thought, Paris it is when I'm through in America, whether I like it or not. Only . . . at that moment, Paris seemed so far away, so . . . foreign. . . .

It was a long night. Neither of us slept. I crawled into my berth and tried. Mike poked his head through the curtain several times during the night, not to say anything, but simply to look at me.

We got off the plane next morning, still without speaking. I went to a hotel, he to his Park Avenue apartment.

I should have let it go. I should have known he had to come to me if we were to have any kind of meaningful relationship at all. That the reason for this estrangement was a deep-seated and basic difference between us which would never be rectified unless Mike was able to come to some terms with himself.

But guilt insisted on pushing me around. It was I who had thrown a sour note into a smooth operation. Greed and creature comfort played a part too: I had so quickly got used to his taking care of me, watching over me with such loving care. I wasn't ready to give it up.

So I was the one who phoned. "Please," I said, "can't you get over it? I'm the same person, the very same person I was before I told you. Whatever happened to me before you doesn't count, you've told me that, it all adds up to make me into this combination of things that you say you like. . . . Please. . . ."

He let me persuade him. He drove me next day to my first theater engagement in upstate New York. We stayed overnight in a motel on the way. We undressed, quietly, sedately. I used the bathroom, got in bed. He used the bathroom and joined me. At first we lay there stiffly, each on his own side. I wouldn't reach out; I had reached out twice. It was his turn now.

A hand slid over. Touched and lay there. Finally he rolled over toward me; an arm slid over me, but it was lifeless, a dead weight.

I waited.

With no preamble, no caress, not even a kiss, he shifted himself and stretched his body out on top of mine, and then lay still. Without expression, his eyes, six inches or so above me, gazed down into mine. And then he started to cry again. "I can't," he wept, "I can't do it. . . ."

It was true. He couldn't. He lay there on top of me like a dead man, except for the tears that fell on my face.

At last I asked him to remove himself—smothering and drowning me wasn't the answer. We moved to our respective sides of the bed and stayed there. I knew now we were through. If our sex life was destroyed, then we had very little else. Over and out. I could do no more.

He dropped me at my theater next day where we said our first words since the night before, and they were good-byes. "Good luck, Mike," I said, "with your Todd-AO, and if you're ever in Paris, give me a ring."

Perhaps it was the finality of my tone. Or perhaps it was simply that his infatuation hadn't run its course. Whatever.

He began his multi-calling again. Flowers showed up everywhere; he even arranged cast parties for my cast, in those obscure little towns where I was playing, no matter where he was.

He tried. He really tried to forget, to take it in his stride. He knew he was wrong, part of him was ashamed, but another part reacted without his control. Sometimes I would find him looking at me sadly. He couldn't stop from asking, "Did you have to do with—" He would throw a name at me. "Was he the one?"

"Do you really want to know, Mike?" I would say.

He found himself a running joke. "If I didn't make friends with your ex-husbands and lovers, who would I talk to?"

But the nature of this particular coupling had been established, the course embarked upon. . . .

CHAPTER 40...

"You're getting to be a habit

with me. . . ."

Mike's new camera and lens were ready for a trial run. He gathered a crew, me, the actor who was my leading man on tour, and took us out to the amusement park at Far Rockaway outside New York City. There, they secured the mammoth camera to the front of the roller coaster, and we two performers sat in the front seat with the camera pointing down at us. Mike, the cameraman and an assistant climbed aboard behind the camera, and we were off.

Up, up, up . . . slowly over the top, and wheee! Dooooown we go, catapulting through space, zooming round and round at a hundred miles an hour. I giggled and squealed and clung to my companion in girlish terror for the new lens's benefit, determined to help make its debut as exciting as possible for Mike.

He got more than he bargained for.

While I was busily simulating roller coaster joy, the camera had loosened from its moorings on the very first ascent. Mike and the two men spent the entire time we were being catapulted along, struggling to keep the massive piece of equipment from hurtling through the air and smashing into the faces of two innocent play-actors.

So now I owed him my life. He did very well by it.

Getting to know Mike Todd's New York was simply marvelous. We saw every show in town. Sometimes we would just walk about the theater district, popping in first one theater, catching a piece of an act, going on to another, catching a piece of that, standing in the back. Then there was the Latin Quarter with Tony Bennett, the Stork Club with Walter Winchell, Sardi's and everybody, Luchow's on Sunday nights, Lindy's, Dinty Moore's, El Morocco, downtown for Italian, up and down for Chinese. There was Peter Luger's across the Brooklyn Bridge, with its sawdust on the floor and great steaks. The Colony and "21" and Voisin and The Little Club and Le Pavillon.

There was good talk and good food and through it all, Mike, wheeling and dealing, reaching for this, planning for that, going after *Oklahoma* for the first production to be done in Todd-AO, sandwiching in between an extravaganza called *A Night In Venice* at the Marine Stadium at Jones Beach. And playtime woven among all that, a racetrack, a gin game, a stretch in the sun, with a phone, to be sure, at his elbow.

I loved it all, Mike's boundless energy and verve, the buzzing excitement that never stopped, the feeling of going-somewhere, getting-something-done. A future with Mike began to look rosy indeed.

Until the night we went to the Copa to see Joe E. Lewis, and the shit hit the fan all over again. I was leaving next day for the West Coast, to start preparing for my Hawaii picture, costume fittings and such. Mike would be flying out the next day to spend the week with me in L.A. before I went on to Honolulu.

At least, that was the plan until we got to the Copa.

A gorgeous black man was sitting at the table next to us. At least eight feet tall, dressed in some bright African robe, and no Americans were doing that in those days. He had to be the real thing, a Masai, maybe? What did I know from Africans, and I didn't dare even look; I had to pretend I hadn't noticed this most unusual sight.

Mike's whole manner changed. He withdrew behind his cigar, narrowed his eyes and watched me instead of the floor show.

He was downright surly in the cab on the way home. I didn't ask why. I didn't want to hear it. He said it anyway. "So who was yours?" he finally came out with.

"My . . . what?" I snapped, knowing full well.

"Your . . . you know . . . the . . . the—"

"You are a pain in the ass, you know that, Mike?"

"If I knew who it was, I could forget—"

"Like hell you would forget, I'm not falling for that bullshit, I'm not telling you anything, so forget asking, that's the thing to forget!" I was outraged that he would begin this shameful racial business all over again.

"Why don't you just tell me who and get it—"

"Oh . . . my . . . God!" I cried, "you sound like a broken record."

"Why won't you tell me—you liked him too much, is that—"

"Of course I liked him!" I cried. "What do you think, I go to bed with people I *don't* like?"

The picture conjured up was too much; Mike grabbed for his chest. This was a little trick of his. If I drop dead of a heart attack, it implied, it will be your fault. The first time he had done it, it scared me half to death—until I found out his heart was a powerhouse. I didn't need somebody shoveling guilt at me, I had an ample supply on hand already. This chest-grabbing made me furious. "I'm never going to tell you anything ever again," I shouted. "This is all too stupid and I won't go on with it anymore. I mean it, this is the end if you don't shut up about—"

"You're covering up something, aren't you, that's why—"

"Stop this cab, driver!" I yelled. Actually we *had* stopped at a red light. I leaped out of the door and ran. Mike got out too, but before he could pay I got in another cab and drove away. I was absolutely livid and trembling with anger.

Only, as usual, it didn't last long. By the time I reached my hotel I was crying, sick at heart and utterly miserable. My life had come to an end. Again. I wouldn't answer the ringing phone, though. What good would more of the same do?

I made my plane next day in spite of a broken heart, and slumped, inconsolable in my seat all the way to Chicago, where I had to change planes.

He was waiting at the door of the terminal. He was holding this five-foot sausage cradled in his arms.

Where he picked up a thing like that I'll never know. I do know it was a very funny sight, and broke me up. Laughter is as good a way to make up as any other.

With Cornel Wilde in *A Thousand and One Nights*.

Between Charles Vidor, left, my second husband and my brother Sam.

Harry Cohn, the
czar of Columbia
Pictures.

With John Huston, my third husband.

Domestic interval with John.

With John on the ranch.

With Paulette Goddard in Mexico.

Water skiing with Kirk Douglas in Acapulco.

On location with Mike Todd.

Walter and John Huston each win an Academy Award for *The Treasure of the Sierra Madre.*

My cameo role in *Around the World in Eighty Days*, with David Niven and Cantinflas.

My best performance (I think), in *The Prowler* with Van Heflin.

With husband number 4, Artie Shaw.

Artie Shaw.

In the road company
of *No, No Nanette*.

Scarlett O'Hara's younger
sisters today . . . with Ann
Rutherford.

The current me.

CHAPTER 41...

"Who's afraid of the big . . . bad . . . wolf. . . ."

We flew on to Los Angeles together. Mike managed to keep his counsel until I took a plane for the islands.

Hawaii must have been truly paradise before the Americans came along to muck up the shoreline with their endless hotels. The sands are white, the air soft to the touch, and the water an incredible blue with long rolling waves perfect for surfing, if that's your bag. Or just lolling, if that's your bag. I tried surfing—until a board whacked me on the head after I had fallen off and gone under, swallowing most of the South Pacific. It seemed wiser to stick to lolling if I wanted to finish the picture.

None of it was conducive to work, but since all the world's a stage, and most of the shooting was done at night, leaving us to our golden days, we managed. Beach, bar, restaurants and streets of Honolulu were our sets, the Hotel Surf Rider was our home. Not a bad way to go.

Lotus living lasted about a week before a snippy cable arrived from Mike—from Venice where he had gone when I left Los Angeles: SO YOU DON'T WANT TO MARRY ME WHY AM I THE LAST TO KNOW. . . .

The day before I left Los Angeles, Sheilah Graham, the columnist, had called me to ask if I was marrying Mike Todd.

It was one of the milder questions a columnist might ask. I've been asked about my sex life, how many times a week my husband and I made love, my bank account, my insurance policies. Sheilah, Hedda, Louella, wielded tremendous power in those days; able to advance or seriously hurt a career, believing they were the watchdogs of our morals, with the right to run our private lives. Not only read by fans, their columns were the entire industry's Bible—Harry Cohn being a case in point. It was how we could keep track of what everybody was doing, where, and with whom.

One didn't *not* answer. "Oh Sheilah," I said evasively, "I'm not marrying Mike or anybody else just now. Don't you think I've done enough of that sort of thing to last me for a while?"

I read her reporting of the conversation in Honolulu, Hawaii; it was hardly surprising Mike had read it too, in Venice, Italy, where a film festival was going on.

It read a bit harsher than I had intended, and I decided it best to talk to him in person.

Footnote: If you want to talk to Venice, don't start from Honolulu. Mike made it more difficult by disappearing altogether. I was to find out why much later. He had himself a little fling so the trip shouldn't be, as he would say, a total loss. How did I find out? Because he told me. If he had done it either for revenge or one-upmanship, or both, and I had never known, what good would it have done him? But it worked out nicely for me: When he brought up his pet self-inflicted hurt, I had an answer. Mine was before, yours was after we met. For shame!

Hedda got me on the way back, calling me at the Beverly Hills Hotel where I was staying. "Are you marrying Mike Todd?" she asked too.

"Hedda, I haven't seen the man for two months."

"Marry him," she told me, "he's mad about you."

The ladies always knew what you should do, and told you, too. It isn't easy going through life with somebody looking over your shoulder at every move. Was it she who told Mike I was back? When I stepped out of the elevator into the lobby, he was there. Without sausage. He stood before me, unsmiling, silent, inches away, tragic-eyed, as if the world had died, oblivious of people trying to get past us to get on or off the elevator. One of the bell captains came along with a mountain of luggage on his cart. "Excuse me, Mr. Todd," he said cheerily, "don't want to run you down."

Mike took my hand then, and led me to the nearby Polo Lounge, not jam-packed in midafternoon as it would be later. The captain gave us a corner booth. "A drink, Mr. Todd?" Mike looked at me. I shook my head. "A lemonade with two straws," Mike told the hovering man, by way of dismissal.

His eyes never leaving me, he reached in his pocket, took out a small, gold-wrapped, bow-ribboned package and slid it toward me. "What is it?" I asked.

"Only one way to find out."

The paper crackled as I pulled it apart. A pin nestled inside a velvet-lined box. A flower carved in old ivory, its petals sapphires and diamonds. "Oh Mike," I said, "it's beautiful."

The intake of breath, and the grunt, as if he were in great pain. "I . . . missed you." I will never know if it was a characteristic of Mike's, but for the rest of the time I knew him, when he made any declaration of affection for me, it was as if a confession were torn from him, a feeling he would give anything not to have.

I reached over and placed my hand on top of his. "I missed you too, Mike, I really did."

He didn't respond beneath my hand. "You gotta know. I . . . did it in Venice."

"Did what—oh. You mean—?"

The focus of his eyes never wavered, as he watched for my reaction. "Why do you tell me, Mike?"

"We got to start out fresh, no secrets between us." I withdrew my hand, but then he grabbed it.

"Don't start that, Mike. I'm not going around on that merry-go-round again, ever. Look here—" I slipped my hand away from his and reached in my bag. "See this?" I showed him my plane reservation for Paris on the weekend. "I had given up on you, and maybe I'd better use this."

"No." He took the reservation out of my hand and slipped it into his pocket. "I'll turn it in . . . I tried, it didn't work, I can't . . . we got to try again, I'm . . . your fella, what can I do. . . ."

I wanted to believe, I guess, Irresistible me. Femme fatale par excellence. His "Human Bondage." Once you've tasted my wares, my boy, there's no escaping.

"Let's go upstairs," Mike whispered huskily. . . .

He told me his latest plan. It wasn't bad. Peace forever in the world is what he had in mind, and he, Michael Todd, would singlehandedly bring it about. How? He would make a deal with the Russians. His new lens was ideal for the scope of a classic like *War and Peace*. The Russians would see that. He would go to the Soviet Union to film the story where it should be filmed, in its own backyard. And the two ideologies would love one another from then on.

In 1954, few Americans had entered the Soviet Union, much less made a picture there. A very chilly, if not cold, war was still very much in evidence. "I need you with me," Mike said, "You can help me do it, be my partner. . . ."

I had visions. Ambassadress-at-Large. My fantastic charm, my mere presence would win the war, change the course of history.

The moment we arrived in New York I rushed to Berlitz and enrolled in a Russian language class.

My state of euphoria was suddenly shattered by a rude shock.

My passport needed renewing, so I hurried down to the State Department offices at Rockefeller Center to take care of the matter quickly. Mike had the habit of deciding on the spot to go somewhere and grabbing the next plane out. I didn't want to have to stay behind on a technicality.

I handed my document to a man behind the counter and explained I was in a rush. He took it and went away. I waited. And waited. And waited. He was gone for what seemed an unconscionably long time. It was on the tip of my tongue to tell him so when he finally returned. What he said to me startled me out of my wits. "You," he said, raising an eyebrow, "have been a bad girl, haven't you?"

I knew instantly what he was referring to. I had been expecting it somehow. Those secret blacklists were everywhere. I had to be on one. Had not the House Un-American Activities Committee cited the Hollywood Democratic Committee as a tainted group? I had attended their meetings. Had I not gone to Washington on the protest flight? Paris, London, and Rome were filled with refugees from Hollywood who weren't allowed to work in the States anymore, and I had freely associated and worked with them all and had made it all too clear where my sympathies lay. Now it was my turn. I knew too that passports were being withheld (proven later to be an illegal ploy) when one's status as loyal citizen was questionable in their eyes.

The man before me seemed suddenly to have shot to twenty feet tall, sprouted fangs, a horrible sneer, and wore a black uniform with a crossbones insignia on the sleeve.

I began to tremble. "Wh-wh-wh-what d-d-do y-you m-m-mean, sir?"

"They want an affidavit from you." He shoved a piece of paper and a pen toward me. "I'm out of forms, you'll have to write it in longhand. Put down there—" The sneer deepened, "—if you can, 'I am not now, nor have I ever been, a member of the Communist Party. . . .'"

This so-called "Loyalty Oath" was making the rounds of government and corporations—including movie studios. Employees had to sign if they wanted to keep their jobs, or obtain new ones. And now it was obviously required by the passport division.

This government official had no right to question my political affiliations—or lack of them. I knew that. Yet I eagerly reached for the pen and paper. I was trembling, scared out of my wits. I, the orthodox coward who crumples at the very hint of danger, had folded again. I was particularly distressed when I had to write that, to my knowledge, I didn't *know* any Communists either. If one did, it was considered one's patriotic duty to inform on them.

I did know one. One person had actually told me that he had been a Party member. The only reason I have been able to hold my head up at all after signing that dastardly piece of paper, is that at least I didn't squeal on a friend.

Even so, I was given a passport limited to only three months.

So much for selling your soul.

I was shaken to the marrow that my country was treating me like a criminal. Mike told me not to worry; he knew somebody in Washington; he would try to get my passport in order with the correct number of years. I was grateful. I clung to him, afraid to move.

CHAPTER 42...

> *"And then they nursed it . . .*
> *rehearsed it . . ."*

When the Russians were slow in coming around, Mike flew off to Yugoslavia to shoot *War and Peace* there. I wouldn't go. That's all I needed, I thought, to have a three-month passport stamped with a visa to Communist Yugoslavia. They would come for me on a dark night and throw me into a dungeon. But I received a cable—printed in red!—from Belgrade. MISS YOU EVEN IN YUGOSLAVIA. I wondered if inquiring eyes had seen that, and what they had made of it.

On Mike's return he pulled his Washington string, and when a brand new shining passport arrived—as if I were a Michael Todd production—we were off on a life of perpetual motion, Mike wheeling and dealing, and I . . . well, I was his now, wasn't I? Whither thou goest. . . . And I felt safe with him.

London and back, Rome, Venice, and Rome again. Beverly Hills and back to New York. *Oklahoma* was about to be made in Todd-AO; in Hollywood Oscar Hammerstein was explaining to a studio what the new lens was: "There are little spacemen created by Mike Todd in the camera doing extraordinary things. . . ." Palm Springs for sun (and gin rummy with Sam Goldwyn), Las Vegas for crap tables. Mike still had suits made with a tiny secret pocket in the back for his "getaway money," he called it. Havana for Christmas and New Year's. It was like carnival time in Rio, with the cruise boats arriving by the hundreds and people dancing the night away in the streets. And gambling, too, of course.

It was fun, it was exciting, but my increasing dependence was making me uncomfortable. Mike had insisted that I move into his apartment, and I had in my moment of panic. It was the only place I had. But camp following lost its charm from time to time, and seemed so aimless. When I mentioned work Mike would ask, wasn't I happy being a "woman"?

He had explained what a "real" woman was, how she behaved. How she was devoted to "her fella." Supportive. There, at his side, *always,* when he needed her.

"The classic arrangement between the sexes," I had answered, "went out of style along with high-buttoned shoes."

"Your trouble is, you won't accept rules."

"Ha," I scoffed, "Where would you be if you accepted rules?"

". . . won't accept being the weaker sex or that you need to be taken care of, it's why women and children . . ."

"Now there's an antiquated rule, women and children first in the lifeboats. What if Albert Einstein were on board? You'd take some fool woman off the ship and let him drown?"

Teasing Mike about man-woman relationships was irresistible; he was like a throwback to the Diamond Jim Brady school when pretty girls were toys to have hanging on your arm and decorate with baubles when you were in the money.

Outwardly I scoffed, but secretly I wondered if maybe he didn't have a point. Those couplings where the roles were clearly defined (he worked, she didn't), seemed to last better than any I had had.

So I hung around and played "woman." And tried to pretend, even to myself, that living openly with a man, unmarried, was the only way to go.

But people poked. "Why don't you marry the girl?" said David Selznick at El Morocco one night. "Is Mike marrying you?" my ex-husband, Charles Vidor, asked when I ran into him. All of us caught up in the same moral code. "Don't be silly," I would answer. "Marriage is old hat." They didn't believe me. I didn't either.

"Why don't we, Mike?" I said lazily.

It had been a good evening. Dinner at "21" with friends. We had seen *My Fair Lady.* Gone dancing at El Morocco's where we had run into David. We had come home quite late, got into robes, and were watching the Late Late Show, two sleepy people. "Do what?" Mike murmured.

"Get married."

He stirred. "How do I know you're ready to settle down to one guy?"

Back to square one. My head began to throb quietly. A wave of hopelessness, gossamer thin, settled over me. I knew what he was hinting at. Had he not referred to it, skirted, implied, alluded to it in an infinite variety of ways since our first plane trip east together? That the black experience had been such a potent and mind-blowing one that I would have to have an encore sooner or later? But for a long time he hadn't mentioned it. Not since I had moved in. Foolishly I thought it was gone and forgotten. Wrong. Very wrong.

I had assured him too many times. I was too tired, too disheartened to do it again. "Yeah," I murmured, "you're probably right."

He sat up abruptly, the peace gone. "Ha! It's true!" he cried. How easy it was to have a fight with Mike.

"Oh Mike," I sighed, "I make jokes because you never stop that same theme—"

"Jokes can be to cover up the real—"

"When would I have time to think of anybody but you—" I put my hand over his mouth. "Shh. Don't make a *geshrei*."

My pronunciation of Yiddish words usually made him smile. "You mean *tsimmis*," he said behind my fingers.

"I mean shut up." I kissed him.

He let it go for once, watching me, though. I could feel the wheels in his head go chug-a-lug-lug.

Was it some Machiavellian plot of his that got us up to the Apollo Theater in Harlem to see Sammy Davis do his stuff? Several weeks had passed. We had been to the Coast and back, Palm Beach and back, Boston twice and back. Shifting cities and living quarters has a tendency to make one feel (me, anyway), as if all the *tsouris* has been left behind, like molting. I am better than an ostrich; I don't even have to stick my head in the sand. I don't want something should *be*? Presto. Wiped out. Sammy cavorting on the stage down there had nothing to do with anything except pure artistry.

I had *thought* I had heard Sammy do "Birth of the Blues," but I hadn't, not till that night, in front of that audience, all black except for Mike and me, who rocked with him, clapped with him in a solid, swinging beat unequalled anywhere else in the world. The very walls quivered. It was a happening, with a superb artist at top form.

Knocked out (I was), thrilled (I was), we went backstage to tell Sammy so. Sammy hugged me and kissed me on the cheek. Mike got a hug too. Sammy Davis hugs everybody: men, women, children and Nixon. All America knows that. But none of them counts. Only the one he gave me had hidden meaning. "It was him," the broken record began, "wasn't it, I saw how he—"

"Oh God. Oh dear God." Mike was driving his white Eldorado. The lights of New York flickered across his grimly set jaw as we headed downtown. "Not again."

"I saw how he hugged you."

"He hugged you too, Mike."

"But he hugged you different, you have an affinity for—"

"Stop it, Mike, just . . . stop . . . it. . . ." I could feel myself getting hot. I wasn't going to be able to handle it. . . .

"It was Sammy, wasn't it, he's the one—"

"I can't stand it, Mike, I really can't stand—"

"I know now, don't I, I know who it—"

I cracked. "You don't know *anything* and you will *never* know anything, because I cannot take this one second longer, you are a bore and a boor and I will not tolerate—"

"So it was Sammy, I knew it all—"

I started to scream. I wouldn't stop. Every time Mike opened his mouth, I screamed again. He finally shut up. The hostility in the car was a living, breathing thing.

We went up to his twentieth floor Park Avenue apartment in silence. I went straight to the closet, got down a suitcase and began throwing things in. He watched, lips pressed together, eyes angry, two laser beams strong enough to melt mountains.

He didn't stop me. He didn't believe I was leaving. I slammed out the door, lugging my case. He never moved, knowing I would be back. My pre-Columbian collection stood all about his apartment, my paintings on his walls.

My anger actually took me all the way to the airport. I asked for a ticket to Paris, like a returning lemming. Waited, smoldering, until departure time.

As we rose, tilted and slid away toward the Atlantic, I thought, drop dead down there, all of you. Especially you. But my heart wasn't in my defiance. Fear had rushed in to take anger's place like a cold tidal wave from the North Pole. Shit, I thought, shit shit shit. You can't even hold on to anger very long, much less a man.

I was depressed. It was an aimless move, going no place, for no good reason. Was this my life, I wondered, this suspended existence in the middle of nowhere? Come come, I said to me, you're going back to Paris, isn't that what you had in mind all along? Pull yourself together!

Orly Airport loomed up in no time at all. I would have preferred to stay in my flying cocoon. The nice fellow from Transylvania (or some place) who met the VIPs rushed up.

"Miss Keyes! I only just learned you were on the plane, I did not know!"

"It was a last minute thing. . . ."

I was glad to see him; he could help me call the Hotel Lancaster for a reservation. He led the way to the VIP lounge. A tall man rose to his feet. "Colonel Lindbergh," Transylvania said, "this is Miss Evelyn Keyes."

The Colonel nodded. "I saw you on the plane coming over," he said.

It seemed I had crossed the Atlantic Ocean with Charles Lindbergh, all the way to Paris—his famous route—and hadn't known it, tightly wrapped up in my own tiny universe.

It was food for thought. Can self-preoccupation grow blinders so large that the whole world slips by and you'll never know? Wondrous things under your nose, never seen, nor tasted, nor felt? I would have to change my ways.

The Lancaster could and did squeeze me in. A lovely room right at the top of the stairs. The phone was ringing as I walked in the door. . . .

CHAPTER 43...

"I love Paris . . ."

He didn't say hello. Just, "When are you coming back?"

It didn't make me feel any better, only foolish. If he had wanted me there, he could have said so when I was considerably nearer. My flight, his call, it was all so childish. What I felt most was despair. "I . . . just walked in," I said tiredly.

"I know. I told the concierge to let me know."

"Ah." I might have known. He probably had spoken to every concierge in every hotel in Paris.

"Uh . . . I shouldn't of ought . . ." He trailed off. But it was an apology, and that was better than nothing.

"Well, I haven't behaved any too well myself," I admitted.

"I have to go to the Coast."

"Ah. Well, have a good trip."

There was such a long pause I thought we had been disconnected. On the verge of hanging up, I heard his voice, a faint whisper. "I miss you awready."

"What? What did you say?"

"I . . . miss you."

"Do you? Do you, Mike?"

"Listen, I'm gonna come to Paris."

"Oh? When did you decide to do that?"

"Can you wait till I get there?"

"Wait for what?"

"I mean . . . you know, don't do anything you'll—I'll—we'll be sorry for."

"Oh Christ. That. It's the furthest thing from my mind."

"Wait till I get there, we'll talk—"

"When will that be?"

"After the Coast, I'll let you know. Meanwhile . . . don't go to strangers. . . ."

Trying to head me off at the pass was what he was doing, hoping to prevent me from jumping into bed with the first man—black, white or pea green—who came along. The promised trip to Paris—a spur-of-the-moment decision, I wagered—all part of a stall for time until he could make up his mind about me. Well, that was okay, I wanted time until I could make up my mind about *him.* "Okay," I said, "no strangers," but added, so he shouldn't get off completely worry-free, "only friends," and hung up.

Feeling one-up, I left the room to prevent another call. I ran into Paulette Goddard in the lobby. I could always depend on running into somebody I knew in the Lancaster lobby. We had a drink and caught up on each other, but then she was off to dress; Eric Remarque was coming to town and they had a dinner date. I got on the phone to Joyce Buck who had been playing nursemaid to my little Renault; the car was ready to go, but Joyce and Jules had a dinner date. Joyce and I made a date for lunch the next day, and I called Marion Shaw. She was off somewhere with Irwin. The entire world travels the Noah's Ark route, I thought, slightly let down.

Never mind, I'm tired, anyway. After a stroll down the Champs Elysées and back, I returned to my room, took a hot bath, got into one of those delicious oversized peignoirs that hang in Lancaster Hotel bathrooms, and rang for room service.

I was halfway through my entrecôte when the phone rang. "Whatja mean by that—'only to friends'?" his voice demanded.

I laughed, pleased to be part of the Ark arrangement, even if my other half was at the end of a thin cable on the other side of the ocean. "Oh Mike, darling, I was teasing, oh I'm so glad you called."

"I feel awful—"

"Ah, don't—"

"You shunt of gone"—deliberately running words together.

"Maybe it's best, we'll find out how we feel. . . ."

So began a period of tenuous togetherness accomplished with the help of Bell, Marconi and the international postal services. Disembodied voices and the written word. "Write me," he had demanded, "every day." "That goes two ways," I had responded.

Although Mike's style was cables, he did sit down and write:

> *Darling —*   *Mon. nite 9:30 P.M.*
> *I'm in bed alone trying to read—looking at your picture—moping*
> *Horrible weekend hope you had the same—Joe (Schenck) coming tomorrow moving him in here, it won't be so lonesome—and feel you would like it somehow*
> *I look for a letter from you every five minutes—really paniced wanted you to come home*
> *See why I don't write letters I can't spell*
> *but I can spell I luv you*
> *I can't be funny I miss you too much—*
>   *Your fella Mike*
> *woke up 4 this morning nightmare about you tried to call you no circuit where is a letter from you.*
> *2 trunks came one marked per. affects one box silverware I will keep both here right?*

I had forgotten I had sent for those trunks. They had been in storage in California for years. I had stuff stashed away in so many places I could hardly remember where, anymore. Bits and pieces of myself scattered all around. Would I ever be able to get Humpty Dumpty together again?

I was immediately depressed. It all seemed so utterly ridiculous. What was I doing in the middle of Paris all alone? His letter was so dear, without punctuation, but it had shape and style, and was so terribly touching. How could I have gone off and left him, what a fool

I was. I too "paniced" and sat down to write that I was homesick, that I longed for him terribly.

His next was a cable: MISS YOU TERRIBLY. TRIED TO PHONE YOU. I LOVE YOU. TO COAST SUNDAY NIGHT. . . .

That was good news. After the Coast he would be coming to Paris, and I could end this suspension in time, this "Waiting for Godot" sort of existence and get on with my life, whatever it was to be.

But the next cable wasn't from the Coast. It was from Boston, where American Optical was. Mike's plans had always been mercurial, the one constant about them.

YOUR GOOD LETTER RECEIVED TODAY. KEEP WRITING. MAKES ME THINK. I LOVE YOU. YOUR FELLA MIKE.

Then back to New York. CIRCUITS OUT OF ORDER WILL PHONE YOU FRIDAY MISS YOU ALL MY LOVE MIKE.

Then finally Los Angeles. WILL DEFINITELY WRITE AFTER RECEIVING YOUR LETTER MISS YOU LOVE MIKE.

My spirits soared considerably. The end was in sight. I felt that the separation had been a good thing, cleared the air, perhaps. At least we would find out.

He wrote his longest letter from Los Angeles. It should have made me happy, but it didn't.

> *Dearest Darling Evelyn,*
>
> *I have started to write you so many times, but when I read my own letters back I tear them up—you might as well know I can't spell I can't write—I am sure that if I sent most of my classics you would say to yourself— this is what I am pineing away for—*
>
> *So many times I want to pick up the phone or cable, come home—but I am scart—about everything I do think of you and miss you real much—once in a while some one puts in a dig—like—*
>
> *Evelyn is a wonderful girl—real gay—remember Paulette—Lawford and Keyes living together at the beach? What was that 3 horse parley? etc.—I hate this fuckin' place—I want things that are for real—for real. People work, happiness—I think I would be ready to forget the past at least I hope I am man enuf to—but the present I mean since us—Gilbert Roland (which was really tossed up to me here—people want us to be happy eh)*
>
> *I think there is a lot of real good in you—am I big enuf to extract all that good and add any good that might be in me in the closed corporation*

Zimmerman and I had a quiet personal talk—Freddy liked what I said about having a 5th column in your midst with the wrong kind of babe for a bed partner—oh the word bed—makes me think of real good thoughts the kind I think of every nite about us. What we have done in bed and what we must get around to—as I write this classic my "thing" is reading and getting ambitious. . . . I will not re-read this letter—I may tear it up like the others—I will just send it—

I love you terrible—fierce—good—quiet—I love you why am I so god-damn scared—

I love you
Your Mike

P.S.
I read your letters over and over—also never go to bed without picking a favorite one—have brought out all your letters. See I am a silly type tycoon—

Oh yeah—biz things are coming along and I think you would like them. . . . my fucking silly chest. . . . I think I like me better than most of your ex's

In spite of his obvious attachment, that communication thoroughly discouraged me. I had never lived at the beach. I had never lived anywhere with Paulette. I had had a few dates with Peter Lawford years before. I don't know if Paulette had ever met him. And Gilbert Roland was an old friend. All pure invention, I didn't know if it was Mike's, or somebody in Hollywood knowing the way to get at him, and I didn't care. I did not propose to go through my life denying past affairs real or invented.

With heavy heart I decided to stop the whirl and get off. But what to do, where, how? One thing at least was clear. I was finished with Hollywood, the letter had achieved that if nothing else. The last clinging, binding threads fell away. Not only had it turned into early Salem with its ugly witch hunt, it was so enchanted with its own gossip that it gorged upon itself. I wanted no part of it.

Paris, then, was it. Sophisticated, urbane, wise and worldly Paris. So be it.

Joyce Buck, dear dear friend, helped me find an apartment, a sweet place in the very heart of Paris, in the Place Dauphine on the Ile de la Cité, two stories with a spiral staircase connecting them, and the glass-enclosed creaking elevator to reach them. And there was room in the *Place* itself to park my tiny car.

I was back in business. . . .

" . . . right back where I started
from . . ."

Joyce and I settled down to seriously grasp the French language, taking lessons, attending the Comédie Française, reading newspapers and Camus in the original. We found a ballet class taught by a displaced Russian princess, eighty, arthritic, who could still show us a thing or two about a *jeté.* We found an indoor swimming pool for a few freezing, chlorine-filled daily laps. Of a snowy morning the lawyers on the way to the Palais de Justice with their tight suits and thin briefcases helped me push my baby *voiture* to get it started. I practiced my French on them, the fruit sellers, the wine merchants.

Any rebirth is joyous, as refreshing as spring.

But then, summer will come along, followed by autumn, the dying time. Newness has a way of becoming routine, giving thought time to creep in again.

When the preoccupation of moving, fixing, fiddling and settling in was over, my old uneasiness returned. Had I done the right thing? A good man is hard to find. . . .

Mike had accepted my move as if he had planned it, insisting on referring to the apartment as "ours," a pied-à-terre for "us" when "we" were in Paris. He sent flowers. He sent a case of champagne. He was so pleased I was perfecting my French, I could act as his interpreter when "we got to Moscow." French, he said, was spoken there as much as Russian.

It was a tempting morsel to dangle before me. I wouldn't be able to resist a trip to Moscow, and why should I, I told myself. *Au contraire,* the project was terribly exciting.

He sent a pin of two entwined gold hearts adorned with rubies, for Valentine's Day, and a cable: HAPPY VALENTINE TO MY VALENTINE BUT MAYBE EVERY DAY SOON WILL BE VALENTINE DAY. . . .

The truth is, I hadn't met anybody else with Mike's glorious energy and verve and spunk. His ability to get things done, to go after something against all odds and to come out on top, his incredible never-say-die spirit. He shared a Scarlett O'Hara philosophy when things went wrong: Said Scarlett as Rhett walked out on her, "I'll think about it tomorrow."

So what if his grammar left something to be desired; he was alive and running. Dead-asses and whiners have never been my cup of tea.

And so I bided my time.

WOULD YOU JOIN ME FOR A WEEK IN ACAPULCO, read the cable from Los Angeles.

I knew I should stick to my decision to make Mike come to me. But I can't say no to a trip. What if, the voice said. What if, this time, it really is the end of the rainbow and you're not there, you will have blown it!

Besides, I reasoned so sensibly, shouldn't I see the man again if I wanted to make a final decision?

The journey was horrendous. All night over the Atlantic, five hours' wait in New York for another plane, a half-day in New Orleans for yet another. Forty-eight hours passed before I was deposited in the middle of the night on the Mexico City tarmac dazed with fatigue, ears still roaring with the sound of motors, off-balance, feeling as if I were still floating, the world, including the man come to meet me, all seeming to be on the other side of a dense fog.

My greeting must have been less zestful than Mike expected, because he immediately withdrew, circling me, watchful and wary as a big cat. I knew it, felt it, but couldn't do much about it.

At the hotel I fell exhausted on the bed. Mike made some excuse about going out for a bite. By the time he came back I was dead to the world.

Not exactly an auspicious reunion after such a long separation.

But by midmorning when we woke . . . and touched . . . and smelled each other's nearness, it was all right once more. For the moment. Thought held once more in abeyance.

Before catching the plane for Acapulco, we had lunch at a restaurant I knew just off the Paseo de la Reforma, Mexico City's main drag. At another table were my old Acapulco playmates, Jacques Gelman, Cantínflas's partner, and his wife Natasha. After much hugging and kissing I introduced them to Mike. It was this chance meeting that led to Mike's deal with Cantínflas to play Passepartout in *Around the World in Eighty Days*. (And it was I who suggested David Niven for Phineas Fogg. The "ex's" right under Mike's nose, and he never knew.)

In Acapulco we took a house high on a cliff overlooking the ocean, not far from the Gelmans and Cantínflas himself. He and Mike became fast friends and the deal for the picture was soon made. Not speaking Spanish didn't stop Mike from wheeling and dealing.

There was swimming and waterskiing, there were lunches and dinners on the beach, in restaurants, and each other's houses. Kirk Douglas showed up unexpectedly and stayed a few days with us. "Why do you have such sad eyes?" he said to me. "You've always had sad eyes."

We gave a party with a mariachi band that went on most of the night, and then it was time to go.

Mike took it for granted I would go back to California with him. We avoided specifics but declared our passion.

"God, how I missed you," he said.

"I missed you too."

"Do you love me?"

"Oh yes. Do you love me?"

"Oh yes."

"Aren't we crazy to be apart?"

"Never again."

"No, never."

"I want you by my side, always."

"Always."

He said he didn't know how he had gotten along without me. I said, me too.

"Let's try again," he said. "I grew up while you were away. Be patient with me. I'm learning, I'll learn. You're good, and you're on my side, I know it, a stand-up dame, I want to be equal to you."

I buried my head in the sand and agreed. To go back to wintry Paris to—do what? Another French lesson? Another creaky ballet class? Ridiculous. It could all be done in Beverly Hills and with Mike, where the action was. With a man who loved me. Who was going to make a picture in Moscow. Probably *China* after that. The possibilities were endless, I wouldn't want to miss out on any of it.

So there we were, back at the Beverly Hills Hotel, together this time, in the same suite. Where everybody knew us.

I must not, I told myself, care about such nonsense as a marriage license. If two people love one another, what else counts? How petty and narrow-minded to be embarrassed. That's what I told myself. And anyhow, you've got him. You'll soon marry and live happily ever after—if you play your cards right, and learn to be a proper woman.

So when a picture offer came along, *The Seven Year Itch*, with Marilyn Monroe and Tom Ewell (I would play Tom's wife), I didn't know if I should accept. "Actresses," Mike often said, "don't know how to be a woman to a man. They want hairdressers who follow 'em around." Look at your contemporaries, he would tell me, Lana, Rita, Ingrid, Ava; what a mess they've made in the "happiness" department. And, he would add, you're not getting any younger, ha ha.

God. I didn't want to be like them; I wanted to be "happy." I would have to break with my independent liberated ways, devote myself to one man and tend his needs for the rest of my life. I must show Mike, my last chance, that I could do it.

But he surprised me by saying, "Ah, go ahead and do the picture, it'll do you good. I'll be running for the next month anyway."

And while I worked, he did just that in a display of perpetual motion. On a plane more than on the ground, making deals for stock, for money, for the rights to *Around the World in Eighty Days.* Off the plane he was on the phone. Between the "I miss you's" he seldom talked of anything but his business. It grew tiresome, and when I would wonder if that's all there was, guilt would stab me for thinking such "unwomanly" thoughts. Being bored by your "fella's" business was surely unwomanly.

I enjoyed making the picture, enjoyed working with Tom and the super director, Billy Wilder. But I kept that shameful secret to myself. And the fact that it was nice being off the treadmill for awhile. It was interesting to see Marilyn Monroe again too, after all the success. I had often met her at Sam Spiegel's house and around on the arm of Johnny Hyde, the William Morris agent responsible for getting her started. I had never seen what Johnny saw, or the camera picked up. I had only seen one more little blonde with the preferred size tits and a funny walk. Success had given her a nice patina, a certain glow. Or perhaps I looked with different eyes.

While I was at it I did another flick for United Artists, some foolish thing called *Top of the World,* which I've never seen.

Then Mike scooped me up and we were off. . . .

CHAPTER 45 . . .

> *"I've got rings on my fingers . . . and*
> *bells on my toes . . . and I shall have music . . .*
> *wherever I go. . . ."*

That summer with Mike was like a montage. Venice. Click. London. Click. Beverly Hills. Click. Mexico City. Rome. New York.

Click, click, click. Christmas and New Year's found us in the Palm Springs California sunshine. Mike gave me a glorious choker, an inch-and-a-half wide, of solid diamonds. Plus five thousand shares in some new venture of Bing Crosby Enterprises. I took it as a sign of true love.

Havana, again. We went there to meet with John Ringling North, who owned the Ringling Brothers and Barnum and Bailey Circus. Mike was to supervise the opening night in Madison Square Garden.

We didn't see too much of Mr. North, who never got up until four or five in the afternoon. Unfortunately he wasn't with us the night we went to a nightclub where a singer of a certain color was performing. His beat and style were terrific. I was enjoying him before I remembered I shouldn't. Too late I looked over to see Mike's eyes glued to me.

Feigning indifference, I picked up my drink, one of those lethal rum things, clicked it against Mike's glass, indicating we should toast our good fortune to be together in this most exotic of places. I smiled lovingly into his eyes.

He picked up his glass, all right. He drank the whole thing in one gulp. He didn't return my smile.

He was instantly drunk, since he seldom drank very much. He ordered another, and quickly drank that down. And another. He never took his eyes off me. The floor show and the black singer went on and on and *on,* obviously planning to continue their good work for the next hundred years. I leaned over to Mike. "What do you say we cut out of this joint," I whispered, "and go find John?"

"Can' face it, can you?" His speech was not only a mess, it boomed out over the voice of the singer and his accompanying musicians.

I was embarrassed. "Please, Mike, let's go—"

"Can' face it—" He reached out as if to give me a push, toppled off his chair, and fell to the floor. Since we were ringside, we instantly became the floor show in place of the one going on.

Two waiters hurried over to help Mike to his feet. He sat, tilted, ready to go again. "Can' face it, can you—"

"Excuse me," I whispered, "I've got to go to the ladies' room."

The practicing coward rushed away and kept right on going. We had a car and chauffeur waiting. I had the driver take me to the hotel and told him to go back for Mike.

For the longest time I stood at the Hotel Nacional's window gazing into Havana's night, heartsick, knowing it was never going to work between Mike and me. Really truly knowing. He had a festering sore inside him that was never going away. I knew I had to make a move.

When he came stumbling in much later I pretended to be asleep.

The next morning he apologized so profusely, so poignantly, that I succumbed, again. "I love you like I never loved anybody," said he, with tears in his eyes. "None of it would be worth anything without you."

The ability to cut my losses escapes me to this day. It plagues most relationships. You've spent this much time at it, you tell yourself, you can't give up now. He/she will change. It's easier to stay with what you have than venture into the unknown.

The circus came to New York as a Michael Todd Production. He got Marilyn Monroe to ride around the Madison Square Garden ring on a pink elephant. People cheered and Mike glowed.

Click, Palm Beach. Gifts of rings and bracelets of amethysts and pearls the size of boulders set in twisted gold. Click, London and Noël Coward, witty and urbane, finding the rough American diamond Todd amusing, as most people did.

Click, Las Vegas, and hundred-dollar chips flowing in, flowing out at the crap tables. I never knew which way, or how much was changing hands. And gin rummy games everywhere, while I watched. Feeling emptier . . . and emptier. . . .

My dreams had turned into monster movies, I woke each morning with pounding heart. "Look, Mike," I said, "I think I'd like to go to an analyst again."

"A head-shrinker?" He frowned. "Whaddaya need one of them for?"

"I don't seem to know where I'm going—"

"Where I'm goin', that's where you're going. . . ."

I went to one, though, this time in New York. It was like the old joke. You get analyzed on one coast, go to the other, and have to go through it all over again, since you've got a whole new set of problems. I went to Dr. Daniel Schneider, author of *Psychoanalysis and the Artist,* figuring he ought to know a thing or two. "Stick around for awhile," he told me, "get off the treadmill, find out what's troubling you."

I did for awhile. The East Coast analysis was the same old shit I had learned on the West Coast. Looking for your father figure to replace the one who left you at two, you want love, but you expect him to leave you again, and blah blah blah. Jesus, Doc, I know all that, but what do I do about it?

Dan had a bum ear; he would put his hearing aid microphone next to you to pick up your little gems. God, I would think, these miserable complaints were being *recorded?* It made everything I said seem twice as silly. What in God's name did I have to worry about, didn't I have everything in the world? Listen, Doc, I can't hang around this dark office of yours, I've got to go, go off with Mike to Milano, he wants to photograph the ballet at La Scala. . . .

Sitting in a darkened box in the theater, watching Mike onstage talking to the prima ballerina, a woman whispered to me, "How do you manage to get all these fascinating men?"

I turned, startled. I didn't know her; a newspaper woman, I suppose; the place was overflowing with press watching the proceedings. (Mike always saw to that.) I had this desire to say to her, "I'm a great fuck." I didn't. I've regretted it ever since.

Men, she had said, in the plural. As if they came in prides. One at a time was all I could handle, lady, and not even that very well. And I never *got* anybody. They just let me hang around for awhile. And why was that, Ev, why did they let you hang around at all? Well, see I've got this great skin, smooth as marble, and you can take me anywhere. . . .

In the darkened La Scala Opera House I started to cry. I didn't know why. I suppose if I had let myself think about it, I might have.

Click. We drove to Rome. Piacenza! Firenze! Had Shakespeare been along this route? Lunch on the way in some tiny trattoria with Mike supervising the pizzaiola sauce. He didn't speak Italian, but he managed. He was a delight and joy on these trips, when there wasn't any business, no phones. He was easy, funny, playful and observant, and I loved him then.

Click, Rome. Dinner on the terrace of a restaurant in a piazza with a fountain playing, a table a mile long, white white tablecloth, around which were gathered Ingrid Bergman, Dawn Addams and her prince, various and assorted Hungarian, Italian and French picture makers.

Click. Cannes and the gaming tables. Mike and his cigar in the inner sanctum that spells hello baccarat and good-bye money. I missed the Las Vegas slot machines that were more my speed, but dug the elegance of the European gambling that conjured Dostoevski and quiet tragedy.

"The Duke just leapt from the tenth story window."

"Dead?"

"Rather."

"Pity. Another thousand on red, please."

Click. Deauville. Somewhere I had picked up a lovely Jean Dessès dress, miles of floating yellow chiffon to watch Mike play baccarat in.

It was the year of the *War and Peace* race, too.

No sooner had Mike announced that his next picture after *Around the World* would be the Tolstoi novel, many other producers got in the act, including David Selznick. They were all going to make *War and*

Peace. It became a contest to see who would get to production day first. The trip to Moscow was imminent.

Back in New York Dr. Schneider told me, "Stop this fooling around and go back to work."

"Don't you see," I said, "I don't believe in Hollywood anymore, I have lost my faith. Like in God. Like in roots. Like you wake up one morning and you don't read the funny papers anymore. *Children* make movies. Who wants to be around children all the time? Rat-fink children, too. They chased all the good guys out."

"You must find yourself again."

"What, did I lose me? Did I stick me in a drawer and forget which one?"

"You make jokes. But it is something like that."

"Oh Doc, what do you know?"

"Plenty is what I know."

That made me laugh, and I went out feeling good. For a while. . . .

CHAPTER 46 . . .

"There's a little bit of bad in every
good little girl. . . ."

Mike, the whirling dervish, actually settled down in a house in Los Angeles when the production of *Around the World* was getting underway.

He thrived, he bloomed, he was doing what he was born for. Dealing, plotting, hiring; the writer of the screenplay had to be found, the director, cameraman, stars, assistants, crew, and, above all, money had to be got hold of, large sums, *millions.* To do that he had to sweet-talk, charm, con, bully if necessary. Mike was in his element, exaggeration his stock-in-trade, the talented hustler selling his bigger-than-life dreams, believing them himself, and why not—they had often worked.

His enthusiasm was catching, and people flocked aboard. S. J. Perelman, to write. Noël Coward would do a cameo, as would Sir John Gielgud, Sinatra, Dietrich, George Raft, Red Skelton, Dominguín the great Spanish matador, Fernandel and Bea Lillie. The money was tough to come by, but he got it, ran out, got more, spent that, and would have to wheedle, cajole, yell, promise the sky.

A person like that—great to visit, but hard to live with. Like being in a perpetual whirlwind. Caught up in his busy-ness, he was one-note Johnny. It was impossible to separate truth from fantasy, reality from fiction, and perhaps there was no difference. When he wasn't actually around, he was on the phone to report his latest coup, plan, deal, with declarations of love and lust thrown in between.

Returning, he would call from the airport the instant he stepped off the plane. "S.I.B.," he would say ("stay in bed"). He would have had some kind of meeting on the way in from the airport. He would be reaching for the phone almost before we were finished making love. Although he would have whispered in the middle of it what we would do "the next time." Future shock in person.

I had plenty of time to myself. I played a lot of tennis. I even did a few TV shots, a Faulkner play among them, *Knight's Gambit,* with Paul Henreid and Mary Astor. And I did a lot of hanging around, trying to be "womanly." (When I didn't agree with Mike, I wasn't womanly.) I felt like a fifth wheel, the runt of the litter. Doctor Schneider was right, I had lost me somewhere. I wanted to go away. I didn't know how. I felt ashamed to leave—that would certainly be unwomanly. I felt ashamed to stay, too. I dreamt that all the light bulbs in the house caught on fire. As I ran about frantically trying to put them out, the chandelier burst into flames, long licking tongues. The ceiling buckled and began to fall toward me.

I thought if one more person asked me when we were getting married, I would give up my nonviolent ways and punch him right in the mouth. I felt like punching Mike when he found time in his twirling to stop and play gin rummy with the "guys." "There is never any time for us anymore," I complained, "and you're finding time for cards."

"I've got to have some relaxation."

"My God! You've talked to me so much about business you think I *am* business!"

"You're my partner, my number one partner—"

"The hell I am. I don't have a contract. Everybody's got a contract but me. I feel very insecure."

"What makes you think a marriage license is security? We've both had 'em and lost 'em."

"This time will be different, we—"

"Why is today different from—"

"Stop with the jokes now, I want—"

"I'm up to my ass, where's the time—"

"Las Vegas."

"That fly-by-night quickie stuff, you did that—"

"What's the difference—"

"If we do it, there'll be some strength behind it."

"If, you say, what do you mean, *if* . . . ?"

"Listen." Mike put his arms around me. "You want to be my partner for real?"

"That is exactly what I'm talking about."

"You got some money to spare?"

I was taken aback. It was the last thing I expected. "What for?"

"Give me twenty-five thousand dollars and I'll turn it into a million."

Wow. I'd be crazy to turn down a deal like that. Money is certainly one form of security, and maybe the only one.

"You've got it," I said.

"Partner," Mike said, and kissed me.

So I was hustled too. It probably paid for the week's nut. It didn't buy another spare second of Mike's time, because he had to go on hustling for the next week, and the one after that, and after that. In spite of all his busy-ness talk, he never told me just how hard he was scuffling to keep it all going in those days, I had to read it years later in a book. Downbeat wasn't his style. Worry was hidden behind irritation and a flaring of temper. It wasn't womanly to take umbrage, but I did. When he snapped, I snapped back. Things were tumbling downhill, when we ran into John Huston at a party.

We had often run into John at gatherings, the theater, or the race-track. Not too surprising. We traveled in more or less the same circles. "Evelyn," John said quietly when he had a chance, "I'd like to talk to you." He was rather stiff.

"Sure, John." I thought I knew what he wanted. I still had a painting of his, which he had every right to want back. "You're at the Beverly Hills Hotel?" I asked. "I'll come round tomorrow and have a drink with you." Mike would most certainly be busy, and even if he weren't, it would be more entertaining than listening to him talk on the phone or watching one more gin rummy game.

John was still rather cool when I arrived. No big hug, just a curt nod. "You're looking well, Evelyn." When John used your name instead of "honey" or "darling," it meant the subject at hand was not to be treated lightly.

"So are you," I said. And he did. Always with a flair for clothes, his long frame looked good in them. He wore a pale pink shirt and gray trousers.

"What will you have?"

"Whatever you're having."

"A martini all right?"

"Fine."

He thoughtfully gathered the ingredients without speaking—ice, vodka, with the required soupçon of vermouth—swished them about with total concentration. He picked up two glasses and, bringing the pitcher along, joined me across the coffee table. After pouring the drinks he raised his glass slightly in salutation.

"It's nice to see you, Evelyn." Vamping until ready.

"I'm always glad to see you, John, I really am," I answered. I meant it.

He sipped again. He still hadn't cracked a smile. "Uh . . ."

The cliff-hanging quality of John's "uh's" couldn't be hurried along. He took his time, set the scene. His way. I waited.

Finally he said it. "You've got the Juan Gris *Harlequin*—"

"It's yours, John. I've always meant to give it back."

He was silent for a moment, the wind out of his sail. He had expected resistance, I suppose. "I'm glad," he said simply. "Leslie gave me that picture."

"Yes, I know." Leslie was the wife before me.

"Well!" He took a deep breath, and the warmth came flooding into his eyes. He refilled our glasses, tilted toward me and said, "dar . . . ling!" The melted caramel sounds were back. "How good to see you. Tell me, are you all right . . . ?"

We had three martinis before we were through. It was so nice talking with John I forgot (again) they were poison, hearing about his place in Ireland, an Italian painter he admired, that Pablo had married an Irish girl.

Finally I remembered Mike. And that we had a dinner date with Arthur Krim, head of United Artists, who was giving Mike a large chunk of money and who would be distributing *Around the World*.

Nothing like a girlfriend-roommate-wife dashing in late and drunk. Mike's reaction was no exception. He was outraged. "Where—the—hell—have you been?" he spat.

"I'm sorry, I had a drink with John—"

"John! John Huston?"

"Yes, he wanted to talk to me—"

"So it's true." The words shot out like pointed daggers. "What everybody says. You're still in love with that guy."

"Of course not! Just because I—"

"All he has to do is lift a finger and you go running."

"I do not," I cried. "We had—"

"You forgot me, you forgot we had a dinner date—"

"I'll hurry and change—"

"Don't bother!" His anger was a seething ball, threatening to burst. "I can't wait for you, I'm leaving now!"

He stormed out of the house, slamming the door violently. The motor roared outside, and the car went shooting off down the hill. The dream came back to mind, with the light bulbs and the chandelier bursting into flame, shooting out like fiery tongues. Mike's words were like that, stabbing slivers of fire.

I shivered and ran to the phone. I dialed the Beverly Hills Hotel. His anger was uncalled for. His jealousy was uncalled for, I had had enough of that. How dare he not wait five minutes for me, when I had waited what seemed like a few million years for him. I was through this time, really through.

"John?" I cried when he answered, "I'm leaving Mike this instant. Can I come over and stay with you?"

Always the splendid fellow in emergencies, John took this new turn of events smoothly in his stride. Without a single beat of hesitation he answered, "Sure, honey, you come right along."

I packed a quick bag and called a cab. I don't need you, Big Daddy Mike, I've got Big Daddy John waiting in the wings!

CHAPTER 47...

"A good man . . . is hard to find. . . ."

John had changed clothing. He now wore a jacket and tie, and his hair was brushed down. "Unfortunately I must go out to dinner," he told me kindly, his sympathy wrapping around me like a warm blanket. "Will you be all right?"

"Oh yes. Fine." I *was* disappointed.

He gave me another martini, ordered some food, showed me the room he had gotten for me adjoining his suite, and went on his way, promising to check in later to see if I was okay.

The fourth martini really set the world spinning. The steak on the plate wouldn't stay still, the hash browns refused to make the journey from table to mouth. I finally gave up, and with careful aim and the help of furniture, made it to my new bedroom and flopped in bed. I couldn't begin to figure out what I was doing there. It was all I could do to keep the bed from wandering about the room. True to his word —and in his best good-in-crises manner—John did check in every so often, as if I had a terminal disease. "Are you all right, honey?" he would ask. "Just . . . fine," I would answer bravely.

Like a broken record. Like a recurring nightmare I woke to the monstrous hangover, full of shame and guilt, horrified at what I had done. Will you never learn, I thought through the pounding head. You want to call it off with Mike, do it with a little dignity, like a mature person, not drunken and sloppy and running off crying to an ex-husband.

I lay on my bed of pain until 8:00 A.M. Then, with superhuman effort, I picked up the phone and called Mike. I wanted to say how sorry I was, how ashamed, to ask forgiveness. I never got past, "Mike—"

"I don't want to talk to you," he said, and hung up.

I lay for another hour, jungle drums agitated, threatening to split my cranium in two. When I thought I heard stirrings in the room next door, I got out of bed, weak from the effort, shakily got into my clothes and crept to John's door. He was up and still solicitous. "How was your night, honey?" he asked gently. I could have sworn his concern went deep.

"Mike won't talk to me," I whimpered.

John frowned. He blinked. "Won't he now," he said. "Well!" he said, "let's see what I can do about that."

He called Mike. Mike didn't hang up on him. "I've got an upset girl here, Mike old boy."

Mike's response must have been of an accusatory nature, because John then said, "No, no, it was nothing like that, Mike. Just thought she shouldn't be roaming the streets in her condition. . . ." There was firmness in John's tone, and, I suspected, enjoyment in what he was doing.

There was a chuckle. Or was it merely a twinkle in John's eye. Something Mike said? The shift was subtle, but there it was: man-to-man understanding all at once and a closed corporation. Oh, I got the gist even if I heard only half the dialogue. We glorious males, we superstuds, so superiorly wise, so thoroughly solid citizen and adult, we must have patience and tolerance (the kind you reserve for *all* inferiors) for the foibles of the little woman.

They had a point, I thought through my agony, this little woman certainly had *her* foibles. Having anything to do with either one of them was the super-foible of all time. If I had had the strength at that moment, I would have walked out on them all.

I sat like a zombie during the morning as people came and went, friends of John's, I forget who, I didn't care. Mike even came over to say good-bye. He and John continued their charade, so amused by the whole caper, ah, the dizzy, laughable dame, prone to these rash decisions, never mind, these strong men brave and true, would take care of, look after her, all the way to Paris, which is where she has wanted to be all along, right? I'm going that way myself, Mike, don't worry. I'll see her to her door, safe and sound.

All so goddamned civilized you could throw up.

I didn't know how to get out of it. Didn't know if I should. If I wanted to. If it wasn't actually for the best. But why did I feel so awful? I was too miserable to think it through, so without any will of my own I found myself on a plane that night with John, flying to New York, to continue the following day to Paris.

With the moan of the motors driving boulder-size steel bullets through my aching head, John took it upon himself to entertain me. It seemed a kindly enough aim to relieve someone in obvious anguish. He told me a story, tilting toward me in his inimitable manner, the melted caramel curling around me, bathing me in its flowing warmth. There were the familiar pauses, the blinks of the eyes. It seems that a girl who had worked on a picture of his, an extra, playing a bit part, had taken herself so seriously—the crime in John's book—that he began to tease her, and soon, with his encouragement, she had become a figure of fun for the entire cast and crew.

But then—he told me—he felt rather badly about it and a little ashamed to have picked on such an easy target. So when she asked him to her house for a drink, he went, to try to make up for his ill manners. (So he said.)

It was a small house in Culver City, doilies on the arms of the chairs, cellophane on the Sears Roebuck lampshades. She lived with her mother, a nice plump woman, nervous at the gentleman caller-director her daughter had invited over. After all, maybe he could make her daughter into a star!

When asked what he would like to drink, John said, "Scotch," without thinking. The daughter disappeared, presumably to get it, and he sat making idle talk with the mother. "You have a lovely daughter." "Thank you." "Have you been here long?" "Not too long." It was heavy going. The girl was gone an inordinately long time. He realized why when he glimpsed her slipping into the back of the house with a paper bag under her arm. She had obviously run out to buy some Scotch. She reappeared, carrying a glass and a pint of whiskey.

John took one very small drink and got out as soon as courtesy permitted. End of girl, and duty toward her. He thought.

A month or so later, she called. Her mother had died, and she desperately needed help. She didn't have the money to send her mother's casket (Mom inside) from the funeral home to the family plot. John, forever dependable in crises, said he would be most happy to help her out. What could a hearse cost to drive from Culver City to Forest Lawn, across town. A hundred, perhaps, worth every penny to cleanse his conscience for good.

Too late he learned the truth—that the family plot was in upstate New York. That single weak drink of Scotch had cost him nearly a thousand dollars.

I listened to it all through the beating tom-toms in my head, appalled. My God, I thought, that's the sort of thing he was doing when he was married to me; going off to have drinks with some girl around the studio, getting involved, sending her money. Money that was mine, too. And he's not telling the whole story, either; he must have slipped it to her to get so caught up in drinks and caskets.

God. I wished anything I hadn't come. Who was this man beside me, turning on his charm, telling me what-was-supposed-to-be-an-amusing story. A perfect stranger.

I felt too lonely for words.

When we got off the plane in New York I was feeling even worse than the day before. John had taken a suite at the St. Regis for the day, and when we arrived there I went straight to the bedroom to lie down. I was in a bad way.

As the day wore on, I heard voices in the next room coming and going, deals being discussed. John getting his life arranged. I wished I could. Marilyn Monroe's name came up. John wanted her for *Lysistrata*. Yeah, I thought, yeah. . . . Once he came in to check on me. "Going to be able to manage, honey?"

"I may have a fifty-fifty chance."

He smiled—with his mouth only; he had something else on his mind. "Uh . . . we've got to do something about the painting, dear, I'd like to get it on its way to Ireland, if I could . . ."

"Yeah," I groaned, "Okay. I'll get up in a minute and take care of it."

I watched him go back to the living room. I thought, the son of a bitch! That's why he's brought me along, to keep tabs on his painting. That's the only reason he's bothered with me at all; why he's telling me phony stories, pulling his phony charm on me, just to get his precious painting back.

My dander rose and pulled me up after. My head popped out like a blown-up balloon, then shriveled violently as the air receded. I managed to make it to the living room. John was talking to somebody. I didn't—couldn't look to see who. It took all my concentration to walk upright toward the front door. "I'm leaving, John," I whispered as I passed him by.

"What's that, honey?" He had turned toward me, smiling.

Just keep your fucking charm to yourself, you bastard, I thought. At the door I gathered my strength together for a smash exit. *"I am not going with you, John, I have changed my mind,"* I said, then turned and started walking down the hall, placing each foot carefully before the other.

John had jumped to his feet and rushed to the door. "But what about the painting?" he called after me.

Lousy bastard. All he wanted. I was right. I turned around. I stood very still. It wasn't easy. I spoke clearly and with impeccable diction. "I have changed my mind about that too." Then I turned around again, and started walking.

Hell hath no fury like a thwarted male. As I turned the corner at the far end of the hall, John shouted, livid, "Keep it then for all I care, and hang it on a whorehouse wall!"

Whatever that meant. Susan B. Anthony would have instantly spotted an adverse connotation there for the entire feminine mystique, I suspect.

I made my way to Mike's apartment (and my paintings), called him in California to tell him where I was. In the taxi over I had remembered the money I had forked over to him. I don't think that's why I went back. But I'm not sure. It may have been why he only chuckled and said, "Stay where you are, I'll be in New York in a couple of days."

But the relationship had altered in spite of what happened afterward. With John too, even after I sent him his painting.

One thing I never did again was drink a martini.

CHAPTER 48...
"Moon . . . over Miami . . ."

Click, Rome. Click, click, click, Milano, Mexico City, Las Vegas, Acapulco. "Hey!" said Mike, "let's spend the holidays in Miami."

"Hey!" I answered, "terrific idea."

"While I wind up things here you go on ahead and charter us a boat. . . ."

What did I know of boats. On Christmas Eve it didn't matter, I took what I could get. I found a grand old tub, a fifty foot, topheavy houseboat with a crew of four, that plied only the inland waters.

Which is what we did, along the Keys. We were actually in one place for an entire week on our floating island, just the two of us, without a single phone to Mike's name. It was lovely. I wanted it to go on forever. We read, swam, made love, sunned, even fished. I might have loved him then, I don't know. My God, he even played gin rummy with me. (I lost.) Sometimes we would pull into a marina for a stroll or a meal. It was at one such stop that I encountered an old acquaintance.

The restaurant on the edge of the water was one of the most attractive we had come across: glass and stone, green plants and low lighting, cool and inviting in contrast to the dazzling sun outside. I thought the owner-host who greeted us looked familiar, then promptly let the thought slide by. I moved from place to place so much, the world and its inhabitants were melding into one.

He showed us to our table and lingered. "Used to see you in that place over in Jersey," he said to Mike.

"Yeah," Mike nodded, "it's closed."

"I know. It's why I came down here."

I suddenly got it. It was the reserved way they were talking, the unsaid stuff that passed between their eyes. I knew exactly where I had seen this man before.

He was John's old betting buddy from the Key Largo sojourn, when John made the bet about the Immaculate Conception that had cost him a few thousand dollars. The gentleman had obviously branched out, moved to another key, and got himself a swanky setup. With the money, I wondered, he had raked in from John and Richard Brooks?

"Got a setup upstairs," the fellow then said. "Want to see it?"

"Why not?" shrugged Mike. Their exchange was unsmiling, mysterious, as if I had missed the gist of their conversation in the middle somewhere.

He showed the way to some rather narrow back stairs, carpeted but otherwise unadorned, as if they led to an abandoned attic. Halfway up the guy said, "Look." He pointed to a spot up near the ceiling above us.

There, through a hole in the wall, was a fellow's head looking down at us. The gun in his hands pointed our way too. *Jesus Christ,* I thought. I froze in my tracks.

"You're ready," Mike said.

For what? I thought.

"In here," said our host, and opened the door at the top of the stairs.

About a dozen men and women in evening dress were lounging about talking, smoking. Their heads whipped around, startled as we entered. Then with a great show of casualness, they tried to recover, their eyes sliding away as if they hadn't noticed our entrance, spreading out in a strolling gait, grouping themselves with studied indifference around the several tables in the room.

I recognized the various gaming tables at once. They were the same ones that had arrived in the large van on Key Largo: roulette, crap, blackjack, et cetera, et cetera. The dealers at them could very well have been the same.

"It's okay," the owner called, "relax."

As if they were puppets on the end of strings, these dozen folk in their glittering raiment flopped back down into chairs and sat in their original tableau.

"Shills, eh," said Mike.

The owner shrugged. "Gotta have 'em."

Jesus H. Christ, I thought. Poor, dumb novice John. He never had a chance.

After we dined and sailed on our way, a lingering uneasiness persisted from this behind-the-scenes glimpse of the gambling world, where Mike had been treated as "one of them." Was I bobbing along my innocent way, surrounded by the unknown, the unseen, carefully veiled off, though they could look at me, as the gunman had done? Like a one-way mirror. Did I really ever know what Mike was up to? Or only what he wanted me to know? His fast talk and eternal movement, was it all camouflage to cover . . . what?

When I finally did leave, the true reasons were safely hidden behind all sorts of pretexts. "I'll be mostly in Europe from now on in," Mike had said. "I'm gonna shoot in London and Paris, and Spain too."

"Oh. Well then," I told him, "why don't I just go on back to Paris, perhaps there are things I can do for you there. . . ."

I really believed that.

"Yeah, that's a good idea," Mike enthused, "I'll be running like crazy here."

Neither wanted to face that this affair was over the hill. Neither wanted to admit there were too many irritations, too many fights.

We were nicer to each other after the ticket to Paris was bought. Mike left me on Fifth Avenue to run into Cartier's to buy me a going-away gift.

I was thrilled. I had visions of yards and yards of diamonds and emeralds. He came out with a gold picture frame with a color photo in it taken in Venice. The two of us on a gondola, in which *I* was hugging *him.*

The Place Dauphine again. Ah, it felt good to be home. There was such a solidness about it, a comfort in its oldness after Hollywood.

I began French lessons again, and swimming. I took up with a Frenchman—just to break Mike's spell—and didn't they always say the best way to learn a language is in bed? But he was uncircumcized. That untidy foreskin was a complete turn-off. Sam Spiegel, in town for some reason, got around to making a mild pass—a sort of, oh why not, nobody-else-is-in-town thing. I told him about the uncircumcized gadget I had just seen, and that turned him off.

The cables started coming again. I MISS YOU. HAVE WE MADE A MISTAKE. YOUR FELLA. I didn't pay much attention to any of that anymore. A game I was tired of. He would call and fill me, his "partner," in on how things were going. We were still quite connected; since he had borrowed my money his office had turned into my business managers. "I don't see how I can live without you," he said one day.

"You seem to be doing just fine."

"It's lonesome here."

"Ah, Mike," I said, "you know it's over now."

"Bite your tongue. It's not over."

It was all too *déjà vu.* I couldn't play anymore, "Ah, Mike, you like me best when I'm somewhere else."

"You sound like you don't love me anymore."

I sighed. "Do you love me?"

"You're my partner, you got to care what happens."

"Oh I do care." You bet I cared. I was spending the million dollars already.

"Will you do something for me?" he said.

"Sure. What?"

"Fly down to Cannes—"

"Cannes!"

"Just for the day—or stay on if you like. I'll send you some newspaper clippings to take along."

"Clippings! Of what?"

"Stories of what I'm doing, from the trades, the *Times.* I want this guy down there to know what I'm doing. You can tell him I'll be along soon."

"Mike. Why don't you just send them directly?"

"A personal touch is needed."

The same old wheeling-dealing, I thought, the half-told tales, and I must read between the lines. It's a guy he's trying to con into some deal, and my going to see him will make him think that Mike really cares enough to send somebody in person, which should keep him dangling until Mike gets there himself. Well, Mike had done, still did, endless things for me. What the hell. "Sure I'll go. Who is he?"

"That will be with the clippings—" Mike paused. "I get a pain in my chest, thinking about us," he whispered huskily.

I wasn't buying. "Then don't think about us."

"You're so cold."

"God. I hope so."

"Don't . . . get lost. Don't fuck around and push us apart—"

There it was again. Somebody telling me not to fuck around. He sent a fat manila envelope of clippings all about the making of *Around the World in Eighty Days,* what it was costing, the people involved, the glorious cast, the excitement it was generating, and just what the fabulous grosses were going to be. Millions, naturally. The name of the man I was to see wasn't French but rather one of those Baltic sounds that I couldn't quite place. The origin of his accent, in English, escaped me too, when he met me at the airport.

He was dark, neatly dressed, a thin moustache, hair precisely clipped; the kind of man that gets lost in crowds.

We went to his apartment for coffee, to discuss our "business." A wife appeared who matched his fadeability. She smiled nicely, brought coffee, and disappeared. The apartment itself, on a side street, was neither small nor large, as innocuous as its dwellers, not a magazine nor book nor dirty ashtray in sight. "Mister Todd," I began, "is absolutely up to his ears—"

"I beg your pardon—to his . . . ears—?"

"I mean, he is very busy at the moment, as these newspaper articles will tell you. But he will be here in the very near future."

He was looking over the clippings, so I didn't feel the need to continue. The weather outside was lovely. I thought I just might check into the Carlton for a few days when I was through with this gentleman. I waited politely for him to finish, sure he would like to ask questions about what he had read. What I didn't know I would invent.

He raised expressionless eyes to me. "Very interesting," he said in his undefined accent. "Let us go over to the casino and show these papers to the manager."

"W-what?" I stammered, taken aback, then tried for a quick recovery. "Ah . . . yes. Of course. *Bien sur.*"

So, that was it. I might have known. What a dope I was. Mike was in some bind with the casino, meaning he owed them money, what else. He knew I wouldn't have come if I had known. What was I in? I thought of the pointing gun at the top of the Florida Keys steps. But France was different . . . wasn't it?

The bright sun was sharply cut off as we entered the eternal night of the casino world, at three in the afternoon. We settled in the sparsely attended bar, and I accepted a glass of Chablis that was offered, something to hold onto. The manager was thick-set, brown-suited, with tie and hair to match. *"Vous venez de Monsieur Todd?"* (pronounced "Toad" in French, and highly apt at the moment, I thought).

"Yes. *Oui. Il est . . . occupé avec . . . cette cinema en ce moment."* I gestured at the clippings. Vamping until ready à la française.

"C'est lui qui j'attendais."

Him I was expecting? "Ah, *oui,* well, *lui . . . il arrivera dans quelques jours. Il est tellement occupé en ce moment avec—"* But I had already said that, hadn't I. My vocabulary was shrinking by the minute.

There was this machine gun rattle of French between the two men. I got maybe half. Fifty thousand. Promised. Vous arrangez, the manager said to the other. Arrange what? Fifty thousand what? Francs? Dollars? *Dollars?* Mike had lost my $25,000 twice? Was this how he was letting me know I was never going to get it back?

The manager turned eyes sans emotion to me. He waved the clippings in his hand. "This is true?" he said to me in English. Son of a bitch, he could speak English all the time.

"Oh yes," I answered, "every word." If he didn't know how show biz propaganda worked, I wasn't going to be the one to enlighten him.

"Bon," he said. He turned to the man who had brought me there. "Then you have nothing to worry about." He rose to his feet, kissed my hand. I rose, gathered my things together, tilted my head to them both in what I hoped was a grand manner, and made my retreat.

To my surprise the sun still shone on the rest of the world. I headed straight for the airport and got on the first plane out of Cannes headed for Paris.

And to the phone.

Naturally Mike wasn't to be found. En route, his office reported. They didn't know to exactly where. He stayed that way several days, long enough for me to simmer down. I finally decided not to ever mention it at all; he would never tell me the whole story. But I began to be more concerned about my investment. When he checked in— from Los Angeles—I asked him, "Mike, how is my money protected in case one of those planes you're always in falls down?"

An exasperated sound came through the wire. "Dope. Don't you ever read the things you sign? You have five percent of the Michael Todd Company! You're going to be a millionairess one of these days!"

I hoped he was only a little bit right. . . .

CHAPTER 49 . . .

"Ochi . . . chorn . . . ia . . ."

The trip to the Soviet Union was finally and truly on. "Hooray!" I shrieked into the phone when Mike told me. "When? I'm going too, right? You wouldn't dare go without me, would you!" I could say "hello," "good-bye," "I don't understand," "This book is red" (what else), and "Greetings, citizens of the Soviet Union," in Russian. I didn't know just how to put it to use for Mike, but I was willing to try.

"You'll need a visa," he told me, laughing, "and hurry, we'll be leaving next week."

I rushed that very day to the Soviet Embassy, expecting them to be thrilled that I wanted to visit their country, happy at this reaching out for friendship from an American at last.

A welcoming committee it was not. The room was large and threadbare, uncarpeted, no pictures on the walls except a photograph of Stalin at one end. Word hadn't gotten to Paris yet. An official sat behind a desk on one side, with a row of spindly chairs facing him where we, who had come for something, sat waiting our turn.

The other "waiters" were without exception poorly dressed, wellworn coats and shoes, the women with scarves around their heads, looking like those long lines of displaced persons wandering Europe after the war. I suddenly felt uncomfortably conspicuous in my fur coat and my new platinum hair. (I have always bleached my hair between men. My years are interlaced with light heads and dark, like a chess board.)

When it was my turn I explained in French to the bored official that I wanted a visa because I was going to Moscow. And I gave him my most enchanting smile.

No response. The good man had obviously never smiled in his life and he wasn't about to break the habit for me. "I hope," I continued anyway, "this won't take too long. I need it for next week."

That got his full attention. His eyes shot up at me in utter astonishment. *"La semaine pr-r-r-rochaine!"* he roared.

The Russian "r" rolls on forever in every language, most particularly French. Had he spotted the American in mine? And learned that all he had heard about the arrogant capitalist nation was true? Here was one of its citizens demanding instant entry to the promised land. *"Ce n'est pas possible!"* He stated with the most emphatic period I have ever heard at the end of a sentence. Walter Huston would have been proud of him. And just in case I hadn't got the message, he called out, "Next!" (Actually what he said was, "Vous," and pointed.)

I was brokenhearted. What good were all these adorable ways I had learned if they didn't serve me in the clinch.

My reunion with Mike in Paris was scarcely observed. It was so overshadowed by my wails of frustration. "I haven't got a visa!" I cried out when Mike got off the plane, instead of embracing him. There was no time to waste. He was continuing on the first thing in the morning, and it was already late afternoon. "Can't you go the day after and see what you can do?"

"Kiss me, for crissake," Mike said.

"This schedule I can't screw around with," he told me in the car driving to town. "It was too tough to arrange." His French partner, in charge of the future shooting of *Around the World* in Paris was present too. Mike, as usual, was jamming his business and personal life into one squeezed-in time slot.

We had dinner at a small Basque restaurant across from Notre Dame. After a bottle of Montrachet-Bâtarde, a piperade and mousse au chocolat, interspersed with his catching me up on what had transpired since I left two months ago, and what was going to, we fell into my apartment and to bed, as though there had been no interlude.

I took him to the airport the next morning, fuming all the way. "At least bring back pounds of caviar," I snapped at him.

Early the following day I was awakened by a ringing phone. *"Moscou vous appelle,"* the operator said in my ear. Instantly alert, nerves tingling, I bolted upright. Mike had managed to get on a phone, even from Moscow. I laughed out loud as I waited for the buzzes and bleeps to sort themselves.

It wasn't the whiz kid in person, however, but rather a female voice, and she was speaking English. Sort of. The connection sounded as if she were coming from twenty leagues under the sea in an electrical storm. Her accent was thick, the "r's" rolling like thunderclaps.

What I thought she said was this: "Mees Eveleen, go to R-r-r-russian Embassy tomor-r-r-row mor-r-r-rning at nine o'clock for-r-r visa. Get air-r-r-r plane ticket for-r-r-r after-r-r-r-noon tomor-r-row. Get blond hair-r-r-r nets, get nylon stockings, come to Moscow, Mister-r-r-r Toad meet you."

Whether I had heard right or not, it was worth a try on all counts, including blond hair-r-r nets. I leaped from my bed, dressed, and went rushing about Paris buying the nets, stockings of various sizes, plus a plane ticket to Moscow on an afternoon flight. "You need a visa," the girl at the desk told me. "Of course," I said, "I'm getting it tomorrow."

She lifted her head from her scribbling. "Tomorrow is May Day. The Russian Embassy will be closed."

My heart sank. It wasn't to be. All of Europe would be out parading and dancing around Maypoles. I hadn't heard correctly.

Nevertheless I showed up at the Embassy at nine o'clock May Day morning. The airline hostess was right; the place was closed. But one gentleman was there, waiting for me. Ah Mike, I thought, you really are incredible. Is there anything you can't do if you set your mind to it? I was in and out in fifteen minutes, my passport properly stamped.

The plane was Czech. I was the only non-Russian passenger. The others were a returning delegation that had attended a convention in Paris. They wore flat shoes, large-brimmed hats pulled down to their brows, coats to their ankles and shapeless jackets and dresses underneath. They made me feel frivolous in my high heels and simple white Christian Dior, the hemline just so in the middle of the calf, topped with my platinum Italian cut hair. All the women had a good thirty pounds on me too. Their eyes slid over me, past me, anywhere but at me, my smile unreturned. At each other they smiled, though, so it wasn't against the rules. And they all seemed to know each other. There was laughter and chatter (r-r-r-r-r-r-r) around me and walking up and down the aisles, while I sat all alone, the leper with the bell around her neck. Détente wasn't on the agenda.

We landed somewhere in Poland for gas and dinner. Our passports were taken away as we left the plane. There would be no defecting today, Comrades. Someone escorted the rest of them into the terminal building. Someone else escorted me. Just me. My very own watchdog. "*Bon soir, Madame, suivez moi.*" Did he think I was French?

He escorted me to the ladies' room. He waited outside. There were no windows, I noticed. They took no chances this alien would jump ship. Asylum is not so quickly offered, it would seem, going that direction as it is coming this.

The forms were long. Did I have any firearms with me? Elks' horns? Reindeer horns? Fortunately I had none. Dinner was at one long table, the laughter and chatter continuing around me. The large amounts of caviar were most hospitable, however, and vodka flowed like the Volga.

Mike was waiting at the airport. "Welcome to Moscow!" he called out over everybody's heads. You would have thought he owned the place.

"You do get around," I giggled happily. "Boy, am I glad to see you!" My bags were pushed on through without inspection. A fellow from the Ministry of Culture was with us, but it was Mike who was my guide as we entered the city, as if he were a Moscovite born and bred. There's the University, here's the entrance to the subway, the Kremlin, the Bolshoi.

The streets were super-wide and empty of traffic at two o'clock in the morning. As we approached Red Square, football coliseum in size, a line of people was coming toward us abreast, strung out across the entire street, their arms linked, singing at the top of their voices, weaving drunkenly and happily along.

When we got to the hotel a band was wailing out the "Saint Louis Blues," the musicians' enthusiasm far outweighing their lack of skill. A few more drunks tottered by us on the stairs. The hotel was ancient if a little shabby, but its former elegance was intact. Our suite even sported a grand piano.

Mike and the Russians became instant soul brothers. His vigor, his enthusiastic rough-and-ready quality matched theirs. We had a splendid first few days. We visited a film studio and watched a woman directing a picture. Hooray for our side. Women were busy everywhere. Women doorpersons. Women policepersons. Old women persons sweeping the streets. How splendid, I thought, still useful members of society instead of being stuck in homes or hanging around St. Petersburg, Florida to rot your last years away.

We saw *Romeo and Juliet* at the Bolshoi, with a sixty-piece orchestra *onstage*. Sitting in the fifth row, Mike whispered to me, imitating Joe McCarthy, "Everybody in this place is a . . . Communist."

We heard Isaac Stern in concert. Walked in circles in the lobby at intermission, drinking tea out of glasses encased in silver. Mike had meetings to talk about picture production, while I went about with the wife of a newspaperman, she who wanted the hair-r-r nets and stockings. Mike had gone straight to the American press when he arrived. He never missed a chance to get in print. His eagerness to have stories datelined Moscow caused dissension in our happy Moscow interlude.

He gave a party in our suite, inviting the composer Katchaturian and his wife, Soviet directors, actresses, ministers of state, all the people he had met, and of course, the press corps. When one of the reporters came in, he said to Mike, "Sorry I couldn't complete that call to Marlene Dietrich for you, Mike."

Mike's eyes jumped to me. I wasn't supposed to have heard that. He didn't like getting caught at such an obvious play like having a newspaperman try the call to insure a story. "Todd calls Dietrich from Moscow to make *Around the World* deal!" That would surely make its way to the news broadcasters and columns.

My eyebrows lifted with just a touch of scorn. "What a show-off you are," I murmured, when the press fellow was out of hearing. "A woman in every port, eh?"

He flew into an immediate rage. He held it too, until everybody had left, then strode about our suite sizzling like a Fourth of July sparkler. "There's never any peace around you," he fumed, "you're always after me—"

"Always? I've been in Paris, Mike, minding my own business."

"You wanted to come here!" he yelled accusingly.

"I can't deny that—"

"I'm sorry I brought you—"

"Then I'm sorry too—"

"The first plane out tomorrow, you'll be on the first plane—"

"Oh really?" I snapped, getting sore, "just like that, eh, the emperor speaks, and his word is law? You happen to be in a very foreign country, and there just might be—" I stopped, suddenly remembering exactly where we were, that we were indeed in a very foreign country, and that our hotel suite might very well be bugged. At least that's what everybody had warned me about. Someone, somewhere in Moscow, could be listening this minute to this silly outburst of the two Americans. I put my finger to my lips, and gestured wildly around the room.

"Don't—tell—me to shut up!" Mike snarled, enraged. "I'm going to tell you just what I—"

I started toward him. I was going to whisper that there might be a bug in the room. He recoiled as if I had the plague. "Don't come near me! Just don't try that, it won't do any good."

It was ludicrous. Two sane (supposedly) people suddenly behaving like lunatics. What must it seem like to that eavesdropping outsider. It struck me funny, and I giggled.

A grave error. A red cape at the bull. Mike's outrage rose to heights. A torrent of words issued forth like a river in spate. I had an actress's mentality and I always would, I wanted to lead him by the nose, a docile eunuch is what I wanted, a hairdresser to follow me around, that's what I should have, and blah blah blah. The words blurred but the sound went on . . . and on . . . and on. . . . I tried to escape to the bedroom, but he wasn't having that; he followed, the words tumbling out, Jacks and Jills. I mean, he went beyond the line of duty.

I wondered what was really bugging him. I remember thinking that loneliness is being in Moscow getting yelled at by somebody who had been a big mistake from the word go. Having to face the fact you have been trapped against your better judgment into continuing the partnership for no better reason than one more lousy trip offered you. And the whole *mishigas* was probably being recorded somewhere. If our entire lives, all the words we ever uttered, could be transcribed somewhere for later replay, I wonder if we would change anything.

His snit quieted the next day and we flew to Leningrad to see an opera of *War and Peace* (and the Hermitage). In the plane, trying to fasten my seat belt and unable to locate it, I asked the stewardess where it was. She answered, "*Oh, il ne vaut pas la peine.*" (Oh, it's not worth the bother.)

Was she trying to tell me something?

CHAPTER 50...

"Falling in love with love is falling for make . . . believe. . . ."

Parting in Paris was uncomplicated, with no necessity to find the right note, the right attitude; he would be returning soon to shoot in Europe. I told him I had read a French play I would like to produce. *Produce,* I said, not act in. I would get behind the scenes. Would he help me begin?

Come help me for awhile when I come back, he said, you'll learn all you need to know.

That made sense. Oh, we kept it impersonal.

First it was London, Mike and his company recreating the turn of the century, turning square and street into yesterday with horse and carriage and costume, Mike running the show, in his element. I watched and listened. I took photographs, helping Mario with his English. David Niven was about too, none of us admitting, even remembering, that we had ever met before.

Then it was on to Paris, where Mike managed to take over the entire Place Vendôme without the police permission he couldn't get; just rushed in of a quiet Sunday morning with masses of people already in period costume, the necessary horses and carriages, set up the cameras and got out before the police showed up. He got away with it too. He even stuck me in a little walk-through. Oh, we were busy, busy—who had time to think of anything else!

Then it was Spain, and out to the great torero Dominguín's ranch, where he raised fighting bulls, to choose one for the sequence of his fight with Cantínflas. I sat on a stone wall, quiet as a mouse, as the rest of them went on horseback to round up the bulls. I watched—and smelled—them thunder by just below me, near enough to touch the dust they stirred up.

We all met again, the men and bulls, in a little village outside Madrid called Chinchon, where the entire center of the town was the bullring, and the entire population of the village became the extras in the film. Dominguín made a few passes, Mario in his Cantínflas costume made a few. The camera whirled, recording it all. And then they were gone, back to America to finish the filming in the studios, back to where the stars were who would do their bits throughout the picture to help make it the big success it turned out to be.

And I? Back to my island in the middle of the Seine. It took Mike a week or so to realize we were apart, he was so preoccupied. And then the whole thing started again like the merry-go-round going round and round. The cables, the phone calls, filled with affection, with love, with longing. It's not the same without you. What am I doing it all for? I got no one to share it with. Are you sure you want to be there? Won't you come back?

"Ah Mike," I said sadly, "you just want me to hang around, don't you, and nothing more. Without any real commitment. Don't you see, I can't go on doing that. As you have often pointed out, I'm not getting any younger, I've got to get on with my life."

"Come back. We'll . . . we'll . . ." the pause was interminable. As if he were trying to get something out, and choking on it, "We'll get . . . engaged."

I couldn't believe my ears. Engaged! Closing the barn door after, and all those other jokes? I began to laugh. This was the funniest thing I had ever heard. Engaged after three years of living together! Hilarious!

Mike was not joining in with my lightheartedness, "Please come back." His tone was deadly serious. "I'll give you a ring to seal it."

My God, I thought, he's in earnest. A chill went through me. He means it. He's trying to tell me something. Marriage is what follows engagements. I stopped laughing, touched. I realized it was his way of saying, "Okay. You win. Here's my commitment, really and truly. We're in this together and we'll work it out somehow, grown-up style."

Well, damned if I didn't go along once more, ashamed of the vague disappointment that I wouldn't be turning onto a new road. But it made sense; it was the only logical thing to do. Wasn't it what I wanted, what every woman wanted, the live-happily-ever-after ending? Hadn't I spent too long aiming for just this culmination not to stick around to see the grand finale?

The fact was, I *wasn't* getting any younger. Fear rustled along my nervous system every so often like a warning from the future.

I burned my Parisian bridges. After all, that part of my life was finished, wasn't it? I gave up my apartment, sold my little car. I said good-bye to the Bucks and the rest of my friends, told them I would most certainly be back on visits like the rest of the tourists, and off I went back to Hollywood.

The getting together wasn't like the other times. This one was quiet, sensible, like two old shoes. A ring was on the way, he said, a fifteen-carat diamond, from his jewel contact in New York (the "I can get it for you wholesale" one).

A diamond is forever, as any fool knows. I found it all so charming, so utterly old-fashioned and quaint. Like part of Mike was. Although he struggled against it, he really still thought there were "good" girls and "bad" ones, virtuous and not. His problem with me had always been that I didn't seem to fit into either category. He had at last made up his mind.

While this symbol of eternity was en route, this substantial evidence of love and faith, scenery was being swung into place for the last and final scene.

We had dashed off to Mexico City and to Tijuana for more bullfight shots. But the big excitement was over a Japanese sailing vessel that had arrived in the Los Angeles harbor.

It was the *Kaiwo Maru,* a 436-foot training master for Japanese sailors, an anachronism in today's world, but perfect for the Singapore sequence in Mike's *Around the World.* What extraordinary luck that it had come visiting just at this particular time. What a golden opportunity to grab some exciting, authentic footage instead of the alternative of miniatures being enlarged.

Mike, the genius arranger, called somebody who knew somebody who called somebody to fix it for Mike and his crew to meet the *Kaiwo Maru* up around Santa Barbara, off Point Conception, as she headed for home. At which time she would be under all plain sail.

To bring about this thrilling coup Mike chartered a boat—a

117-foot twin screw job—and, never one to do things alone, piled a number of us aboard to keep him company. Me. Ketti and Kurt Frings. Art Cohn, a writer who was doing Mike's biography. Assorted secretaries and assistants, among whom was Kevin McClory, who had supervised other sequences of the picture in Pakistan, Thailand, Hong Kong and various points east. He had come along to help Mike with the capturing of the Japanese full-rigged ship.

Kevin brought two other guests on board with him, Michael Wilding and Elizabeth Taylor.

To say that I noticed anything between Mike and Elizabeth wouldn't be true. It never even crossed my mind. Elizabeth was everything Mike professed not to care for; she was the epitome of movie star in dress, attitude and demands. And she never stopped drinking champagne from the moment she stepped on the boat until she got off two days later. Besides actresses, Mike didn't like women who drank a great deal. And she had a husband.

No, there was no possible way I could have got a clue. In retrospect I tried to figure out why my antennae, usually quite sharp, had been dulled. Perhaps because of all that was happening. The sight of that beautiful, three-rigged schooner, sails billowing in the wind, slipping out of the fog that Sunday morning, like a leftover from another century, was a sight never to be forgotten.

The sea was rough; we tossed and bounced as Mike, Kevin and the rest of the crew got into a small boat with the camera and went off into the fog to circle the larger vessel and photograph it from as many angles as possible. After the first glimpse we on the motor boat had to move on so they wouldn't catch us, the twentieth century, in their lens.

They returned in a couple of hours, the work done, and that was that. The trip back to L.A. was leisurely: sunbathing, chatting. More champagne. A lot more. A stop somewhere for dinner. Mike kissed Elizabeth good-bye. But then, so did I.

The ring arrived.

It certainly *looked* like an engagement ring. A square emerald cut, showy, but not too. After all the big deal about it, Mike was strangely indifferent as he slipped it on my finger, I thought. No kiss, no hug, no declaration of "with this ring, it's you and me, babe, from here on in." I attributed it to his preoccupation with his picture. I knew he had a million and one things on his mind.

I was certainly right about that.

I wore it to a party Mike gave for Edward R. Murrow, a noble man who, singlehandedly on TV, had stood up against McCarthy. He had become something of a folk-hero for it. Mike had gotten him to do the introduction at the beginning of *Around the World.*

The Wildings were there too. Mike was a good host, paying attention to each guest, seeing to their food, their drinks. I didn't notice that he did more for Elizabeth than he did, say, for Mrs. Murrow. Later in the evening when some of the men settled down for a bit of gin rummy, Elizabeth might have stayed in the room where Mike was for most of the time. But I couldn't actually vouch for that.

My ring didn't fit. It was far too big and kept slipping off. Mike said it was too dangerous to wear like that, I could lose it. He took it and said he was sending it back to be resized.

When he asked me to run down to Caracas for him I was delighted. I don't have time to do it all, he told me. Check on a theater there for us (us, he said), the size, the shape, see if it would accommodate Todd-AO. "You know what we need. I don't trust anybody else to make the right decision. You've been in on enough discussions, and you can take a copy of the blueprints with you. You'll be my—our—representative. What do you say?"

I was thrilled. Here was full partnership, no more hanging uselessly around. I could try my wings at executive decision down Caracas way, finally use the experience I had gathered from watching and listening to Mike in action.

After Caracas I was to fly to London, meet with Noël Coward and Robert Morley, give them some added lines that must be dubbed in, supervising it, explaining whatever was necessary. Then on to Paris and the Lancaster Hotel, with added lines for Fernandel, and repeat the process with him.

Off I went, pleased as punch, happier than I had ever been. Here was the beginning of a new career, one that incorporated all the things I knew. And I would be working with and for my man. Which is how it should be.

He waited until I got back to Paris to give me the word. I suppose he felt it would be easier if I were on home ground. Though why I had to make such a large circuit remains a mystery.

When he called I blathered on excitedly. Caracas was a long strip of a city. The theater was handsome, and Morley was too darling for words. "Listen," he said, "I have to tell you . . . I've fallen in love with Elizabeth."

"What? What?" What was he talking about? A piece of film, a place?

"I've fallen in love with Elizabeth." Ah. He was teasing. He was always doing that. If I weren't jealous, I didn't love him. "Elizabeth who?" I asked, going along with the joke. Too much had happened in the interim to be remembering a small run up the coast.

It took him the longest time to make me understand it was no joke. I was stunned by the revelation. The earth is flat? The moon really is cheese? "Well sure," I finally said calmly, "I understand. Listen, good luck to you."

Luise Rainer revisited. She had won an Academy Award. What was my prize?

I hung up, and went to pieces. I had been . . . taken. When I wasn't looking, I had been delivered a knockout punch. I felt jilted. There was no other word. Mike had set it up that way. Why? I kept asking myself, why? I had been in Paris, set up in my own apartment; it had been over between us, why ask me to come back? Why go through that farce with a ring—*and take it back*—and send me off on some wild goose chase making me think it was legitimate business, letting me be so excited and pleased about it. All of it, every bit of it, his script. From beginning to end.

I felt I had been set up like a group of tenpins and knocked down with rather more than necessary violence. Why? And don't give me this bullshit about finding love, because I won't believe it. You find love too easily, you find love too fast.

I felt doubly wretched because I knew I should have known better. I should have—nay, I *did* see all the signs along the way. Like the phone call from Moscow to Marlene Dietrich when she was still big news. And I knew in my heart at the time that when he did the circus and had Marilyn Monroe ride the pink elephant, in her glorious hey-day, that if she had beckoned with her little finger he would have gone running. And he would have called it love, and believed it, too.

But what the hell; you play around with the big time, the rewards are high. So you have to be prepared to take your lumps.

Finally I was able to look at the positive side. I wouldn't ever have to hear "S.I.B.," or "prepartee" or "walk-around money," "rootin' interest," "calling from the police station," "where's it written on Mount Rushmore," or smell a cigar, or watch a gin rummy game again. Ever, never again. . . .

It wasn't quite the end. The cable read: ONE OF THE GREATEST SHOWS EVER SEEN . . . OPENED LAST NIGHT AT THE RI-VOLI . . . TRIED TO PHONE YOU . . . LOOKS LIKE WILL SEE YOU NEXT WEEK. LOVE . . . MIKE.

It was more like two months.

Meanwhile I found an exquisite apartment fairly creaking with history. On the Quai de Bourbon of the Ile St.-Louis, it sat on the point of the island facing upstream, and the waters of the Seine flowed past on both sides. The cobblestones below were the same ones poor Marie's cart had rolled over when they carried her to her doom. I hired a Chinese cook and a Spanish maid, and began to give dinner parties in my elegant, gold-draped dining room, with the money flowing in from the Michael Todd Company.

He arrived in January, keyed-up as usual, bursting with plans as always. His next was going to be *Don Quixote,* with those two magnificent comedians, Cantínflas and Fernandel. The success of *Around the World* and heaps of money flowing in hadn't changed a thing; that was finished and done with; tomorrow was here!

It was there in my beloved Paris that Mike made the remark that made it undeniably clear what made him run. "They," he told me, "think I can't do it again. I'll show them."

He stayed overnight with me, as he always had. It would have seemed silly not to. Were we not friends? Family, as he insisted? His "partner" in the company? Once in a while he would get mixed up and call me Elizabeth, but that was understandable. He would have liked to keep us both. That was understandable too. I would have liked to have kept all mine, too. Why does the new one have to knock off the old? Why can't we all love one another?

Some time after he had gone, my friend Joyce Buck called. "Artie Shaw is in town. He talks about things with the same approach as you do. I think you would like him. Are you free for dinner?"

I knew who Artie Shaw was. Who didn't? "Sure," I answered. What did I have to lose?

BOOK SEVEN

CHAPTER 51...

"Oh . . . let them begin . . .

the beguine. . . ."

He came in talking. "Good-to-see-you, what's-with-the-hair?"

"Oh, I change it from time to time."

People who've been filmed can never have a blind date, they've seen each other's pictures. He had less hair than in the last one I had seen, a clean-shaven, lean face and computer-sharp eyes under thick brows. "I-don't-know-if-I-like-it-yet, you-finished-with-Mike-Todd?"

"Him with me is more like it."

"Best-thing-that-could-have-happened-to-you. Good-looking place you have here, I thought of settling in Paris but changed my mind, it's more of the same with a French accent. . . ."

The Bucks and I managed to exchange greetings and embraces, but it was Artie who dominated the room with his flow of animated, inquisitive talk, wanting to know everything instantly, his vibrancy ricocheting around the ancient walls like sparks off a flint.

Yeah, I thought, feeling the first stirrings of interest. Dynamos were my bag. None of this languid, slow-moving life force for me. Or is it that once you've known a sprinter, a trotter won't do?

We all walked to another corner of "my" island, to a restaurant called Le Bossu (The Hunchback), so named because of the nearness of Notre Dame, across the bridge.

Over *friture de goujons*—thin strips of fish fried in butter—and a bottle of Chablis, the talk spun out like mayflies over water, touching and moving on, wings sparkling in the sun. From politics to books to economics in Hollywood to plain gossip, it was witty, gay and lively. I was having a perfectly splendid time.

Afterwards the Bucks went home to their child, but Artie and I moved on to a club for a drink with Claude Thornhill, the super pianist who had played in Artie's band years before. Against the rattle of glasses and a flickering TV screen in the background unfolding an American western with French subtitles, Artie told us how, after looking everywhere, he had settled on the Costa Brava, was building from scratch, that the walls were up and the roof was just going on. That there were only fishermen and their families in his village who spoke nothing but Catalán and a little Spanish if they had to, which was why sometimes he got hungry for the sound of English and would drive to Paris or London to see some American friends. It all sounded exquisitely romantic to me. I hung onto every word.

The two men began reminiscing of those days when the band went to war. A bunch of muscle-soft musicians with little exercise other than blowing their instruments suddenly found themselves on a battleship crossing the Pacific, with Japanese torpedoes hurtling toward them; under fire on obscure tropical islands, diving for foxholes while bombs and shrapnel fell about their heads. "Survival seemed remote, so I made a run at increasing my odds," laughed Artie. "I learned the Japanese national anthem. If they landed I would greet them on the beach playing their song."

Getting shot at seems to bring about a special togetherness among men and a fondness for remembering—inspired, no doubt, by the relief that it's over and they're safely out of it. In any event the two men were enjoying themselves and I thought it time to leave them to their memories.

Artie walked me to my car. The evening had been impersonal until then, the conversation general. That changed as he opened the door to my car and let me in. Leaning down toward me he said softly, "Drive carefully. I wouldn't want to lose you now."

The next night we went to a nightclub in St. Germain de Prés where a jazz violinist was playing. It had been my idea; I wanted to entertain my new friend, and isn't music what a musician would want to hear? "He's absolutely terrific!" I told Artie with conviction. I knew what was good, hadn't I studied piano back in Atlanta?

Watching Artie Shaw, one of the world's foremost clarinetists, listening to a fellow craftsman in the smoky, raucous basement Parisian joint, a revelation came to me.

Mike had often said, "Everybody's got two businesses, his own, and show biz." That was after a civilian, as he called non-show-biz persons, would have told him what was "good" in a picture or play. Watching Artie listen, I knew that music should be added to Mike's remark. For he listened as I had never seen anybody listen before. I mean, the man *listened,* he was swept up in listening until it became a physical thing. It soon became clear that we were tuning in with different sets of ears, this music man and I.

Just how different I had no idea, but I knew I wanted to find out.

When the show was over, his talk was dazzling, his subject matter making wide sweeps round the globe, his vocabulary soaring in infinite variety. His grammar, I couldn't help noticing, was thrillingly impeccable. The reputation, then, that had preceded him—the multimarried (and who wasn't) brilliant, well-read intellectual—was true.

My heart quickened its beat. The life within that had taken a nose dive began to surface once more. Here was a presence. A strength I hungered for. Someone who could take me somewhere I had never been.

It wasn't a question of should or would; we simply returned to the Quai de Bourbon and my bed as if we had lived that way all our lives, our consummation as natural as the morning dew. It was coming home after a long absence. As if our lives, varied and chaotic as they had been, had led us to this incredible and perfect moment.

A great peace descended on us both; we knew we were going to be all right from here on in.

He moved into my place next day since he would be in Paris for another week, and then we would both head for Spain. We would not part again—not even for an hour. It was settled without further thought. When your prince comes along, you know it. (Every time.)

Otto Preminger, in town to make *Joan of Arc,* took over my lease. A Simca station wagon, larger than the tiny Renault, was purchased to handle the Spanish backroads. Our packing included a very large case of Tampax to avoid a repeat of the Palermo scene. It was a busy week.

And through it all the dialogue begun between us would spin out unceasingly through the years. The searching, the delving, looking into each other's corners and crevices, wanting to know the hows, the whys, wanting to understand each other. We must learn everything about each other, leave no stone unturned. Perfect and total communication was our goal; this was the way to avoid the mistakes of the past, the way to benefit from our errors in order to make this the most perfect relationship of all time.

He told me that he had left America the previous year. Packed up, bag and baggage, and come to Europe to live. He had been rejected, abandoned by his own country. From favored son, beloved of millions, earning some $30,000 a week, he had been kicked out of the only society he knew, overnight. Dragged from a band tour down in Texas one day in the fifties by the infamous Un-American Activities Committee, he too was thrust before their Washington klieg lights and cameras while the illustrious congressmen demanded to know why he had joined the Committee for the Arts, Sciences and Professions.

He wanted peace, Artie told them, and that organization had been for peace.

Didn't he know it was *communist fronted?*

"Listen," Artie told them earnestly, "if there had been a Republican organization for peace, I would have joined that."

The inquisitors half-heartedly joined in the laughter of the spectators and said, well yes, they had been amiss in that respect, called him a dupe, and let him go.

But his phone stopped ringing overnight. Tax people closed in to say he owed $80,000. He didn't, but to fight the government he would have had to pay a lawyer at least as much. (Since Watergate times we've learned that the government was never loath to get at people through the IRS.) Artie, his feelings and his pocketbook gravely hurt, sold his beloved dairy farm in New York State where he had settled down "forever" and left America for a new way of life.

He had found his way to the Costa Brava, as far a cry from his former life as possible. He had spent this last year there all alone, reading, studying, thinking, summing up his life; what he was about, where he was going, and why. *Completely alone.*

America's loss was my gain.

I never knew anybody who had done a thing like that. How could I not have faith, not believe that somebody who had done something like that knew what he was talking about?

"Are you sure," he would ask me every so often, "you're going to like Spain?"

"You'll be there—"

"I'll be writing, you know, a good four hours a day; a separate wing is being built for that purpose, you'll be on your own while I'm holed up—"

"Four hours without you?" I teased. "I don't know if I can stand it!"

"I just want you to be sure, it's a long way to go without being sure—"

"I've never been so sure of anything in my life."

It was true. This glorious turn of events was not unexpected. I had always known some wondrous thing would happen to me. And now Spain, but of course Spain, the most romantic, mysterious and passionate of all countries. A "castle in Spain" is part of our language, symbol of our dreams and our longings. And now I was going to one with the love of my life, found at last by a most circuitous route, off to live the contemplative life. No more running around the world, the dream had really and finally come true.

Just one thing bothered me, a tiny cloud lurking that could rain on my parade. It had to be got out in the open, I could not go on carrying this ridiculous secret, nothing at all until Mike had made it hang in my head in Capital Letters, too heavy to go on enduring. "Artie, there's something I must tell you. . . ."

I told him of my black experience. I told him why, how, of telling Mike, of Mike's reaction, and my reaction to Mike. He had looked at me as I told my tale, listening as he had to the music, a frown between his eyes. Oh God, I thought, another one, he's reacting the same damn way. Well, to hell with him too.

"I wouldn't imagine that's a thing you ought to tell Mike Todd."

What had he said? "Uh, yeah, so it turned out—"

"That particular prejudice—that a black excels in sexual prowess— is so deeply ingrained in the white American male that it borders on superstition. He is secretly feared by most whites—"

"Oh God. Really?"

"You laid too heavy a load on a man like Mike. . . ."

I started to laugh. Oh how I laughed. He hadn't said anything funny, it was just such blessed relief. I got up and hugged him tightly. "Oh Artie, how very much I love you!" I cried. I did, too, in my fashion. I hung onto every word he had to say in those days. . . .

CHAPTER 52 . . .

"In a lit–tle Spanish town . . . 'twas on
a night like this. . . ."

The Bucks, who had brought about this miraculous mating, "married" us in a festive little mock ceremony until we could get around to the real one. Thus firmly united we left Paris in tandem, I following Artie's gray convertible Mercedes in my new pale yellow Simca, both cars bulging with luggage. On through the Port d'Orleans, down through the green rolling fertile hills of France. Limoges,

Brive, Cahors dropping straight south to Toulouse, Carcassonne, Narbonne, and finally after two days on to Perpignan, which sits right next to the Spanish frontier.

The countryside had changed as we neared our destination; the earth lost its coolness and took on a reddish, drier look. Vineyards extended as far as the eye could see. The streets of Perpignan were lined with oleanders, all in bloom, their pink and white blossoms catching the sun, adding a festive welcoming air. Spring had come early that year, just for me.

Crossing into Spain one sensed an immediate change; as if Europe proper had been left behind and we had stepped into another century. Crumbling Roman ruins and ancient villages dotted the countryside, flocks of sheep strolled along and crossed the roads, as did geese and cows. Not yet summer, tourists were rare, and we seldom passed another car, the standard Spanish vehicle being the horse and cart, clumping along at a sleepy gait, usually, I was to learn, without a taillight at night. How we missed hitting one all those years is a miracle, since Artie maintained a demon pace at all times. He did get a few chickens and once an owl.

He timed it, I'm sure, that we come upon Bagur as the sun was shedding its final rays. It was a moment of exquisite beauty, forever imprinted on my mind. The sky was filled with riotous hues that overflowed and spread across the village ahead, splashing against the time-worn ochred walls to make a rich patina that only age can achieve. Our tiny caravan passed between them along a narrow cobblestone street that joined the central plaza. It too was cobbled and ancient. The Romans might have crossed those very stones; the Moors certainly had, a remnant of their earlier presence sat in splendid glory against the blazing sky at the top of the hill just beyond: a crumbling Moorish castle, built in the eighth century when the invaders from Africa still held sway over the land. The village itself nestled around the hill beneath, looking, in that light, like a bracelet of multi-shaded topaz and onyx.

Artie pulled over and stopped, I an echo behind him. He got out and came over to my car. "What do you think?" He smiled.

"Oh Artie." I couldn't speak.

"Leave your car here. We've just enough light left to see the house if we hurry."

Both in the Mercedes then, we left the village of Bagur behind, going up over a rise and down the other side.

And there, as we began to descend, sitting on the edge of the mountain, just before it fell off into the valley below, sat Artie's half-finished house. Beyond, spread out as far as the eye could see, were the waters of the Mediterranean, bathed in the glory of the last bursting rays of the setting sun. Homer's wine-red sea in person.

Home. At last.

It was too much. I wept. Artie, knowing how he had felt the first time he saw the view even without the added serendipity of love, put his arm around me, and didn't speak.

The house itself, whose walls were built from the stone on the land, was placed so that every room would take in this panoramic sweep of valley and water and jagged coastline spinning off to the right. Rocks of rufous-red jutted out into the sea, and green pines were scattered over the land like chunks of emeralds. Full-length terraces would be built on both floors, with glass doors for every room.

But all that had to be imagined that day of my introduction; only the walls and the roof were there, an empty shell waiting to be shaped and filled with plaster and paint, tiles and beds, lamps and bidets and books and the sound of music and voices; all the things that would make it our everlasting, dream home-sweet-home, love-nest come true. "Oh Artie!" I cried, "what a perfect time to arrive on the scene!" Our laughter, uncontained, slipped through the empty spaces and toppled down the mountain.

Back in our cars, I followed the gray one down to the water's edge where Artie had taken a house while his own went up. In a sandy cove, he had told me, just large enough for a few fishermen and their families—and the stranger in their midst who, as everybody knew, was a very famous *músico americano*. Dark when we arrived, the boats had already departed for the night's catch. Their tiny lights were twinkling in the black stretch of water, the only illumination around. It would be morning before I would see the miniscule beach where the women sat in the new day's warming sun mending the nets damaged from the night before. "*Buenos dias,*" they nodded, smiling at this new blonde apparition among them, not unduly alarmed. A friend of the señor's was a friend of theirs. What peace. What uncluttered serenity. How pure and clear the air was. I took in a lungful and let it out with a contended sigh.

Super-chameleon me fell quickly into Artie's established routines. Breakfast prepared by his housekeeper, a walk on the beach— "*Buenos dias! Buenos dias!*"—then a run up to check on the progress of our future home. Ah, it was gorgeous playing house, grown-up style. Decisions, decisions to be made by the second. What tile here, brick there, which light fixture and where, and what about the sliding doors. These had to be made by the ironmonger, no such thing as readymades in sight. Look at this phenomenon, Ladies and Gentlemen, an actual made-by-hand house!

My drawing-room French soon gave way to a more practical Spanish vocabulary consisting of mortar, pipe, wire and/or faucet. Soon we were dashing into Barcelona a couple of times a week, a two-hour drive of dodging sheep and carts, to see about drapes and rugs, beds and chests, locks and keys, hooks and hinges, pots and pans. "You'll know what we need for the kitchen," Artie said.

"Who, me?" I laughed uproariously.

We were walking down the Calle de Paja back to our hotel, our shopping brought to a halt by the Spanish midday siesta. All doors were closed tightly at one and stayed that way until four. The snooze was necessary; most Barcelonians, including the kids, would have been up the night before until two, three or four in the morning.

Artie glanced over at me thoughtfully. "I think it's time we got something else straight, Kesi," he said.

"Ah? What now?"

"Let's go up to our room and talk for a minute before lunch."

"Of course."

The trick, Artie had told me, is to speak up immediately when something is on your mind, straighten it out before it has time to fester. Don't assume the other person feels the same way you do. "Assumption," he said, "has been the mother of a lot of fuck-ups." Keep talking things over, that was the only way two sensible people could hold onto a perfect understanding.

Well, I certainly wanted to be half of a sensible pair. It's probably why it hadn't worked out before with me and the others; nobody ever spoke up.

We always stayed at the Hotel Colón, they knew us, we knew them; they had even given me my new name when some nearsighted clerk mixed up the spelling of my last name. "That's it!" Artie had exclaimed, "Kesi!" He had been searching for a nickname for me. The maids were also used to the crazy American señor who insisted that the *matrimonio*, the double bed, be put in his room, even if it was for one night only. Twin beds were out; we were together at last, together we were going to stay.

We sat down in two chairs facing each other, like Laurel and Hardy in a rowboat. He had to wait to speak until the church bells across the way finished bonging out the hour. It was the usual Spanish accompaniment, no matter where you were. I wondered what was bothering him this time.

Finally he leaned closer and began: "You know, Kesi, it doesn't even seem to occur to you there's anything untoward about not knowing what is needed in the kitchen."

"Well I don't. I don't know thing one about a kitchen, I've never cooked in my life!"

"*Not* knowing something doesn't seem much to brag about."

"Oh." I was taken aback. "I see what you mean."

"To run a kitchen, run a house, those are responsibilities, and you have sought out men who would do those things for you, you even moved into their houses and apartments to avoid that responsibility—"

"Good heavens," I murmured, "do you think so?"

"—and you're trying to do it again, aren't you?"

I stared at him. "My God, I guess I am."

"Oh listen—" He took my hands in his. Earnest was the word for Artie. "I'm at fault too. I'm doing the same thing I've done every time —falling for the beautiful gentile lady type who hasn't the faintest idea how to be a wife. But you and I, if we talk enough, we can work it out—"

"Oh yes!" I cried. "Yes, we must—"

"Lana, Ava, you, any pretty girl, you've been raised to think you're doing a man a favor by merely saying hello."

It was a funny idea. I laughed. He ought to know what he was talking about—Turner and Gardner were the last names of his non-wifelike selections.

"It's true," Artie said (earnestly). "Ava, even after months of marriage, would come bouncing in at the end of a day, saying, 'What's for dinner?'"

Artie rose to stand by the window. "Well, one day, I had had enough, and that night when she came in and repeated her question, I said, 'Ava. Sit down. I want to talk to you.'

"'Of course, darling,' she said, 'what about?' and dropped on the couch beside me with a pretty little flounce. Ava was very winning, you know."

I chuckled. "Oh yes indeed, I know that."

"'Ava,' I said, 'look. I do certain things for you, do I not?'

"'Darling!' she cried, 'you do everything!'

"'No, wait,' I said, 'not everything. But certainly some things. I pay the rent, the utilities, the gardener, the help, I buy the food, your clothes, take care of all the business—'

"'Oh darling,' she said, 'I know you do—'

"'Ava,' I said, 'what do you do for me?'

" 'I love you!' she cried.

" 'And I love you,' I told her, 'so we start even there. What else do you do—'

" '*I love you!*' she repeated, as if I hadn't heard her the first time."

I leaped up and went to him. "It's exactly what I've been doing, isn't it, oh my God, isn't it, just . . . lending my darling person to the man I was with, expecting it to be enough for him—"

"Where would you have learned any differently, you never saw a married couple interaction while growing up. You only saw your single mother, and your adult life has been handsomely rewarded because of your looks."

"Surely a little more?" I murmured.

"Try," responded Artie, "to have managed the same things without them."

I flung my arms around him. "Oh Artie," I cried, "it's not too late, is it, I haven't come to my senses too late, have I, I can change all that, must. Will you help me please? Show me the way?"

"What would help a lot is if we defined our roles, spelled them out, to avoid head-on collisions."

"How do we do that?"

"Well," Artie said, "for example, someone has to be the captain. We can't have two, is that not so?"

"Oh yes, absolutely," I agreed.

"I know figures, you don't, it is usually the man who runs the business part—"

"Oh yes! Absolutely!" I cried, relieved to get out of that part. "You are the captain! My God, of course, you're the leader of the band!"

He laughed. "And the kitchen is normally the woman's dominion, unless you want to fight that?"

"No no. God, no. I've fought being a woman long enough, I'll run a kitchen like it's never been run before."

"By instinct it is the female who is the nest-maker."

"I never was." I shook my head. "What in the world was wrong with me?"

"You never trusted men since your father died and left you. You didn't want to take a chance another man would do it to you, and of course arranged it so they would. . . ."

On and on it went, these analyses, these diggings-in, through lunch, through the years, the endless takings-apart in order to re-shape (with such honorable intentions), ignoring Humpty-Dumpty's fate, logic and reason being the name of the game. And who could argue with groovy things like logic and reason.

That afternoon I began to look at kitchen pots and pans with new eyes. . . .

CHAPTER 53...

"How much is that doggie . . . in the window. . . ."

Where to begin. Well, for starters, see what a kitchen looks like. What is that, good God, a wood-burning stove? Artie! *Artie!* "They're very good to cook with, I hear," he comes up with.

Oh, you hear, do you. But in the new house surely we'll have a gas or electric one? Well no, where would we get gas, and the electricity is very weak, there's a shortage, it's turned off every afternoon between one and five, and they sometimes forget to turn it on even then. Anyway, when in Rome—we must live as the rest of the natives.

You showed me some natives living in a cave, and should we travel by horse and cart?

Ha ha. Kesi's a card. What are you worried about? The locals know how to use a wood stove, you'll have a handy man to build the fires and stoke them, you'll have a cook, all you'll have to do is supervise them.

When we were served fried pig's blood, the necessity for supervision became clear.

Artie was hungry for American fare (the way to a man's heart!), most especially desserts, lemon meringue pie, apple pie, and coconut custard and rice pudding! An American cookbook must be located, then. I sent word to New York, London, I wrote to Joyce in Paris to see if she had one lying about. We scoured the bookshops of Barcelona. In the process we picked up a third member of the household.

Our captain had said during one of our talks that a house is not a home without a dog.

"But Artie," I had protested, "I've told you about this allergy of mine—"

"Nonsense!" scoffed he. "You won't have that anymore. You feel safe now. That was a protest against the man you were with, you knew you shouldn't be there and you wanted to get away. You've no need for it now. . . ."

I bought it. Because I wanted to hear it. (I love dogs out of all proportion. To this day when I pass one in the street, my pulse leaps forward with delight. A hunger that won't go away. But neither will my allergy.) It wasn't a simple matter, this allergy of mine, but my leader said it would go away, and he ought to know.

The doggie in the window, in the Avenida Generalisimo Francisco Franco, was a three-month-old Alsatian, black with blond under-markings evenly distributed, two perfect blond eyebrows, the tail wagging, oh please rescue me and I'll give you undying love. Who could resist?

Artie named him Machito.

Kesi and Machito, Artie's creations. How many people get a chance to be reborn? With Artie's help I was going to conquer this most important role of my life: that of Woman, Compleat Mate to Man.

The process wasn't always smooth going. Areas of showing love or not showing it, signs I wasn't thinking of him, popped up where I would have least suspected it. Like the filter tips of the cigarettes in the box at Artie's elbow being in the right direction so that when he reached in, the filter end would arrive at his mouth first. Not disturbing the angle of the dictionaries he had placed on the end table beside every chair he sat in. Nor the ashtrays. The two bed pillows for reading had to have the loose ends turned toward the right side. His bottles in the medicine chest, sox, shorts, shirts, sweaters, all had to be arranged just so. Any of these things out of place was a cause for irritation. "Isn't order better than disorder?" he would say.

Could I disagree with that? And I did have this inclination to leave things where they landed. "You're one hundred percent right, Artie."

"Then if you agree," he want on, "that order is preferable, isn't it better that you go along with me than I get sloppy along with you?"

"Yes. Absolutely. Only Artie, sometimes when the maid dusts, she doesn't put things back in the right place."

"You are in charge, Kesi, it's still up to you."

I couldn't help wondering if these thoughtlessnesses of mine had been the downfall of my former relationships. I had paid no attention to the direction of John's cigarettes. I *had* carried Mike's cigars around in my purse; it had seemed sufficient, but what did I know.

"And Kesi," Artie continued, "since you have agreed that order is better, and since I have told you how important it is to me, and then you forget, it means you are forgetting *me.* In which case do I not have a right to be hurt and angry?"

Artie's boiling point was low. He prided himself on it. One of the Last Angry Men, he called himself. "If people got angry," he had told me, "instead of behaving like sheep and putting up with the shit they do, the world would be a better place." As an example of what he meant, he told me that when he came back from the South Pacific, having survived the Japanese attacks, he was having lunch at the Plaza Hotel in New York and asked for butter. "You can't have butter," answered the waiter righteously, "there's a war on, you know." And Artie, who knew the Plaza was taking advantage under the guise of patriotism to charge the same high prices and give less for it, answered, *"I know there's a war on, I was just in it, now bring me some fucking butter!"*

He got the butter.

I gazed at him in awe. How brilliant he was, the way he thought things through, not accepting half-truths the way most of us did. How lucky I was to even know him.

"Don't you see," he told me, "I have a duty to us both to point it out when you slip back into your messy ways, since your life has been nothing more until now than a series of flounderings about, never knowing what you were doing next?"

Oh my God, was it ever. I had never even thought of order. How grateful I was to him for bothering to take so much time with me. He really cared. Obviously.

"The trouble is, Kesi, anger seems the only way I can reach you, the only thing you respond to. . . ."

That would certainly seem to be true. The trouble was there were so many things to remember and the list grew daily and I would lapse into forgetfulness, unaccustomed as I was to thinking about another person. Then he would yell as promised. After which I would remember that particular thing so he wouldn't yell again. A raised voice scares me. And when it happens in public I am so embarrassed I actually can't hear. My ears close up in shame. That really pissed him off.

"That's your southern genteel what-will-the-neighbors-think upbringing," he would say contemptuously, "worrying about appearances, about what those strangers over there are thinking rather than what is happening between us." He said it's why I had the allergy, this tendency to poke things under the rug. He himself was of the "let it all hang out" school. He had no allergies.

Ah, I had a lot to learn. I couldn't fail this time. How many more chances would I get? I was ashamed to tell him that sometimes little red welts appeared on my skin after I had petted Machito. Anyway, I didn't care; he was such a dear animal I wasn't going to stop petting him no matter what. And the welts didn't *always* appear. Perhaps Artie was right; perhaps the intruding allergy would finally disappear altogether. Doesn't love conquer all . . . ?

CHAPTER 54 . . .

"Be it ever so hum . . . ble, there's no
. . . place like home. . . ."

In midsummer the three of us moved in, ready or not. Mostly not: screens weren't on windows, nor glass panes either, doors were still missing, fireplaces unfinished, with ropes instead of railings on terraces. But never mind. The beds had arrived, custom-made sofas and chairs from Barcelona, antique chests and tables from the Calle de Paja. And my precious kitchen, heartbeat of the house, with its yellow tiled walls, rust tiled floor, white marble counter tops and handsome black iron and chrome stove (wood-burning) was ready to go!

When Artie settled down in his study to sort out his papers, anxious to recreate his famous order once more, I decided to make a solo flight, initiate my domain and surprise him with my considerable cleverness by making a lemon meringue pie! A cookbook had arrived with simple enough directions for a beginner like me. Armed with rolling pin, measuring cups and spoons, bowls and saucepans, I began.

Measure carefully, that's the secret, here's the flour, just so, the butter worked in . . . there . . . so much sugar, and squeeze the lemons. . . .

A fly landed on my nose; I brushed him away with an elbow, my hands full. Another made a dive for the sugar. I fanned him away and covered it up with a piece of napkin. Now the eggs must be separated most carefully. . . . More flies were coming in through the unscreened windows, but I couldn't do anything about it. Timing was all-important, these yolks had to be beaten. . . .

I stirred, I poured, caught up in the excitement of creation as the filling thickened nicely as the book had promised.

In went the egg yolks and the mixture was set aside to cool, covered to keep out the circling flies. Then I whipped the egg whites, filled the finished crust with the yellow mixture and spread the fluffy meringue over it.

It was . . . beautiful! I was carrying it toward the oven with one hand, waving away the flying objects with the other as Artie walked in. "Look Artie!" I cried, "I made this! You didn't think I could do it, did you!"

"My . . . God!" I heard him say as I bent down to place my work of art in the oven. I smiled, pleased he was overcome at the sight of my pie. I closed the door and straightened up to receive my deserved accolade.

He wasn't looking at me. His eyes roamed the kitchen. "I . . . have . . . never seen so many flies in my entire life!" he growled. "Get out of here!"

"W-what?"

"I am going to spray this kitchen." He reached in a cabinet and pulled out a can of DDT (still thought a miracle, except by Rachel Carson). "Go on, get out of here, I'm going to kill these little bastards right now!"

"No!" I was shocked. "You can't do it now! Didn't you see me put my pie in the oven, I've got to watch—"

"Pie or no pie, these flies have got to go—"

"Can't you wait—"

"No. Get out." He pushed me out the door and began to squirt the stuff around.

Nobody wants to be in a room with that spray flying around. I went into the dining room and sat down, broken-hearted. My first pie, down the drain. I wouldn't look at Artie when he came backing in, squirting as he came. I hated him. "How could you stand all those flies," he said. "I've never seen anything like it."

"I didn't notice them," I muttered sullenly.

"No, I suppose you didn't." Artie chuckled and patted me on the head. "Little Kesi," he said tenderly, "your ability to block out your surroundings is astonishing."

Singleness of purpose is a quality Artie admired almost as much as sweets. How often people would say to him, How nice it must be to have your talent. He told me: "That's a cop-out, an excuse for not having to work, as if talent was all that was needed." Somebody said it once too often. "I tried to play the clarinet," this man told him, "but I didn't have your talent—"

"Just how hard did you work?" Artie snapped.

"Ten years," the man said, "I played ten years."

"Around the clock?" Artie glared. "All twenty-four hours?"

"Well, no. . . ."

"Did you live, think, breathe the clarinet?"

"I—"

"*Did you learn how not to take a shit* if it was going to interrupt your practice?"

The man stared, silenced, taken aback by the passionate outburst.

"Look, you want to play, say, the violin. Then follow Jascha Heifetz around, *do every single thing he does for thirty years,* then we'll talk about talent!"

It was my turn to glare. "Would anybody have chased Jascha out of the kitchen, just answer me that?!" I yelled. He stood there baffled as I dashed back to rescue my first-born.

It tasted only slightly of DDT. Artie ate it with *mucho gusto,* anyway.

Food, to Artie, I was to learn, was love. For me it had been nothing more than careful calorie counting, strictly supervised intake for health and weight-watching. For him it was a refrigerator overflowing with tasty tidbits to choose from, any kind, any time he liked, from his beloved desserts to cheeses and roasts, quiches and breads, soups and casseroles. A full larder meant he was cared for, that somebody was thinking of him.

"Jews appreciate good food," he grinned. "What else was there to do in the ghetto but eat? If Hitler had been clever he would have opened free delicatessens on all street corners and the Jews would have eaten themselves to death, and Hitler would have gone down in history as a big benevolent hero."

No refrigerator big enough to hold all Artie's love was available, so we had one built. Then we got our own generator to run it when the drizzle of Spanish current conked out on us. To its deep whirring thump, our house became a home: panes and doors got installed, fireplaces made to function, all at a snail's pace since workmen would lay down their tools come fiesta day (and there is one of those in Spain for every blink of the eye) and hie themselves down to the plaza for a session of Sardana dancing. It is the Catalán dance, done in a circle to the music of an instrument called the tenora, plaintive and sad, not unlike the clarinet.

Our social life took shape too. American friends were just down the coast at Palamós, the Robert Ruarks, he the famed journalist and writer of the best sellers, *Something of Value* and *Uhuru!* A kind of poor man's Hemingway with his animal heads on the walls and planted elephants' feet and tiger skins and little stuffed dik-dik. There were Spaniards too, with their rambling haciendas and flowing pesetas and servants who always wore little white gloves when serving. Ours didn't own a pair, which probably showed some sort of cultural gap between our nations.

We took time off to get ourselves legally hitched, flying down to where England sits on Spain's southernmost tip, Gibraltar. It was anticlimactic to be sure, but still what a great place to begin the rest of your life, on the Rock of Gibraltar.

Our guest rooms ready, friends began to show up: Marcia and her successful writer husband, Frederic Morton, came along. What fun it was to show them "our" Roman and Phoenician ruins, potters, weavers, and hey look, our own olive trees here, wine comes from right down there. They succumbed, and bought land next to ours. We would start our own writers' colony!

Mike was still in touch, buzzing around the edges. Cables came in from New York, California, London, St. Jean Cap Ferrat, Cannes, and then nearby Madrid. It was natural, I was still his "partner," and his office was still handling my affairs. Artie wasn't happy with the arrangement and told me to dissolve it when I could. I had written to Mike when I moved to Spain, and suggested just that.

He wrote back: "What the hell are you doing in Spain? Please write immediately . . . I hope [it] doesn't revolve around Artie Shaw, but of course, I could mind my own business, but I won't because you are family to me, and therefore it is my business . . . regarding your investment, I strongly urge your doing nothing to jeopardize your investment . . . I am going to do a very big production in Spain next year, also which we will take up when I see you. . . ."

He backed away when he heard the truth and sent a cable: ELIZABETH AND I WISH YOU ALL THE HAPPINESS FOREVER THAT WE ARE HAVING . . . AND DO HOPE YOU WILL INVITE US TO SAY HELLO WHEN WE ARE IN SPAIN. . . .

Absolutely. Why not, everybody must love one another. And maybe he would bring a big suitcase chock full of money with him. We kept hearing how his picture, *Around the World in Eighty Days,* was raking in million after million. We also kept reading how he was spending them. Extravagant parties, baubles for Elizabeth, including a thirty-carat diamond ring (ha!), priceless paintings, a private plane, called *The Lucky Liz.*

"That guy is going to blow your money, Kesi," Artie said.

"No no. He wouldn't do that. He promised me a million." But I was secretly worried. It wouldn't be the first time Mike Todd had blown a fortune; he was famous for it. He had been up and down the money ladder many times in his life, sometimes teetering on the edge of bankruptcy. I knew about his gambling. He had done that when he *didn't* have money, how he must be throwing it around now that he did. Where were the dividends from my five percent that should be coming in?

In the fall Artie's lawyer, Noah Rosoff, and his wife, Sophia, arrived for a visit. They were warm and alive. I liked them immediately. "Noah," Artie said, "I think you ought to look into this Todd thing. She has no one looking after her interests there, why it was even Mike's lawyer who drew up the papers of his agreement with her."

I laughed. "I don't pay as much attention to these things as I should. Yes. Someone should find out what's going on. Would you, Noah?"

He said he would look into it when they got back to New York. I felt better. I always felt better when somebody else was worrying and I didn't have to. Daddy Noah.

For my birthday Artie gave me a Spanish guitar, a Fleta, and showed me a few simple arrangements. How nice it was, having my very own bandleader in residence.

For Christmas the Bucks, our matchmakers, came down to see how we were getting on. For me they brought a sweater and for Artie some funny piccolo. Although he never touched the clarinet he would doodle around on every other instrument, recorder, bagpipe, fife, and make a fine sound. He entertained us royally with his new little gadget, playing anything we requested, and when the notes weren't there, filling in with his voice, and going on. He was enchanting, and I was enchanted with him.

Again and again he would ask, "Are you sure you are happy this isolated from the mainstream, are you sure you don't want to go back, are you sure you're not growing restless . . . ?"

I was so sure that when passport renewal time came round, I insisted "actress" be taken off under occupation and "housewife" put in its place.

No, it was not I who was the restless one. . . .

CHAPTER 55...
"Vaya con Di . . . os. . . ."

The study was reasonably ready for Artie to begin work; the bathroom was finished in deep blue tile, the floors laid with cork ones, the private terrace enclosed. True, the corners and shelves were still jammed with cartons and boxes waiting to be sorted, but his desk was in order, *his* order, the typewriter set up, pencils in their jars, lights arranged just so, clips, paper, reference books on the shelves above, the scene set for the great American novel to unfold.

But no. Not just yet. First we must get up to London for dental appointments. Well, okay, sure we had to see a dentist from time to time, I agreed without much enthusiasm. Travel had lost its charm, whereas staying in our very own house was exciting.

We stayed at the Westbury Hotel, where instead of the modest digs we asked for, they gave us, on the house, their bridal suite. Next day we found out why: free advertising for them. A lurid story appeared in the paper how "pasha" Artie Shaw had come to town with his zillionth wife and had set her up in the style to which she was accustomed, in the plush suite with the red velvet-lined walls, satin sheets and queen-size beds. (It sounded like John's whorehouse.) Meantime he was building—for her—a luxurious castle on top of a Spanish mountain.

It read well. Especially the "pasha" part. We laughed at the story, but I was beginning to notice that the title fit Artie quite well. He was a wiz at finding ways to be waited on. "Ah, Kesi, you're nearer than I am, do bring me the cigarettes (book, plate, coat, cup, keys)." "Ah, Kesi, you're younger than I am, do bring me the cigarettes (book, plate, coat, cup, keys)." To serve another, be concerned over the needs of another, he told me, that is true love. "Do you know that Mrs. Darrow never served chicken to Clarence for thirty years because he didn't like it, although she herself loved it?"

"Fancy that," I murmured, impressed.

"Nor did Mrs. Blake talk around William when he preferred silence."

"My my." I shook my head in wonder.

The least I could do for my man, then, was to get things the way he liked them. (If they are to be done, why not the *right* way, he would say.) His morning egg to the exact degree of hard/softness, the freshly squeezed orange juice without seeds or pulp, toast buttered to the edge and not a fraction less, coffee poured to the exact quarter-inch below the rim, no more, no less. It was nerve-wracking, the constant surveillance of these minute measurements that extended to all foods, to all parts of the house, inside and out.

I was pleased when he finally settled down to work, disappearing faithfully at nine each morning into his study. Four blessed hours to myself, oh, there was so much to do! Those recipes in my new cookbook called for herbs, I was planning a garden, a greenhouse, I knew the perfect place for it, below the house where there was a southern exposure. I must see the carpenter, the nursery man—"Ke—si!"

So soon he had finished? The mornings rushed by. Artie had a bad ear, loused up in the war when he was standing too near a big gun when it went off. He couldn't hear if I answered back. I had to go to him. "Ke—si!" rang through the house a dozen times a day.

The first time it scared me half to death. I rushed madly in the direction of the sound. "Artie!" I cried, "what is it?"

"Here," said a calm Artie, "hold this for me." He held out a fishing rod. "I want to glue this broken end together."

"My God Artie, you frightened me yelling like that!"

"I didn't know where you were."

"You could look—!"

"Hold it still," he murmured, concentrating on his repair.

Finished with his work quota he would want to go. To shop. See the tile man, the ironmonger, buy clothes. Artie was a great clothes buyer, anything new from belt to socks to everything between. "Ke—si!" It soon became the pattern, my running to the sound of his voice. But when *I* wanted *him,* I had to go to him too. He couldn't hear me if I called. Resentment began to flick its ugly head. "Do you have to yell like that?" I finally snapped.

"How else can you hear me?"

"I come to find you when I want you, why can't you—"

"You should be pleased I care enough to want to share something with you—"

"Oh I am! I am!" *What's the matter with you, selfish, self-centerd creature that you are.*

"Ke—si!"

"Yes, Artie, coming!"

"Let's go fishing."

Never one to do things halfway, he owned enough fishing equipment to open a sporting goods store. We built a special fishing room off the garage to house his many rods and reels and lures and their cases—plus his giant library on fish, which told where they lived, when and why, what they ate, and all about their love lives. There was very little Artie didn't know about every goddamn fish in the world.

I didn't fish; I was never going to. One dead deer was all the wildlife I ever wanted to bring to heel. But if he wanted to fish, then he had every right. And if he wanted his wife to accompany him, why then he should have her. We had this miracle of togetherness going, didn't we? It was my duty, as a woman, to go with my man whenever he wanted me to.

Many an afternoon saw us beside the local streams, me with a book and a writing pad, my husband casting his line over the waters.

Then there was the daily chess game. Artie even made several chess boards himself, out of wood and cork. He designed a chess set out of two shades of silver, a modern flat affair that came apart, easily packed for traveling. He liked to use his hands. He carved, he painted, he made his own flies, he fixed electrical appliances when they broke. There didn't seem to be anything he couldn't do, or didn't know the answer to. My very own walking encyclopedia and dictionary. He bought books and charts of the stars and planets, and a big telescope. Nightly we gazed up at the heavens to find Venus, Saturn and its rings, Jupiter and its moons, and the worlds beyond.

Yes, where we could go, the things we could do, seemed infinite.

When I read in early March, 1958, that Harry Cohn had died, I was surprised at the wrench I felt, the sense of loss. As if a big piece of my life had slipped from view. It is one thing to choose to leave; it is another not to have it there to ever go back to.

The worst was yet to come.

Artie was in his studio that morning of March 23 when the call came. Our telephone, at best, was never much more than an intercom to the village, three minutes away. A frayed thin wire that connected us with the outside world and blew down at the slightest hint of breeze. On top of that, all calls between cities and countries went through Madrid, which was considerably south of us, even if we were calling France, considerably north of us. So it was with difficulty that I recognized through the crackle and pop the voice of Bud Ornstein in Barcelona. Bud was the head of United Artists there, for whom I had made several pictures, through whom Mike was releasing *Around the World.*

It made me laugh. Obviously some message from Mike, or he was already in Barcelona. Only he, who had managed to get a call through from Moscow when nobody else could, would attempt to wrestle with the Spanish telephone system. "Yes, Bud," I shouted, "I can almost hear you!"

Through the static and buzzing I heard Mike's name and the word "plane."

"What was that, Bud, he's there? Coming? Flying in?"

But then, as if the world stood still for one brief second, Bud's voice came through loud and clear. ". . . was killed yesterday. . . . ."

I stopped breathing. I couldn't have heard right. He couldn't have said . . .

"Hello? . . . Hello?"

"Yes, I—I'm here, Bud, what did you say? . . ."

Bzzzz, clkclkck . . ."plane crashed". . . . eeeeeeh . . . "New Mexico . . . sorry . . . tell you. . . ."

"Yes. Thank you for calling. . . ."

I was stunned, not believing. Mike Todd *killed?* In a plane crash? That was a long way to go, I thought crazily, to promote Todd-AO. That's what it was, some spectacular publicity gimmick; he would reappear like Houdini.

I went into Artie's study without knocking. He frowned until he saw my face. "Mike Todd's been killed in a plane."

"Good God." Artie rose. "And Elizabeth, was she? . . ."

"Oh my God. I don't know. . . ."

We soon heard the details from other people calling and on the radio. Elizabeth hadn't been along. Mike had been on his way to New York from California to attend a Friars' Club dinner in his honor. He had been flying in his own private plane, *The Lucky Liz.*

Noah Rosoff tried to phone from New York, failed, sent a cable followed by a letter. He told us he had written Mike requesting a get-together to talk about my situation with his company. Two days before, on March 21, Mike had phoned from California, saying he would be in New York the 23rd, and if it suited Noah, they could meet that afternoon. "Fine," answered Noah.

"I'll call you when I get in," Mike said, "at one o'clock."

"That's Saturday," Noah said, "I'll be at home." He gave Mike his home phone number.

At a quarter to one Saturday, Noah was still at the Racquet Club having lunch, so he called home to tell his wife Sophia where he could be reached when Mike Todd called. "I'll wait here," said Noah. "Don't wait," Sophia answered. "He won't be calling." She told him the news.

Noah went on to write that he would be getting in touch with somebody of the organization soon; it had been strictly a one-man operation, and we ought to make a move to protect ourselves as soon as possible. It was uncertain what would happen next, without Mike.

Without Mike. What a thin, transparent veil is between being "here," and . . . obliteration. About-face, over and out. Poor Mike. All that running around, struggling to win the battle, and whap. If we knew the end, would we run the race?

Another tie gone from my life, like cutting away the ballast in his *Around the World* balloon. I sat on the terrace looking out at the sea, and I thought, Mike gave me this. He set me free to go on to another life, and look what I found. I could easily have been in a falling plane with him and I would never have seen this panorama of sky and shoreline and water that was mine each day. Never tasted the freshly baked bread, the just-plucked mussels. I listened to the pleasant sound of a maid singing while she polished the tile floors. I sniffed the tang of fresh sea air. Felt the sun warm on my skin. And I thought, remember this moment. It will never come your way again. . . .

"Ke—si!"

"Coming, Artie. . . ."

CHAPTER 56...

"You may not be . . . an an . . . gel . . .
but angels are . . . so . . . few . . ."

In April Noah had a meeting with Mike Todd Junior. I knew the young man well. His father and I had spent many, many evenings with him. He was a quiet, reserved fellow, not yet thirty, subdued probably from growing up in the shadow of his flamboyant father. He wasn't in show biz, didn't plan to be. He was, according to Mike Senior, going to "spend the next ten years writing a very important book." Mike was promoting his offspring's work before it was written. But now here he was, all at once in charge of Dad's kingdom.

Noah reported that the meeting was pleasant enough, that Junior had told him that his Dad always said that Evelyn was a "stand-up dame," so why, he wanted to know of Noah, was I trying to give them a hard time now that Mike was dead? I had never made a loan to the old man; Mike had merely given me some stock out of the goodness of his heart.

Well.

I will never know the truth. Whether he had decided that on his own, whether it's what Mike Senior had told him, or whether it's what the lawyers in charge of the estate had told him. Or whether they were all trying to pull a fast one.

I did know a couple of things, though. That Mr. Todd *Junior* was behaving like a prick, and a chintzy one at that, something his father could never be accused of, because if it had been true that Mike gave me the stock, then he should be paying me what his father intended me to have without question.

I also knew that I had a lawsuit on my hands. If these unclever people, low on imagination and high on greed, trying to inherit the world Mike had wrought, had sunk so low as to try and gyp me not only of any profit but of the loan itself, they had a fight on their hands. Beware of the wrath of the rabbit. Did they think I had been stupid enough not to have saved the documents indicating where my money came from, and when?

When I read that they planned to release their next picture in something called Smell-O-Vision, I knew I was in bad trouble.

Noah wrote that five percent stockholders held a special position, that Mary Pickford had had five percent of United Artists, and look how rich she was. I didn't think that Michael Todd Productions had attained such lofty heights as United Artists, but what the hell, let's go. Noah said he knew a lawyer that specialized in just that field, the five percent stockholder, one Abe Pomerantz.

The plot thickened. All those hot emotions, love and hate, passion and anger, longing and ambition, began turning into long legal documents written by people who hadn't even been there. It was depressing.

Artie, masterminding it from the Bagur end, got restless come May. "Let's get out of here for a while," he said one day.

I was dismayed. The garden was in, the greenhouse started. Machito had grown to such a handsome large dog, full of wit and wag and zest, and he looked so sad when we left him behind. "But, what about your book?"

"I need a rest from it, time to think a bit."

"Where will we go?"

"Salmon fishing."

He knew from his books where salmon could be found in Spain. Off we went, west to the Atlantic side, through Pamplona, on up through the Basque provinces to Santander and the Oson River, two people straight out of *The Sun Also Rises.* Under Hemingway's influence every step of the way, we lunched on cheese and wine alongside the road under spreading shade trees, by pond and stream, our books propped before us.

Then it was "real civilization" he wanted, and off we headed for London, driving all the way; we stopped flying, as if Mike's end had been a warning. We took the ferry across the Channel, saw a few shows, and back again to Paris. Benny Goodman was staying in our hotel, Artie's old rival from the big band days, only Benny was still at it.

Seeing Benny in a coldly impersonal hotel room, in his bathrobe at eight o'clock at night, marking time until his concert started, depressed Artie. It brought back all the time he had spent on the road just that way, an isolated, unrelated-to-the-rest-of-the-world existence. And after we attended Benny's concert later in the heart of Paris, Artie said, "Thank God I'm out of that racket. Let's go home."

Abe Pomerantz came all the way to Spain to talk to us about the Todd affair. He was a nice portly man who couldn't eat shellfish, and there wasn't much of anything else. Legal talk flowed. Switching roles, I was now something out of Kafka's *The Trial.* Mr. Pomerantz was preparing my case, but he wanted thirty-three-and-a-third percent of what we collected. Since it was possible that those now in charge of Mike's affairs were rapidly disposing of the profits, I got angry at Sonny all over again. Whatever I got, even my original investment, I would have to give a third of it away.

The Rosoffs came along again, down from Paris, on their way to Switzerland, and Artie insisted on driving them there, reluctant to part with their company. For a man who had spent a year alone, Artie loved conversation; it turned him on more than anything. It was almost magical the way words and thoughts flowed from him in glorious articulateness, those dictionaries on every table springing to life through his lips.

Meantime I had got Machito a wife to calm him down, keep him company when we went off. Her name was Chucha and she was ugly and dumb. Machito didn't mind but Artie did; he preferred good-looking females. It hadn't helped; we now had two sets of sad eyes watching us pack.

We set out, the four of us, in the gray Mercedes, up through Spain and across France, lunching in Aix-en-Provence, along the corniches, to spend the first night in Monte Carlo. The weather was hot and humid and the water in the bay, so cool and blue against all those white ships, looked inviting. "Hey!" I said, "let's go for a swim."

"We don't have swim togs with us," Artie said.

"I do."

"Did you bring mine, then?"

"Why, no. . . ." My heart sank. Why hadn't I thought of bringing his swimming trunks?

The frown. "You thought to bring yours, and not mine?"

I was embarrassed. The Rosoffs were listening. Artie, I knew, had written them that he had at long last found the perfect mate, along with ecstatic happiness. Now they would see I wasn't so perfect. Love is swimming trunks too, and I had failed. "I'm sorry," I muttered. "I wasn't thinking—"

"You can't seem to get it straight, Kesi," he said hotly. "There are two of us."

"I know, I know." I hoped the ground would swallow me.

"If you thought you might like to go swimming, you could have thought I might like to—"

"Oh for Crissake, Artie." It was Noah cutting in. He had a big deep voice that boomed with authority. "Who wants to go swimming, anyway, let's have a drink instead. I could use one about now, what about a nice *fine à l'eau*."

"You don't understand, Noah," Artie said to him, "she does this sort of thing far too often—"

"Well then," boomed Noah, "maybe you could kill her off and start over with another wife, but first let's have a *fine à l'eau*."

What with Noah's cool interference, checking in at the hotel, dinner and a few *fine à l'eaus*, l'affaire swim trunks got cut short. I knew Artie had not liked not being able to go on, he always liked to gnaw and thrash and dissect every little altercation. But he was charming at dinner, making us laugh with stories from his youth, using hilarious accents which he was so good at. I thought the Last Angry Man had gotten over something quickly for once.

Wrong. It came out in Milano in the damnedest way, like the lashing tail of a storm, to take me by utter surprise.

Artie had this incredible sense of direction. He could descend on the most foreign of cities and find its center, like a homing pigeon. Milano, where we would spend our second night, was no exception.

We were excited, planning where we would go. We never tired of Italian food. And there was La Scala: Should we see an opera? "The shopping is great here too, I understand," Artie said. "Let's look in the shops before they close, I could use another sweater."

We all laughed. By count, the number of Artie's sweaters had to be in the hundreds. We had checked in to our hotel and were walking down the first street we found. Artie suddenly came to a halt. "I've got a button missing here," he said, fumbling with the little pocket just under the waistband of his trousers.

"It doesn't show," I said indifferently. I had spied a handsome shoulder bag in a window. "Look at that, you know, I really could use—"

"I don't want to go around this way, it ought to be fixed."

I turned back to Artie. He was still pulling at the pocket. "We can give it to the valet when we get back to the hotel," I said, "and he'll sew a new button on for you—"

"Don't you have a button?"

"Me?" I laughed. "What would I be doing with a button in the middle of—"

"Don't you carry a button box with you?"

"A—button box!" I stared at him. "What the hell is a button box?"

Artie was getting annoyed. "It speaks for itself, does it not—and obviously you don't have one—"

"Of course I don't have one!" I snapped. Annoyance is not a one-way street. "Do *you* have a button box?" I asked Sophia. The smallest of head-shakes indicated she didn't, her eyes on Artie: if he pounced, she was ready to run. She shouldn't have worried; I was the target.

"What Sophia has or has not has nothing to do with you, you are my wife, and *you have failed me!*"

"Artie," Noah began, in a gently chiding tone, "don't you think you're making a mountain—"

This time Artie was not to be put off. "I will take care of it myself," he spat, "as it seems I am going to have to learn to do!" He stalked off down the street in angry strides. His voice had risen and heads were turning. The three of us shut up, embarrassed. I was, anyway. We followed him at a distance, not knowing what else to do, while he stormed into one place and out. Then another. And another. Somewhere along the way the Rosoffs decided to go off on their own, and I couldn't blame them.

I fairly seethed. Why, this man was a raving lunatic, totally unreasonable, absurd in his demands. What a dreadful, dreadful mistake I had made. I would have to get out instantly, I would not put up with his monstrous behavior one minute longer. . . .

My anger suddenly deserted me. Black depression seized me as I thought, dear God, what am I into this time, following a crazy man looking for a button through the streets of Milan, Italy! Who would have believed it? Was this what it had all been leading up to? This then was my destiny? Fate's little joke? And where do I go from here? Home? And where is that, pray? Hollywood? Where blacklists held sway and people cringed and pretended it wasn't so? Anyway, I had lost my taste for donning makeup and speaking stupid lines to somebody else's stupid lines.

So what was left. To go somewhere else and start life again with yet another man? The very thought was appalling. A terrible sense of failure rattled my very bones. Other people around me managed to achieve lasting togetherness; the Bucks, the Ruarks, the Rosoffs had been married for years and years. Why not me? Was I not brought up on Cinderella too? Had I not been promised a happy ending too? From every song, every book—*even my own movies?* It was my birthright, for crissake! *Why not me?!*

Like Sandburg's little cat feet, a new thought edged in from another part of my brain, the part that had been observing how Sophia Rosoff had tended her husband, been concerned over his food, his rest, little things here and there. I noted that when there was any hint of disagreement between them, it was handled with amusement and tolerance.

Tolerance. That was the key. I had so little. At the first sign of something not to my liking, I was convinced I had made a mistake. Who was I? Miss Flawless in person, that I could pass judgment on another person so quickly and easily, turn thumbs down like some disapproving monarch?

Would it not behoove me to look further, to see what was behind Artie's present overreaction? Could it be the thoughtlessness of not thinking of his swim trunks, plus maybe other nonthinking acts I might have done?

I looked up to discover I was passing La Scala Opera House, where two years before the woman had whispered in the darkened box, "How do you manage to get all these fascinating men?"

Well, they were. I couldn't deny it. Filled with vitality, imagination, even the word "genius" had been applied here and there.

And now Artie Shaw with his brilliant mind, with his lightning-quick ability for grasping the new, his discernment fast and sure, his intellect bursting across a conversation like a dazzling display of fireworks. Was I willing to throw all that away for a silly button? Sure he was difficult, extraordinary people are difficult. Would I settle for a placid plodder? The thing that had pushed him to the heights didn't go away in between.

Face it, old girl, you can't have it both ways. You may be many things, disturbed, upset, even suffer despair from time to time, but bored you will never be. Make your choice.

Ah, what the hell, I thought, as I stood firmly in front of the last store Artie had entered, to carry a button box around is probably a very good idea.

It was thus I reasoned my way deeper into the quicksand. . . .

CHAPTER 57

"And he swam . . . and he swam . . .
right over the dam. . . ."

Like an addict in need of a fix, no sooner were we back home than
Artie insisted we pop off to Andorra for trout. "A good game fish," he
said.

Andorra is that tiny country above Spain and below France, and the
fish lived in a crystal clear river that cascaded down large boulders
through thick lush evergreens.

I tried to be appreciative, but I had my own desires. *I wanted to be
home.* I wanted us to solidify these roots we were digging for ourselves. We had a staff of four back there, a housekeeper, a cook, a
gardener, a laundress—all to take care of two dogs? So much still
needed to be finished: shelves, doors, painting, my greenhouse; my
herbs were making their debut in the garden. . . . I put a clamp on my
irritation and forced myself to remember how it had come about that I
was in Spain in the first place. Whither thou goest. . . .

When we returned to Bagur there were messages from Pomerantz
saying that the Todd people weren't coming around. It looked as if we
would have to file suit. There was also a message from Fred Morton
that he and wife Marcia would be in Vienna in late October, and why
didn't we join them.

"Splendid idea," said Artie. "There's a great game fish in the
tributaries of the Danube I'd like to go after."

Fish, then, had become the sound of the distant drum my husband
heeded, his Star in the East. The Pied Piper had laid aside his horn to
follow the bait. A search for self? I must try and understand. He had
been dealt a mortal wound by his own country, I knew that. Patience,
patience, and was a trip to Vienna so difficult? I had never been there.
The land of Mozart and Strauss. Who would have thought, hearing
that waltz, that underneath the celebrated blue swam a fish who had a
rendezvous with Artie Shaw.

So, while other people streamed south to warm Spain as November
closed in, we Spaniards took off northward for cold, damp Vienna.

It was nice. Civilization at its peak. Castles and parks, white wine
and Wienerschnitzel. White horses and opera. And best of all, pastries and coffee *mit Schlag* at Demel's, every afternoon. Fred told us
the waitresses used old German when speaking to customers. Would I
have known that by staying in Bagur? Would I have known that the

famous Sacher torte, a chocolate cake with a thin layer of apricot marmalade just under the icing, had been a reason for a famous lawsuit? Somebody had tried to steal Mr. Sacher's recipe. The Viennese take their pastries seriously.

With one last *gugelhupf* under our belts, a few added pounds, and a fond *auf Wiedersehen*, we left to swing south toward the Tyrol to look for Artie's fish.

I endured the search; the scenery was a knockout, the sky a brilliant blue, the snow-capped peaks quite took your breath away, and the thought was consoling that Artie couldn't freeze his ass off forever standing there in the swirling waters of the Drau River on whose banks we had settled for a few shivering days.

Next stop Venice. And the shit hit the fan.

Now, Artie had told me that he had it on proper authority that most marriages breaking up do so at "that time of the month." That women during their periods go a little crazy and cannot be rationally dealt with. He said I must let him know when I was in, or about to be in, said condition. (I wondered just how we could be warned when *he* was going off his rocker.) He said I turned into another person, whom he named "Myrtle." I was to let him know when irritable Myrtle was on the way so that we could avoid any unnecessary clash. The trouble was that one of Myrtle's sneaky ways was not to keep track of the schedule.

I might have suspected werewolf time was upon me when we arrived in Venice, where, when you park your car on the outskirts, you grab a gondola instead of a cab. When Artie insisted on paying less than the gondolier asked, I muttered, "For Christ's sake, Artie, it's not the tourist season. The guy's not getting much business, what difference do a few lire make?"

"He's trying to take advantage—"

"What advantage, we're the only customers—"

"Hush, Kesi, I'll handle it."

I flushed with annoyance. "You've never been here—"

"Italy is Italy!" Artie snapped. "And get off my back!"

I hushed then, but my temple throbbed as we glided our way into the city proper. "Do you know you never stop telling me what to do?" Artie's voice went on over the lapping sound of water, "You're a director at heart; did it rub off from all those directors you knew?"

I felt feverish. "Once in a while I might know something you don't," I said sullenly.

"You're behaving like a spoiled child. What's the matter with you?"

"Nothing's the matter with me."

But there was and I discovered it after we checked into the Danieli.

"Oh Christ," said Artie, "I might have known. Myrtle is with us. You'd better take it easy, lie down for a while."

"No, no, we're only here overnight. I'm fine, let's go."

We walked around town, looking over squares and churches, the Bridge of Sighs, the Doge's Palace, fed pigeons in the Piazza San Marco. It was a desultory walk, me dragging all the way. I felt plain lousy.

Passing the Danieli once more we went in to check on a restaurant for dinner. While Artie spoke to the concierge I sat down in the lobby, my head feeling like an inflated inner tube. It must have shown. When he came back, the first thing he said was, "You look tired, Kesi, why don't you lie down for a while before we go out?"

"No, no, I don't want to lie down. Let's go." I thought if I lay down I'd never be able to get up.

"Maybe you wouldn't be so grumpy if you did."

"I'm not grumpy," I said grumpily.

"Believe me, you are. Go take a nap, you'll feel better—"

"I don't want to take a nap—"

"Then just lie down for a while—"

"I don't want to lie down, now leave me alone, for God's sake!" It was an unfortunate choice of words.

"Is that what you want?" His voice had risen. "You prefer that I don't care about you? Is that what you want?" It was becoming a scene, a public scene. "When I don't care about you I'll leave you alone, is that what you want—*for me not to care about you?*"

"Shh, please," I whispered, "people are looking."

"The neighbors again. Is that more important than what is happening with us?"

"I'm sorry, I'm sorry, I didn't mean—"

"Kick a man in the belly, saying you're sorry doesn't make the hurt go away—"

"I'm sorry," I choked hoarsely, dying of humiliation, "I'm sorry, I'll go lie down—"

"I don't give a fuck what you do, now!"

"Oh please," I breathed, eyes swiveling around the lobby, "please, is it Myrtle acting up? I didn't mean it. . . ."

On I went with what I hoped were soothing sounds. Artie had told me that once a man's adrenalin gets going, I couldn't expect him to turn it off like a faucet, I would have to do what I could to calm him, particularly when it was my fault. And this was; he had meant to help me and I had brushed him aside.

Slowly I was making my way through the maze of marriage, through the difficulties of give and take. Learning to think before I spoke instead of blurting out the first thing that came to mind. Raised as an only child, then a movie actress to whom everybody catered, what would I know of giving? I knew only accepting. That's what Artie said. He also said that marriage was a woman's racket and up to her to make it work.

I had accepted that and also that all errors were my fault. Which is how we got past what happened two days later.

Departing Venice we went west to Torino where we would spend the night, arriving after dark. We dropped our bags at the hotel, and leaving our passports at the desk so they could check us in, went out to dinner at a nearby *trattoria*. Afterwards we strolled around the city and returned to our room around midnight.

Just as we were getting ready for bed, Artie said, "Did you pick up the passports, Kesi?" (Somewhere in our travels it had become my duty to see to the documents at borders since Artie did most of the driving: the carnet for the car, our passports, vaccination records if needed. I would trip out when we arrived at customs, smile charmingly, hopeful they wouldn't slow us down with long inspections, particularly going into Spain when we always had something along we preferred not to be charged duty for.)

"No," I answered, "I forgot to pick them up, I'll get them in the morning."

"You better get them now, Kesi, I know you. In the morning you're liable to forget."

We were already undressed. There wasn't any room service after midnight to send them up. I really didn't feel like getting dressed again and *schlepping* all the way down four flights of stairs. "I won't forget. Don't worry."

The interesting thing is, it didn't occur to either of us that Artie could have gone down for them.

We got up quite early; we had a long way to go. The plan was to weave our way through the foothills of the Maritime Alps, on down to Nice, and back to Spain, hugging the Mediterranean all the way.

It was a lovely drive. The trees had put on their autumn display of brilliant reds and oranges and yellows. The mountain air had a sharp ping to it.

As the French border hove into view, some five hours later, I remembered. Artie heard my anguished gasp and looked over, startled. "What's the matter?" he cried in alarm.

"I—forgot—the passports," I whispered hoarsely.

The explosion of rage had all the intensity of an Arab-Israeli war. The car shook with it, threatening to burst at the seams. Words like bursting bombs showered about my abject head, the ways of telling me what a hopeless dope I was were varied and infinite. I most assuredly did agree; I would never be able to forgive myself.

"I'm sorry," I mumbled miserably as on he went.

He continued, the tide unabating, until finally it seemed useless to say one more "I'm sorry," and I just sat despondent, despairing of my future. I was clearly no fit mate for anybody.

"You sit there," cried Artie, "*silent,* after what you have done."

"I haven't been silent!" I cried. "I've been saying how sorry I am."

"I suppose you think saying you're sorry makes everything all right."

"No, no—"

"You kick a man in the balls and say you're sorry. It still hurts."

"I know, but what else can I say?"

"Better think of something!" he shouted. The car doors rattled.

This outburst had the thin edge of violence to it. I kept repeating "I'm so sorry!" as long as he kept going. Not because I had forgotten the passports. I had forgotten that I had forgotten the passports. I did it only because of the threatened violence.

But I was beginning not to be sorry. I was beginning to find this unceasing tirade rather tiresome. I mean, I had to endure the five-hour drive too, didn't I? It was a stupid thing to have done, but it wasn't something I had done against Artie. And it couldn't be undone, so let's get on to the next project. I would never forget the passports again, that was one sure thing.

If only he would shut up for a while, I thought, let me think, *let me be sorry. . . .*

After a good three hours even Artie Shaw's anger finally ran its course. Followed by an uneasy truce. Then explanations on both sides.

"A man's adrenalin. . . ." and blah blah blah.

"I must listen. . . ." and blah blah blah.

Rumbles in paradise. I refused to take notice. I didn't want to know. I had my castle, I had my prince. There was no turning back; this was it, for better or for worse. . . .

CHAPTER 58

"New York . . . New York . . .
a hell of a town. . . ."

We must go to New York. Noah Rosoff said so, Abe Pomerantz, the five percent expert, said so. My "case" couldn't progress further without personal attention.

New York! Together for the first time there. What would it be like? A great place to visit! Especially if you live in Bagur, Provincia de Gerona, España. The first month we couldn't throw away even the fabulous wrappings the things we bought came in. The delicatessen windows impressed us most, with their mammoth turkeys, giant strawberries, and roast beef slabs the size of Mount Rushmore.

Between seeing lawyers we saw old friends and met new: Terry Southern was making a name for himself, Stanley Kubrick was coming along. We found them highly stimulating, ablaze with talent. We went to hear jazz groups old and new: Gerry Mulligan, Ornette Coleman, Cannonball Adderley, Coltrane and Miles Davis. Artie and Louis Armstrong kissed and hugged at a Joey Bushkin party after a long-time-no-see.

There were old and new drugs going around too. Grass, the new chic thing to smoke, was old hat to Artie. His musicians, he told me, used to grow it in the warm hoods of their cars as they drove about the country. A pleasant high, he said. So when a joint was passed around at parties, no standing by this time, I took my turn. Artie was right. And once when mescaline, new to us both, was passed around we sampled that too, timidly touching the white powder with the tips of our tongues. (Listen, we had read Huxley.) Nothing much happened. We thought.

I don't know how much later it was as I lay in bed back in our hotel that I became aware of the many colors on the wall across the room: vivid reds, greens, oranges, yellow, purples, infinite colors, infinite shades. All woven together, intertwined, interlaced.

As I watched they moved, changed places, went back again. It was lovely; it was—living color, as if some extraordinary painting had been given life and breath. And even as I watched, this mass of color left the wall and hung there in space, trembling, vibrant, just beyond the foot of the bed.

I don't know when I became aware that Artie was awake, that he was watching the phenomenon too. "See that?" he whispered in a soft, dreamy voice.

"Yeeah," I whispered back.

Words were not necessary. Time ceased to exist. A fiery ball of flame left the other mass and hung above us, shimmering and dancing in air. Sounds in the street fourteen stories below rose up to us with crystal clearness, each tone separate, be it human, motor or bell. In the midst of it all we made love in slow motion, savoring each sensation, floating somewhere above the bed, inside the flaming ball.

I don't know when Artie went to sleep. I only know I looked over to find him sleeping and thought, I wonder what he looks like beneath his skin? I began to peel off layer after layer. After the skin came the flesh. Then blood vessels. . . . I went all the way down to his skull. It was scary. I blinked and put it all back in place again before I too finally fell asleep.

The colors stayed there the entire month we were at the hotel.

It made us wonder; are there things there to be seen that most of us are unable to see without aid? That maybe some of us do see without mescaline or other mind-expanding drugs? Like Picasso or Michelangelo or Pollock? Or Artie Shaw when he listens to music in that way of his, is he hearing something we nonmusicians don't hear?

We were very close that month, closer than we had ever been; we had the freshness of a new experience, plus the richness of the full knowledge of each other, including the ups and downs. I have often wondered if it would have made a difference if we could have stayed on a diet of mescaline. . . .

I gave the necessary depositions to the lawyers representing the Michael Todd Company. We sat in Abe Pomerantz's office while two strangers asked me about very personal matters that were none of their business. (Hey Mike, will you come down here and set these impostors straight?) One of the lawyers raised himself up and said through narrowed eyes, his expression aglow with cat-that-caught-the-mouse shine, "Isn't it a fact you are suing this company because Elizabeth Taylor is involved and you can get some free publicity?"

We had a big laugh over that, wondering just what use publicity would be in Bagur. It was the first I had heard Elizabeth was "involved." I was sure she didn't know anything about these cheap shenanigans. The other lawyer had the sense to look embarrassed for his cohort.

Our side presented bank statements, contracts, and whatever other *mishegas* goes with that game lawyers play. I won, hands down, the "case" never went further than that deposition. The only trouble was, one zero had to be taken off the original amount promised. It's a big difference.

We bought up a good portion of the city of New York—everything we thought we might need and couldn't possibly live without—to *schlepp* back to Bagur. And one fine April day, with some forty-odd crates and packages and suitcases in tow, went down to the sea to board a ship: *Queen Elizabeth* (the First), still traveling the oceans, a city unto herself, a noble ship indeed which had transported thousands upon thousands, in peacetime and war. "When does this place get to Cherbourg?" Beatrice Lillie was once heard to ask.

Who should be on board but my old friend, Sam Spiegel. He told us some interesting news: He would be coming to Spain in the near future; he was going to make a film from a Tennessee Williams play called *Suddenly Last Summer.* He hoped Elizabeth Taylor would consent to do it. What he needed, he said, was a little Spanish village near the sea. We told him we happened to be acquainted with just such a place. He didn't seem to pay much attention; he seemed more worried about the fact that we had gotten behind schedule; the big liner had gotten stuck on a sand bank on the way out of New York harbor, and there we were at sea the first night out with the lights of New York still within swimming distance.

Frogmen went down to set us right, and soon we were off, awash in champagne, caviar, chinchilla and ermine, truffles and humming-birds' wings, a monument to the past that would soon go the way of all yesterdays.

We arrived at Cherbourg at four of an Easter morning, in the dark, in the rain, to answer Bea Lillie's question. Artie and I, dressed in jeans, along with a number of other passengers dressed to the hilt, the ladies in flowered hats sheathed in plastic, got off the big job and onto a tender, they bound for Paris, we headed for home.

Nothing is so rewarding as going home, when it's the place you want to be. Machito and Chucha jumped for joy. But no more than I.

CHAPTER 59...

> *"It's a little street . . . where old*
> *friends meet. . . ."*

Not much changes in a place like Bagur. Our cook's wife had twins. The cook bragged so much I dragged out the oldie: "It takes two to tango." It didn't lose in the translation. My four employees laughed until they cried. I was very big in the kitchen.

We had brought back an outboard motor, so now we bought a boat to go with it, a fourteen-foot dinghy, with which we combed our shoreline, popping into inlets and coves for fish, for a swim, to visit the Ruarks down the coast.

Artie wasn't pretending to work on his book. I pretended not to notice. He wanted to run up to London; we ran up to London. He wanted to run down to Barcelona; we ran down to Barcelona. Ava was in town with her current boyfriend, Italian actor Walter Chiari. Both gorgeous, what can I tell you. We all had a drink together.

We had lunch at Bud Ornstein's. Gregory Ratoff was there. He was highly amusing, helped along by his droll Russian accent.

Artie was pensive on the way home. "That's what I've become in this country, in Spanish, a low comic."

"It's because you won't learn the language properly, Artie," I told him.

Artie was fluent, but absolutely refused to learn the correct grammar. "A book, masculine?" he would scoff. "A table feminine? What nonsense!" He said them any way they came out. The result was—well, yes, rather comic on occasion.

"It's more than that," he went on. "If I lived to be two hundred—" (he planned on one hundred without question) "—I would never learn the subtleties of a language the way one understands it by growing up in a place. I am throwing away a big part of myself not living in my own culture, not being able to exchange ideas with people who understand me and whom I understand."

"But isn't it better to know two cultures—or more—isn't that increasing your horizons?"

It was a discussion that would occur more and more frequently as things that had amused him in the beginning began merely to bug him. The telephone not working. Not being able to get things except in season. The vagueness of the Spaniards about time. (They seemed incapable of getting anywhere when they said they would, or finishing anything by the date promised. While we were there it was decided that since so many pupils were late to school, the doors would be closed at nine and all pupils not in would be left out for the day. They couldn't stick to it because too many teachers didn't make it on time either.)

One day soon after we had returned, I went to Artie's study to call him for lunch to find him fitting the pieces of his clarinet together. I had never seen it. I knew he still had it; I had once asked what was in the small black case he kept in the corner under his desk.

I watched with fascination as the instrument took shape. That long black tube was why I had known who Artie Shaw was before he walked into my Paris apartment. The results of those fingers applied to that instrument had been heard round the world. Lay in a deep hole somewhere along with other valuable documents to be protected against annihilation in case of world holocaust. Was the source of revenue that came in nicely every month. "Why are you . . ." I whispered excitedly, "are you? . . ."

"I thought I'd see. . . ." He looked up at me shyly, a condition I had never seen before. "Would you mind going out of the house for a while? I'd sort of like to do this alone. . . ."

"Oh!" I backed away. "Of course! I understand, I'll clear out at once."

I hurried outside, slipped down the steep bank the house was built on, scrambled across the sharp incline past the new greenhouse until I reached a spot just below his study.

Clinging to a scruffy bush on a Spanish mountainside is how I heard Artie Shaw play his clarinet in person. All he did was play some scales. Up and down. Over and over. They were some of the sweetest sounds I had ever heard.

It was the only time; he never did it again. But I was uneasy. I knew something was afoot. His restlessness was growing. Had the New York musicians turned him on again?

But spring was upon us and visitors began showing up with more and more frequency, by car, by boat; even Truman Capote buzzed by wondering if he could rent our house. For a time Artie's restlessness was put in abeyance.

One such visitor was quite unexpected.

It all began one day when I received another of those static-filled telephone calls I had come to dread. This voice told me, I thought, that Sam Spiegel would be arriving at Palamós by boat the following noon. I wasn't really sure that's what the man had said, but since Palamós was only fifteen minutes away, we had nothing to lose by going over to find out.

It was something to see, that white, forty-meter pleasure cruiser pulling into the harbor alongside the small fishing and minor cargo boats. The entire population of Palamós thought so too, and they gathered around to watch. There was Sam on deck in white shorts, his ample belly jutting forward, a captain's cap perched jauntily on his head. He had his usual gorgeous redhead, blonde and brunette with him. He had come, he said, to look for locations and see the beautiful countryside we had promised him.

We swung aboard and off we went, cruising in high style along the shores we knew so well. But Sam? He would never know them; a boat that size couldn't get close, and a bit of haze was in the air. It didn't daunt Sam. He gazed shoreward through binoculars while we were served a tasty fish soufflé, lots of white wine and a tarte aux pommes.

Kiss kiss, good-bye and adios, and better luck next time. We stood waving from the dock as the yacht pulled out to deeper waters.

It was with utter amazement, then, that I went to the village a month or so later to find the place filled with those big unmistakable trucks that carry movie equipment to a location site. And that wasn't all. Emblazoned across their sides in huge lettering was the proclamation, Horizon Pictures, the name of the company that Sam and John Huston had founded when I was with John, and whose name Sam continued to use. As if I had stepped inside a time capsule, I was suddenly catapulted back ten years.

It was an odd sight, seeing them in my plaza, about as far from Hollywood as one could get. Were we all tied together, irrevocably, no matter what? I knew Elizabeth, finished with widowhood and married now to Eddie Fisher, must be around somewhere.

I went looking.

If a movie crew in New York City can cause a stir, imagine the excitement in a tiny village on the Costa Brava. All I had to do to find where they were shooting was to go where the entire population of Bagur had gathered in a tight cluster.

I pushed my way through. And there, plopped down in the middle of a narrow dusty street were the camera, lights, microphone dangling overhead, crew, director, assistant directors, script girl, and movie star. As if they had never left home.

The movie star and I greeted each other like long-lost buddies. Sharing the same guy and meeting in out-of-the-way places can do that. "Come up to the house," I said, "any time you're free, you and Eddie. Anybody can tell you where it is."

Eddie came up first that afternoon with Elizabeth's two small sons in tow. I knew him well; he had been Mike's friend and married at the time to Debbie Reynolds. Obviously merely consoling Elizabeth when Mike died got boring after a while, and further steps were taken. Now here they were. Eddie had been a bouncy, boyish singer, the hottest thing on the tube and enjoying life. But that day he seemed ill at ease, with greetings a bit too noisy, jests labored, as distant as if we had never met. Was he not able to take these shifts of personnel in stride? Perhaps it was just his duties as nursemaid rattling him. Our terraces with their steep drop below weren't designed for small children. And of course that's where they insisted on playing. We three adults had settled in the living room, two of us making an unsuccessful attempt at conversation, the third watching his charges through the window.

One of them ventured too near the edge. When Eddie called for him to retreat, it appeared to urge the child forward. He began to swing on the railing. Eddie rose to step outside.

It was a compliment to our singing maid: the glass panes were so clean Eddie couldn't tell which panel was open. With three-to-one odds, he picked the one that wasn't.

Wh-a-ap! Elizabeth was nearly a widow again.

The explosion of a five-foot wide, seven-foot high, half-inch thick pane of glass shattering is very loud indeed. Where a smooth see-through wall had been, there appeared in one split second a nasty jagged hole with sharp spears hanging like fierce stalactites from its upper edge. Right where Eddie's head had been. Sharp enough to stab a person's eye out. Or cut his throat. The rest of the glass was in splinters around his feet.

Eddie survived with nothing more than a scratch on the brow. He was stunned into incoherence, however. "Oh, señor," cried our cook who had come running when he heard the crash, "today you have been born again!"

True or not, it served one purpose. The kids dropped everything to gather round this more entertaining happening. Elizabeth, on the other hand, couldn't have cared less when she came along later. What's a near miss compared to the real thing that had occurred with her last husband.

They sent the children back to the hotel in a studio car and stayed on for dinner. Not so much, I decided, for our company, but so they wouldn't have to share each other's. One could already sense a strain between them despite the light patter. "She gave me this jade ring for a wedding present, I gave her a Rolls Royce." Or was it the other way around?

I liked Elizabeth the first time I met her; I liked her at this, the second. What she is, she is without pretense. That she happens to be beautiful, that she is successful at what she does, that she has been a movie star all her life and knows no other kind of existence—are the ingredients that make her what she is. Spoiled? Of course. As the Queen of England is spoiled. Would the Queen know how to live like "ordinary folk" after living in a palace all her life? But the same ingredients also give Elizabeth a sense of self that makes her comfortable to be around. It also gives her the courage to fight for what she wants, and against things she doesn't like. That day in Bagur she was not liking something worth a damn.

A French newspaper had run a story that she and Eddie had started an affair before Mike's death. She was hopping mad and wanted to sue. Eddie was dead set against it. "Don't make waves with the press," he said. "They'll only say worse things about us."

Elizabeth was adamant. "I'm not going to let those bastards get away with it."

The underlying hostility accompanying the discussion had the acid smell of disenchantment. She wore Eddie's wedding ring on the left hand and Mike's on the right. Or was *that* the other way around? For the love of Mike is why they were together. Or so she told me after Artie took Eddie into his study. By then a goodly amount of wine had been consumed and the belligerent factor had risen.

Later Artie told me that he had said to Eddie, "Let her sue. She's going to anyway, so why not go along with it, that is, if you want to get along with her. A star of her caliber is in a fine position to sue the press, and should if they're taking advantage." (Artie has always been very good at arranging other people's lives.)

Meanwhile, back in the living room, over further quantities of our native red wine, Elizabeth and I were reminiscing about Mike. Was he like this with you? Or like this? I told her of the roller coaster ride, the funny trips to American Optical, the marvelous time in Chinchón outside of Madrid when both Cantínflas and Domínguín were fighting bulls. She looked at me with those big violet eyes. "I envy you," she said sadly. "You had the best years with him."

I wondered if that was true. It was certainly one way to look at it.

I wasn't surprised that her marriage to Eddie Fisher didn't last. But then I'm never surprised when *any* marriage doesn't last. Only when they do. . . .

CHAPTER 60...

"Someone's rocking my dreamboat. . . ."

Artie was no longer amused at things Spanish.

How we had laughed when the carpenter had shown up with seven different doors that should have been identical since they all opened into the same hall. "Kiku," we cried, "why did you not make the doors all the same as we planned?" "Oh, Señor y señora, it got so boring to make the same one over and over."

Or the time the Ruarks were having a bathroom retiled while they were away. Although when they returned it was beautifully tiled right up to the ceiling, the shower head was now missing. "Why did you take out the shower?" they asked the mason. "Oh, Señor y señora," he replied, "because you didn't tell me not to."

"It's hopeless," Artie would mutter at each new imbroglio, "utterly hopeless."

I found myself beginning to defend "my" Spaniards.

But then the winds began to get him down. We had fierce ones, as we lived on the sea. They even had names. The blustery Tramontana down from the Pyrenees, the steadily blowing Garbi from the south. Wind drove people mad. How could I argue that? Then there was the vagueness of schedules, the closing from noon to four, the slow pace of the carts on the road.

The climax of his discontent came over what should have been a minor trip up to Perpignan, across the border into France. We had to go there every few months (even that had begun to bug him) to check the cars out of Spain and avoid the horrendous Spanish import duty.

It was a perfect day in early September, clear and bright, with a brilliantly blue sky. "Let's take the scenic route back," Artie suggested. "You've never seen that one."

Our usual route was the quicker inland way through La Junquera; we had passed there so often the customs people knew us and always welcomed us warmly. The scenic route wound along the cliffs above the shoreline of the sea, by way of Port Bou. It was a good hour longer; few people traveled it. Ours was the only car to pull up to the customs stations perched on top of a hill in the middle of nowhere. Two little houses, the French on their side, the Spanish on theirs.

I skipped out of the car with the passports and carnet. *Bon jour! Bon jour!* The French passed us out with smiles, with comments on the weather, happy to see us.

Then across to the Spanish frontier. *Buenos dias! Buenos dias!* The police greeted me with smiles, commented on the weather, stamped the passports, and I proceeded to the customs man with the automobile carnet.

The usual procedure was a glance through, a scribble, a stamp on a page, over and out in seconds.

Not today.

No smile, no light banter. The blond, curly-headed fellow remained seated at his desk, didn't speak, didn't even look up. He flipped through the pages of the document, flipped them backward to take another look. Then he snapped the carnet shut, handed it back, and looked up at me for the first time. His eyes were blank and unsmiling. "Your car," he said in Spanish, "cannot enter Spain."

My mouth fell open. "B-but—we live here, we have—"

"The car has been in and out too often."

"B-but we have a house here, in the Provincia de Gerona, this is where—look here, the police have stamped our passports *entrada*."

It was the first time he smiled, the little prick. "You," he said, "of course can come in, the police have given permission. It is your car that cannot."

"That's crazy!" I shrieked. "We're up here on top of a mountain in the middle of nowhere, we can't go anywhere without a car!"

The smile snapped off. "The car cannot enter Spain," he said in haughty official tone, and turned away. It was at moments like these that I missed Harry Cohn and all the power of a big studio to come to my rescue. But I did have Artie. I went back to where he was waiting in the doomed car. "Artie!" I cried, "they say the car can't come in!"

"I'm sure you've misunderstood, Kesi," he answered calmly, "you're always thinking your Spanish is better than it is—"

"No no! Look!" I shoved the carnet at him. "See, he didn't—"

"Son of a bitch," Artie said, "that's insane, give me that thing. You obviously didn't make it clear—" He snatched the carnet and strode inside.

There was quiet for a few moments; I could hear the distant hoot of a ship on the sea below, a cricket calling a mate. Then Artie's voice began to be heard. It grew in force and caused the mountain to shudder as he slammed back out the door with verbal flood-gates wide open. At the top of his voice and in no uncertain terms he told the Spaniards what they could do with their system; unfortunately, with his ass-backwards grammar he sounded like the low comic he feared to sound like.

By then, since they had nothing else to do, the two policemen and the blond curly-headed cause of it all had gathered at the door to watch the entertainment, the discomfort of the two Americans in their power, hardly bothering to hide their smiles behind their hands. The police, with amusement, stamped us out, registering for posterity that our stay for that day in their country was all of five minutes.

The French, who had passed us through such a short time before with smiles, looked at us now with suspicion. They examined our documents with care. They went through our car and luggage. Finding no reason to detain us, they reluctantly permitted us to reenter their country.

"Don't you see," Artie fumed, as we drove away *"don't you see* we cannot continue to live in a country that can stop our *car* from going in. My God, it'll be us next, we're at the whim of every border official. . . ."

I shivered. My world was crumbling. It didn't help matters that we were able to drive back around to La Junquera and to be greeted warmly there. As Artie pointed out on the way home, "It's too hazardous to live in a place where the rules and regulations change from day to day, from border to border! Not to ever know what will happen tomorrow? That's anarchy. No, no, it's too uncertain. Why, we could even lose our house if some government official took a shine to it. . . ."

It was a theme he would continue in the weeks to come. "We've had all we can get out of this Spanish experience, Kesi," he would say. "It's been a good one, but it's Never-Never Land. It's time to enter the world again. We ran away, you and I. But now we can go back to America. I can go back because I have you on my side. You can go back because you have me. . . ."

It's true that he was wasted here; he wasn't using himself properly. The phone didn't work. The winds did blow. The Spanish were impossible about time. And if Artie was no longer happy here, how could I insist we stay?

I knew I had to reconcile myself to the fact that it was over. Perhaps my sense of permanence, or that it existed on this spot outside an obscure village in Spain, had been an illusion all along. Nothing in this world is permanent, anyway, I reminded myself.

But I was heartsick. I still tried to hold back the tide. "Oh Artie, are you sure it's the right move? We've worked so hard, put so much of ourselves into this place—"

"Nothing is ever lost. We've learned a great deal—"

"I do so love it here. It was my dream always to be—"

"Think of it this way. How many people ever have a dream fulfilled?"

"Ah. Yes. That's true, isn't it."

"We'll get another house—"

"It won't be the same—"

"It will be better, you'll see. Things work in America, there won't be the hassles—"

"I love the hassles—"

"Just think how it will be to be able to get everything you want, how you want, when you want it."

"Ah. Well, yes. . . ." It was a nice thought. I tried to hold on to it.

"And we have each other, wherever we go."

Another nice thought. I held on to that one, too. . . .

CHAPTER 61

"Que será . . . será . . ."

Even so, it took another year and another trip to New York before we finally left Spain altogether. I had to admit, the hustle and bustle of the Big Apple was infectious. And the people we met there. Like Lenny Bruce. Some friends brought him around to our hotel after his show.

We already were acquainted with his records, impressed with his humor and wisdom. He was lean and hungry-looking then, in his mid-thirties, and quite good-looking. We all hit it off instantly, and sat around talking until dawn.

Lenny told Artie he had been in the same boot camp with him at the beginning of the war. Their paths had never crossed, of course; Artie was the big superstar then, Lenny a raw eighteen-year-old. "Yeah," said Artie, "it was nightmarish for me being in that position." Half his navy life, he told Lenny, was being treated like a VIP, and the other half being told who-the-hell-do-you-think-you-are-you're-no-better-than-us. He never knew which was to prevail. To illustrate his point, he told Lenny the story of what happened to him in that boot camp.

One Sunday the men were hanging around the barracks, nothing much to do and confined to camp. A sailor came bounding in. Seaman Shaw, he said breathlessly, Commander Somebody-or-Other is on his way to see you!

Well, my God! A commander! Artie had been in the navy long enough by then—five weeks—to be impressed as hell with rank. He scurried around, got into a tidy uniform, shined his shoes, shaved again, checked his nails, his locker, his bed. All the other men hung around helping, giving advice, terribly impressed that a commander was coming all the way to the barracks to see Seaman Shaw.

The barracks formed a semicircle around a plot of grass. Artie went there to wait. All the surrounding windows were filled with the heads of the men, eager to watch this momentous occasion.

Artie stood stiffly at attention as the Commander, followed by a number of aides, strode into the circle. He stopped before Artie. Artie saluted. "Seaman Artie Shaw?" the Commander barked.

"Yessir," Artie answered.

The Commander grinned. "Put 'er there," he said, and stuck out his hand in the classic position of handshake. Artie naturally took it.

The Commander held on, grinning around at his aides, at the heads sticking out of windows, and said, "I've always wanted to shake the hand that patted Lana Turner's ass."

Well.

Artie had read up on the rights of an enlisted man when he began to be abused so often. An officer has no right to bandy about the name of even an ex-wife of an enlisted man. Artie called the Commander every name in the book, beginning with stupid cocksucker, to arrogant bastard, tasteless, crude fool, and going on from there. His articulateness, extensive vocabulary and low boiling-point served him well that day.

The Commander, having read—and obviously forgotten—the same fair-play clauses that Artie had, realized he had made a gross miscalculation in thinking this licorice stick player would be flattered by his attentions. He turned beet red, said not another word, turned on his heel and left. The incident was not reported.

Lenny's bag was anti-establishment. He loved the story.

The following night the phone woke me in the early hours. Artie, who sleeps down in the depths somewhere, hadn't heard the ring. I answered. It was Lenny, just off the floor of the Blue Angel. "I told the story," he said, "you should have heard it—" (It took me a second to figure out what story.) "—They were all ears, you could have heard a pin drop. And then I threw in the part about patting Lana Turner's ass. They gasped with shock. It went great!"

Artie had come to. "Who is it?" he asked sleepily. When I told him he reached over and took the phone. Soon he was involved in animated conversation. I looked at the clock—4:00 A.M.

I lay listening to Artie, his laughter, the extra vibrant ring in his voice, the pleasure he was having. All right, I thought, I'll stop dragging my heels. He should be here. A racing car gets rusty unless it's let out once in a while. A racehorse confined to a stall would soon go quietly mad. We were courting disaster to stay on in Spain. The arguments had become more and more frequent. Artie needed room.

But to my surprise he didn't want to settle in Manhattan, he wanted New England. I didn't care where. I was committed, my role clearly defined, stated on all documents: wife, housewife, dependent. All I knew of New England were the airports, theaters, army hospitals, city auditoriums or broadcasting stations I had rushed in and out of at various times, and those all look alike wherever you are. But Artie knew the area he wanted, he had lived there before.

So we went and found—Lakeville, Connecticut, population 1,200 (a metropolis next to Bagur), two hours from New York, the same distance we traveled to Barcelona, only here there were supermarkets, book stores, even a public library, movie houses, people who spoke our language, and phones that worked, oh how exciting! The house— Artie fell in love with it on sight—was enormous, rooms some thirty or forty feet long and/or wide, some twenty-five of them, give or take a few, filled with fireplaces and hardwood floors and countless bathrooms. We got it fairly cheap, who else would want a white elephant. On water again, 324-foot frontage on Lake Wononskopomuc.

Here then, was the place to do the living happily ever after, to totter on into our dotage, together, till death did us part. Who would have figured that one back in Atlanta? A castle in Spain, yes, but a New England Colonial on Lake *Wo-non-sko-po-muc?*

I clung, not quite ready to let go of my Spanish dream. The dogs must come with us. Machito yes, said Artie, but Chucha no. He was adamant. I gave her to our cook, Ignacio. Anyway, Chucha knew him better than us, we had been away so much. But our couple, Pepe and Montserrat, must absolutely come with us. "Please, Artie," I begged, "you know how everybody says it's hard to get help in America." That they had an eight-year-old girl and Montserrat was seven months pregnant bothered me not at all. The children would go to better schools, babies were always dying in Bagur born at home the way they were, and babies never die in America, everybody knows that. God knows we had plenty of room in the new house. Artie agreed, grown accustomed to the baronial life too.

We packed eighty-two crates, made by the carpenter who had made the seven different doors, plus thirty-eight bags and trunks.

Finally the last day arrived. Off we went, the Simca station wagon jammed to the hilt, Machito wedged in the back. It was late afternoon, as it had been the day we arrived. Once more the sun was fighting the sky in a fiery glow. I broke down again, sobbing my way out of town. I probably would have kept it up all the way to America if Artie hadn't gotten grumpy. "Jesus, Kesi," he complained, "you're being extremely self-indulgent. You think you're the only one feeling anything? How do you think I feel?"

"How *do* you feel?"

"Change is harder on me than on you, you know that, I have it—"

"Then why are you doing it?" I cried.

"You know very well why. But rest assured, this is the last one for the rest of our lives."

I believed him. I actually did.

CHAPTER 62...

"Just a cottage small. .

by a waterfall. . . ."

One hot day in August, with our worldly goods trailing along, plus the pregnant Montserrat, her husband and eight-year-old Maria, *and* a Simca station wagon and a dog named Machito, we *schlepped* to our new abode, and were soon into heavy nest-making once again.

This time I was ahead of the game. I knew about cigarette boxes, pillow directions (so did Montserrat), sharpened pencils, how to run a kitchen. Menus too; I had even made lists—at Artie's suggestion—of what he liked and didn't like and combinations thereof. We took our things out of storage, my art works, his books, musical scores, concert grand piano and a few zillion other things, all happily to be under one roof at last.

I took the eight-year-old Maria off to school and found a doctor to see Montserrat through delivery and the baby afterwards; the hospital was ten minutes away.

Artie explained New England behavior and dress to me. Tweed skirts and flat-heeled moccasins, Brooks Brothers button-down shirts, short hair, unbleached. He himself snipped mine off. Beauty parlors, he said, were a waste of money. And no expletives. Don't say "fuck" or "shit" around town, nor take the name of the Lord in vain.

Gotcha.

Now we were ready to make local friends. We met neighbors, came across an old Paris friend, columnist Robert Yoakum, and became acquainted with John Buckley, older brother of William and Jim. Terry Southern had taken a place nearby, too.

A mixed bag of political persuasion, from America-love-it-or-leave-it groups to tear-it-down-and-start-all-over factions. We were loftily above that. Having lived elsewhere for so long, we were now blessed with a more objective view of America. Sure that we knew how to prove democracy would work, we invited these opposites to dinner one night, the John Buckleys representing the right, the Terry Southerns bringing up the left.

Peace didn't last through dinner. Every subject went awry. Drugs? Chic on Terry's side, un-American on the Buckleys'. God seemed to be sitting next to Mrs. Buckley; I felt guilty not to have set another place. Not believing in Him wasn't patriotic, either.

Terry didn't want to be left out of the patriot bag, and after dinner he went to his car and brought back a rolled-up paper. "This," he told us, "I'm sure you will agree, is the *essence* of, the bottom *dollar* on, patriotism." With that he unfurled a banner about twenty-four inches long and four inches wide. FUCK COMMUNISM! it declared in red, white and blue.

In spite of that the Buckleys invited us to *their* house for dinner. They lived in an opulent house, with an opulent living room in which the first thing I spied as we entered, in an opulent corner, on an opulent table, under an opulent lamp, in an opulent silver frame, was an autographed photograph of the late, infamous senator from Wisconsin, Joseph McCarthy. The murderer of my friends' careers, a blight upon the land of Thomas Jefferson and Benjamin Franklin. "Th-th-that is . . . J-J-Joe McCarthy," I whispered hoarsely.

My hostess misread my shock. "Yes," she answered in hushed and reverent tone, "one of our great, unsung heroes."

Togetherness in New England wasn't going to be easy.

Our menagerie steadily grew. First another dog joined up, a perky miniature schnauzer whom we named Garbo because of her aversion to strangers. Then I came home to find two black cats and their litter pan; it seemed Artie had promised a friend of Terry's we would take them aboard when he departed for California.

And finally a baby.

From the start I had had to act as interpreter between Montserrat and her American doctor. When the labor pains started it was I— Artie considered all this woman's work—who bundled the bulging woman and husband Pepe in the Simca and rushed them to the hospital. There I explained to the nurses how she was feeling, to Montserrat what they wanted her to do, and then went off to soothe anxious Pepe in the waiting room, a stranger in a strange land. "Don't worry," I lied, "nothing can happen."

It was great relief when a healthy bouncing baby boy appeared, with all appurtenances in place and accounted for.

I had my work cut out for me. I had a family of four to take care of, baby clothes, strollers, toys to buy, baby bottles to boil, formula to mix—they knew nothing of these things. There were the animals to look after, the house to run, the shopping. And there was Artie, for whom I must function as cook-companion-playmate-sex object-intellectual sounding board, and assistant in whatever endeavor he was undertaking at the moment.

Yes, I was plenty occupied.

The question was, what was Artie going to do, now that we were installed in our native land? . . .

CHAPTER 63...

"Let it snow . . . let it snow . . .

let it snow. . . ."

His study was set up again—twice, in fact. He began upstairs and decided he preferred down. He used it mostly for reading, reading, reading! He talked a lot of deals. This! That! They fell through. As did an idea for a talk show in California. Open arms and welcome home it wasn't. Artie had been so sure the blacklist was finished. I was beginning to wonder.

BBC called from Toronto. They wanted to do an hour special on Artie Shaw, brimming with nostalgia. He wouldn't play? Never mind, they would have somebody else play the clarinet, they would have an entire band playing in the Artie Shaw style. All he would have to do is narrate.

It was an entrancing experience for me, who had never seen him in action. A big band had gotten ready by listening to his old recordings. Artie only had to sharpen them up a little here and there. And he did it so easily, relaxed, knowing his stuff, doing the thing he knew best. I had never seen this person before. I understood then, that when he had been worrying about losing a part of himself in the Spanish language, he had already lost the biggest part of all when he'd given up his music.

It was the part television shows and entrepreneurs wanted. How about playing something for us, they would say. With his clarinet he could have had any deal he wanted. No go. He would have it his way or not at all.

During that period it never occurred to me to work; I *was* working. Busy with my job as housewife and mother of four—make that five. "Ke . . . si!"

"Coming!"

New York City took the place of Barcelona, about the same driving time away but with considerably better roads, built with American know-how (and money), and made for speed. Which is how I learned the way I was going to die.

Artie had always been a pushy driver, passing everything on the road. It was a cinch in Spain with a Mercedes, with nothing more than horse and cart, bicycle and dilapidated truck for competition. In America, with miles of smooth asphalt unfurling before him, the racing driver lurking in his depths emerged. The Mercedes had been replaced by an Alfa Romeo. When Artie slid behind the wheel the competition was on. When another vehicle hove in sight he pressed down on the gas without thinking twice, with utter contempt for a posted speed. For that reason one eye had to always be glued to the rear view mirror to watch for the fuzz.

Since he so often lost his gamble with them—he could paper a wall with traffic citations—I was convinced he would lose as well on the chances he took with our lives. "Please, Artie," I would plead, "please slow down."

"I'd like to get there, Kesi."

"We might not get there at all if you drive so fast."

"You know I'm the safest driver around."

I would have trouble believing that when we had missed another car by fractions. "Please—"

"Hush. Let me concentrate and we'll get there in one piece."

I was never soothed. I knew we were doomed. . . .

When the snows came he slowed down, to my surprise. "I told you I was a safe driver," he said smugly. He was the only one of us who had lived in Grandma Moses country. It was enchanting at first when the world turned white and the lake froze over. Artie, my God, could ice skate, even do figure eights! Was there no end to his accomplishments? We turned up the furnaces (two), built fires in the fireplaces, and settled in to cope. For a while that winter it looked as if we might.

Eight-year-old Maria was speaking English like a native, the baby gurgled in his crib, the doting parents able to pay a little attention to helping me with the house, and Artie took to his study seriously. He began writing a musical. Everything except the music, that is, the dialogue, the lyrics. "Ke . . . si! How does this sound?"

In between he made geometric sketches, sat down to the piano as if it were a long-lost friend and began to practice Chopin daily. And there was his fishing equipment to attend to. "Ke . . . si—I need a hand. . . ."

It was evident that an audience of one wasn't enough when he finished his musical. We invited the neighbors in for a reading. That was nice. The pressure would be off for a few hours. It wasn't easy being the entire cheering section for somebody grown accustomed to the applause of thousands.

Ten of us gathered around. He began to read his script—all the parts. It hadn't occurred to either of us that I might read some of them. The new identity that I had worked so hard to achieve under Artie's diligent guidance, was complete. I was Kesi Shaw. Artie's wife. To the people gathered in the study at his feet. To Artie. To myself. Evelyn Keyes was wiped out, obliterated. Her nasty alter ego,

Myrtle, put in an appearance occasionally long enough to snarl, "I'm busy, get it yourself," or "For Christ's sake, slow down!" Then there would be an angry outburst, a repetition of Venice and others like it. Nice Kesi. Mean Myrtle.

It was Myrtle who was bothered when Artie would entertain our guests with stories of what had happened to both of us (like the border incident when the car couldn't get in), and use the singular "I," as if he had been alone. He also began to retell little jokes or stories I had told him—things that had happened to me long before I ever met him —and use the singular "I, " leaving me out of my own happening.

I tried not to be annoyed. Doesn't a good wife *like* to take a back seat, watch her husband shine? Down, Myrtle; quiet, Kesi. But— "Artie! That story you told tonight, that didn't happen to you, that was me—"

"What does it matter?"

"Well, Jesus, I don't, I feel as if . . . as if—"

"You're prone to 'feeling something.' You're too sensitive."

"It's as if you . . . deny my existence—"

"You should feel flattered that I identify with you so strongly that it seems as if it happened to me."

"Ah. Yeah, well—"

"Okay? Now be off. I want to read for a while." Yassuh, massuh.

He took his musical to George Abbott, the whiz director of such things. He didn't get any satisfaction there, either. Which is why he went into the gun business. . . .

CHAPTER 64...

"*. . . always chasing rainbows. . . .*"

With the coming of spring things jostled apart, like a jarred jigsaw puzzle. The baby had grown large enough to crawl and, though cute, was becoming an obstacle course. Artie's restlessness, like sap in a maple, spread as the weather warmed. He wanted to be out on the lake when the fishing season opened. So we dashed to the Finger Lakes district for a boat, then to Pittsfield, Massachusetts, for an outboard motor. When the snow was barely melted he rushed down to the lake shore to practice fly casting.

Garbo the schnauzer came into heat. Machito, turbulent, began daily fights with the dog next door. The greening world seemed to remind the Spaniards of their beloved Cataluña. They began moaning that Maria would forget how to speak Catalán, that the baby "looked American." They wanted to go home.

Artie was delighted. He could use their sitting room off the kitchen for the new bug in his bonnet. Guns.

It was my fault, I suppose. I gave him a gun. Poring over a gun digest he had expressed a desire for a certain kind of rifle. I got it for his birthday. That's how far I had made the grade up the good wife ladder. Because I hate guns—hate the ugly sound they make, the smell of gunpowder, the fearful speed of a bullet through the air, the viciousness with which it hits. I despise the violence of a gun's intent altogether, the way it can turn a beautiful deer into a bloody carcass. Artie said that was because I was a female. That violence was inherent in the male; that it was the reason for his force, his drive, the basis of his power, of his accomplishments. A woman didn't have these qualities. He said that violence disturbed me so because I didn't trust men since my father left me. Artie said a lot of things like that.

We put the Spaniards on a ship headed for Barcelona, waved them and another chunk of Spanish dream a fond farewell, and Artie filled up their old room *faster* than the speed of a bullet. Never one to do things halfway, one gun followed another. Soon he was making his own cartridges with a machine he bought for the purpose, along with scales for measuring gunpowder. Before long there was enough of that stuff around to blow up Fort Knox.

It was a short step to opening a gun shop.

His interest in these things took him to places where men gathered who had the same disease. There is a whole subculture in the land formed of people who love guns and what they can do. With some of these men, Artie furnishing the money, a tract of land was bought in the nearby town of Clinton Corners. They quickly built a shop and firing ranges of all kinds and distances, called themselves Shooters' Service, Inc., and opened for business. Gun freaks gathered from far and wide, Artie in there with them.

Artie once told me a story about himself. On tour with his band, they wound up in a place by the name of Palacios, Texas, scarcely noted on the most detailed of maps. Gathered in the dance hall were the local ranchers, still in their high-heeled boots, a rugged lot but enthusiastic. One of them kept winking at Artie as he danced past the bandstand.

At a break Artie went over to him. "Why do you keep winking at me?" inquired Artie.

The man grinned. Nudged Artie with his elbow. "I won't tell anybody," he whispered conspiratorially.

Artie blinked. "Tell anybody—what?"

The man chuckled, nudged him again. "I know you're not Artie Shaw."

Artie laughed. "Of course I'm Artie Shaw."

"Aw, come on," the man said, "I know better than that—"

"Why do you think I'm not Artie Shaw?"

"Come on," winked the man, "what would Artie Shaw be doing in Palacios?"

It was how I felt accompanying Artie to the site of his latest enterprise. How did I get here? Where had the dream gone? Who was this man I was married to? Who, the bigger question, was his wife?

My dreams took on an unnerving quality. I was often wandering, lost, in houses I had never seen before. Once I dreamed I was in a coffin, still alive. I tried to rise up to say so, to find a doctor cutting off my legs in slices.

Flare-ups between us became more frequent, mostly over trivia (perhaps I had forgotten the salt), often rising to full-scale warfare. I would react with boredom almost as soon as it had begun, he with an inability to curb his temper for the rest of the day (and sometimes longer). "Can't you forget it," I'd say after a couple of hours, "and go on to something else?"

That never failed to infuriate him. *"We aren't through with this! How do I know you won't do it again!?"*

"Because I've just said so," I would answer wearily for the millionth time."

"You said it the last time!"

"Try me once more."

Each time I was amazed at the intensity of his anger. It was too firmly fixed in my head that he was a brainy and rational fellow guided by logic and intellect, whose gray matter must certainly have control over base emotion. Had this not been the thrust of our talks through the years? Constructive anger, yes, and necessary if we must correct the world's faults. But wild, insane fury? Because I had forgotten to put the salt on the table?

Years passed before I realized he could have gotten his own bloody salt (or whatever). But then, he had my number. Dining table matters were the wife's responsibilities. When the Spaniards left, my taking over the cooking and getting it to the table was such a natural step that I scarcely noticed the changeover.

Wrapped up in my never-ending chores I barely noticed the brochure on motor homes Artie brought around. "Look here," he said, "it's not a trailer, it's the whole thing in one."

"That's nice," I murmured, stirring the sauce béchamel, one eye on the bubbling escalopes of veal.

"Let's get one."

"Whatever for?"

"There are gun clubs and shops around the country, I could check them out; we don't want another winter here, be nice to get away—"

"We just got here!" I cried, dismayed.

"They come from Brown City, Michigan. . . ."

We were soon on our way to that unlikely spot (Palacios again) and without much ado, a Dodge Motor Home was in the works, made to order for one Artie Shaw.

Some thirty-six feet long and seven feet wide, the back end was turned into a work bench for his cartridge-making equipment, a rack for his guns. There were bunks, bathroom, kitchen and dining table. Extra water tanks were put in, its own generator installed to furnish lights, heat and air-conditioning so we never had to plug in anywhere, a platform was built on the rear to hold a little motor car to get us about at stopovers.

The little woman was allowed to do the curtains and rugs. Also the pots and pans for the kitchen. Or should I say galley.

Whither thou goest. . . .

CHAPTER 65 . . .

". . . everything is peaches down in
Georgia. . . ."

Two days before Christmas, we filled our new home-on-wheels with clothing and supplies, shooed in the dogs, climbed aboard ourselves, and in a blinding snowstorm took off down south, leaving the house and two black cats in the hands of a local woman. Oh-what-fun. Mush!

So here we were before the second year had begun in our new

abode, on a cold winter's day, moving on. Well, heavens, you've always liked to travel, and this is for business, and who could dispute a noble endeavor like busy-ness, right? I wriggled down into my fleece-lined coat and looked ahead.

All day and into the night our bus crept along slushy turnpike and parkway while Christmas lights shone from every lawn and front window, shrub and tree flickered and danced along the way like winter fireflies behind the curtain of falling snow, hinting at warm hearth and hot drink, of gaily wrapped presents and hugs to go with them.

Bah and humbug! We scoffed at such nonsense, this bow to crass commercialism, as we sloughed by in our rolling home. But my thoughts floated sneakily in as I watched the headlights of oncoming Eastern Seaboard traffic flash across my husband's concentrated face over the massive wheel, caught the puzzled eyes of the disoriented dogs huddled nearby. I remembered Christmases past, when I lived in a little house like those we were passing, when trees weren't bought but chopped down in the woods, and strung with popcorn and paper chains and stars out of tinsel that we made ourselves. I remember I wrote Santa for a watch and a red kite to fly. And he brought them, I believed he did, and it was more thrilling than any diamond necklace or Cadillac had ever been—

"Here's a spot we can stay."

It was a filling station closed for the night, somewhere in Maryland. We opened our double bunk—still a double for us—and settled down for the night, bundled like mummies against the penetrating cold, surrounded by gas pumps, Coca-Cola machines, piles of used tires and snowed-in trucks. I thought of the two cats with twenty-five rooms to roam in, two big furnaces chugging away to keep them warm, as I dozed off in a fitful sleep. . . .

We took off before dawn, and soon left the snow behind but not the cold. Nor the trail of seasonal lights and decorations. America was certainly together on that. Christmas Eve was Virginia and the Carolinas, bleak and gray, and a chill to penetrate the bones.

Christmas Day we crossed over into Georgia.

Right . . . back . . . where . . . I started from. . . .

The red clay color of the earth was familiar. The "Enjoy our zephyrs, dodge our heifers" sign had been removed, however. Interstates had finally curtailed the free-wheeling movements of Georgia cattle. The movements of blacks were also still restricted as I discovered when we stopped for gas and to let the dogs run. Restrooms this way: "White" on one side, "Colored" on the other. With the Christmas good-will-toward-men wreath on the wall between them.

The year 1962 was one week away. Twenty-two years had passed since I first became aware of that particular injustice. It still hadn't changed. Depression settled like a gossamer web. Twenty-two years since I had tried to share my enlightenment with my family. They hadn't changed either. Hadn't seen my light, hadn't heard my drum. Hadn't even tried. And I, my conscience pushing, had had to travel my separate path.

The web tightened. To—where? To this bus? Whizzing along a highway, simply going *from* someplace, to some other place? Twenty-two years, I thought with shock, of doing just that. *Twenty-two* years, gone. In the flick of an eye. Like that passing farmhouse . . . whoosh! Billboard . . . whoosh! Tree . . . whoosh! And I still hadn't arrived anywhere. I was still running—no, worse—I was being dragged along by somebody else who was running. And Artie was. Don't tell me he wasn't. I saw now, he had run *from* America to Spain, from Spain *to* America, *from* Connecticut to—where? Oh God, to *where*? Was *there* going to be better than *here*?

With sudden clarity I understood it all.

When things didn't go right, Artie took off like some skittish bird. Hadn't he continually done that? Hadn't he walked off the bandstand at the height of his fame and disappeared from sight? Headlines had screamed, ARTIE SHAW VANISHES.

What an absolutely perfect choice for Daddy. A man who can vanish. My subconscious, Myrtle, probably had that one figured right from the beginning. A man who can be depended on to vanish.

The insight fairly took my breath away. I had really done it this time. Had hitched my wagon to . . . an illusion. Had actually gone along—at this late date—with the entire Cinderella package, prince, castle, happy ending and all. That could disappear like the fairy godmother did, with the flick of a wand. Schmuck. It was to laugh. Miracle indeed.

It was hard to breathe, to get air in and out. Atlanta 14 miles, the sign read. Fourteen miles and twenty-two—no, twenty-five, there were three years prior to enlightenment—since I had gone off to seek my fortune, chasing mirages all the way. I'm a mess, I thought angrily, and everybody helps me stay that way. No, be fair, you do the large share all by yourself—"What?"

Artie must have already been trying to get my attention, because he spoke with annoyance. "I have never seen anything like it! You are eternally off someplace else!"

He caught me at an unfortunate moment. My frayed id bristled (or was it Myrtle's?). I answered snappishly. Answering Artie snappishly was jiggling a muleta before a toro, asking for a charge. Nice

wives didn't jiggle muletas. "There must be some way" (I snapped)
—"you can start a sentence without an implied criticism of me—"

The bus speeded up, a sure sign of anger. "What's the matter with you, Kesi," he said sharply, "are you about to have your period?"

"You are always criticizing me in one way or—"

"Always, always, surely there is another word in your vocabulary—"

"See? There! You're doing it again—"

"Can we never get past your tender feelings to—"

"Isn't 'never' the same as 'always'?"

"Are you trying to irritate me? You have been disagreeable all day—"

"I most certainly have not—" (Had I?)

"Can't you watch that tone of yours?"

"*My* tone! You started this! Did you hear how you spoke to me!"

"*Get control of yourself, Kesi!*" Artie hissed. "Pull yourself together! Can't you do that?"

The dogs, hearing his explosive inflections, moved to the back of the bus. For their sake, for Artie's, for mine, I made an effort to follow his advice. What was I upset about—I had a dream slipping? Big deal. So what else is new? I had other things to think about; Atlanta was coming up fast. That, without a doubt, was the cause of my edginess.

I shouldn't be this near and not call my mother. But then, would she be hurt if we didn't go see her? And would Artie stand still for that? No two poles were ever more opposite than he and my mother. Making small talk with little old southern ladies was perhaps too much to ask of him. Still and all—it was my mother. "Uh . . . Artie, do you mind if I call my mother? I don't feel right being this near without—"

"You haven't answered my question."

I looked over at him, puzzled. "What question?"

Silence. He looked straight ahead, his hands tight on the wheel. "What question, Artie? *I* just asked *you* if I—"

"Can you pull yourself together?"

"Oh that, for God's sake," I muttered. I leaned toward him. "I *am* together, and now I'm asking you if—"

"Your sincerity is touching," he spat sarcastically, "it's extraordinary how you think you can vent your spleen anytime you like—"

"Oho!" I cried, "look who's talking—"

"I'm warning you, Kesi!" I should have heeded the deadly hiss. But no. "Warning me! Of what, pray?"

"I won't take much more of this—"

"Take what? Oh God, here we are. Oh please, *please!*"

"Please, please," he imitated nastily.

"Artie," I begged, "we're almost in Atlanta, look, there's a sign, can't we talk about all this later, I want to know now if—"

"I want, I want. The only words you know."

"Goddamn it, Artie! You're just being difficult—"

"I haven't begun to be difficult, cunt."

"Shut up!" I screeched. For a crazy flash I thought my mother could hear him, she was so strongly on my mind.

Now I had done it.

To tell Artie to shut up was like lighting a firecracker under a herd of buffalo and standing in front of it. As if it were a denial of his worth, as if without words he ceased to exist. In the past I had told him to be quiet a second or to shhh, and those times had been explosive enough. But this topped them all; this was a biggie.

Before I could explain a holocaust burst over me. A stream of words so vindictive, malevolent and vicious it boggles the imagination: Harridan, lunatic, cheat, selfish, unfeeling, blind, dense, unreachable, untrustworthy, were some he hurled, with variations on the theme of the hopelessness of it all, threading the barrage together. All the while going at full tilt, slamming our clumsy vehicle down the highway as if it were a sports car.

When a cluster of lights loomed ahead he jerked suddenly to the right, barrelled into a filling station/restaurant stop and slammed on the brakes. As we jolted to a stop, pots, pans, books, pillows and dogs all shot forward as if an earthquake had hit.

Artie got to his feet and started toward the back. "I've had enough," he yelled hoarsely, "I'm getting a gun and end it all right now."

I died a thousand deaths. I grabbed him. Oh please, oh dear God. No. No. I blocked his way to where the guns were. If I really think about it, I couldn't have stopped him unless he had wanted me to, but I don't care about that, because how can I really be sure that he wouldn't do what he said he would do if I hadn't tried. They say a person can be stopped by a cup of coffee, any little thing, if he can be reached at the right time.

I shiver when I remember that night.

He finally sat down at the big wheel again, that big bus wheel, and he put his elbows on it, and dropped his head in his arms.

For two hours and forty minutes he stayed like that, with me standing beside him. After 4,000 pleases and 2,000,000 I'm sorrys, I quieted down and just stood there, hovering. The dogs too had crept up and were lying as close to me as they could, their troubled eyes watching.

With the motor off the bus grew colder and colder, below freezing, I think. It didn't matter if we turned to ice cubes, I wasn't moving. Artie silent was almost worse than Artie yelling.

I noticed a sign just past the restaurant. East Point, Georgia. So that's where we were. A suburb of Atlanta. I used to go to dances there when I was a teenager in high school. "Good night . . . sweet—heart. . . ." They were all tag dances, with the boys breaking in every few seconds, except for the six "no-breaks," and those you made dates for ahead. I wrote in my diary when I was sixteen: "I will never marry a boy who isn't a terrific dancer."

"Artie? Please . . .?"

Finally he rose with a sigh, got out and went into the restaurant. I could see him through the window, drinking a cup of coffee.

He came back and we moved on. . . .

We spent three months in our rolling home, mostly in the South-west. There were some good times. The scenery was often a knockout, purple mountains hanging in space, towering cactus, flocks of geese taking off in a pink sunrise. Artie saw a lot of gun places. The dogs picked up a lot of burrs in their paws.

The fact that my breathing began to act up again was scarcely noticed.

We returned to Connecticut in the spring and picked up where we left off. Things may have seemed to be the same after that, but they never were. . . .

CHAPTER 66...

"I walked along the street of sorrow
. . . the boulevard of broken dreams. . . ."

I had been raised to believe that being ill was . . . well, not nice. A thing one didn't discuss in mixed company. When I was growing up nobody I ever knew went to a hospital, not even to visit. An occasional sniffle might be allowed, but that was it.

So my struggle for breath was highly embarrassing. ("What's that wheeze in your chest?" "Wheeze! Ha ha! That's just a little frog. . . .")

"What's the matter with you?" Artie would ask.

God, I was sick of that question. "Nothing. Nothing at all!"

But when the infernal racket persisted, when I would have to get up at night and walk around the house for hours to be able to breathe, he suggested I see his doctor. "Better have Leder take a look at you." Leder. A nice name for a medicine man. Take me to your. "And while you're there," Artie went on, "ask him why you're so cold all the time."

I hadn't stopped wearing clothes in bed after we returned from our motor home sojourn. Sometimes I even wore socks. I always wore a nightgown and—more significantly—panties under it. "Jesus," Artie would grumble, "I can't find you under all that."

"I'm cold." I was too, to the innermost reaches. I got colder when he reached over for me. "I'm sorry, Artie I think I·. . . have to get up for a while. . . ."

Dr. Leder told me I had asthma.

"Asthma!" I was shocked. "That's a . . . children's disease, isn't it, that they grow out of when they become adults?"

"You're obviously in your second childhood," winked Doctor.

Jokes our Le(a)der makes with me nearly on my deathbed.

"You're probably allergic to something," he went on, "so you'd best see a specialist in these matters, an allergist."

Doc number two. A fine fellow who made tests and discovered the offending culprit. Mold spores or some such flying objects. "If you have animals around," he told me, "you should get rid of them."

"Fat chance," I told him.

He nodded. "Didn't think you would," he sighed. "All my patients say the same thing."

He made up a corrective serum to shoot into me three times a week. That meant three trips to New York. Artie, too, had an increasing number of shows to do, lawyers to see, discussions of a book he had written before I knew him and wanted to publish called, *I Love You, I Hate You, Drop Dead*. Our hotel bills were becoming absurd. "I think we'd better take a little place in town," Artie finally said.

The minute we were in the big city so often things started popping left and right. More guest spots on shows for Artie. Discussions about other books to be written, a musical to be done (another one!), perhaps a band to be taken out on the road, Artie conducting. A movie to be made. A writer friend had a marvelous script, *The Snow Queen*, perfect for Elizabeth Taylor. "Would she do it?" Artie asked. "Let's go see," I said.

She was with Burton by then, and he was doing *Hamlet* up in Toronto. Off we drove to take the script to her. ("Oh please, *please* don't drive so fast." "*Get off my back!*")

Burton was brilliant onstage, the two of them glowing backstage, in their prime, at the top of their romance. "That was sick," she told me, "that marriage to Eddie. Sick." I assumed she assumed her latest arrangement was well.

Nothing more than the trip came of it, but it didn't matter because something even more interesting was happening. We had taken a larger apartment on East 51st, and were busily giving parties, going to them, running here, running there, suddenly absorbed by New York life. We saw Lakeville only on weekends.

Leaving the apartment one day we ran into my friend Joyce Buck's brother. "Hey hey! Long time no see!" All those noises. "Where are you two off to?"

"I for one," I said, "am on my way uptown to get a fix."

"Oh yeah?" was Brother's unruffled reply. I guess all his friends got fixes. "What about you?" he said to Artie.

"Oh, I was doing some errands, nothing important. Why?"

Brother was in the film distribution business. "I'm on my way to see an English film I hear is great, only everybody's scared of it—a little girl gets kidnapped—so it's up for grabs for distribution in this country. Want to go with me?"

"Sure," said Artie, "why not?"

Which is how he got into film distribution. He bought the film then and there that afternoon. It was called *Seance on a Wet Afternoon*. It would be a smash hit, win awards left and right. He and Brother set up shop, called themselves Artixo— which is Artie Shaw in Catalán— got offices, hired salesmen, bookkeepers, secretaries and all that jazz.

And that isn't all that was happening to Artie.

One day he said to me, "Kesi, sit down. I'd like to talk to you."

I cringed. These talks invariably meant I was doing something he didn't like. At least he was calm. I would try to remain that way. Friction time these days far exceeded the smoother moments.

"Look," Artie went on, "you obviously don't care about sex anymore."

I was taken aback. Was it true? I had seemed to have lost my enthusiasm, hadn't I. . . . "Why . . . no, I guess I don't. . . ."

"It happens to women when they get older."

I didn't like that so much. I wasn't the only one getting on. "You're older too."

His impatience was merely slight. "Age doesn't make any difference to men, they can go on the rest of their lives." He leaned toward me, earnestly. "Kesi, I can't go on this way, you know—"

"I know. I know you can't."

"I never get laid, for Christ's sake."

"I'm sorry, I'm so sorry, I—"

"What if I go elsewhere, would you mind?"

So very early Noël Coward. "Not at all," I said, "not a bit."

"You've noticed I like Marcia."

Marcia was part of an attractive couple we had met at some party or other, and had begun to invite to ours. He was amusing, she was beautiful—and young. All those good things. That she was somebody's wife didn't seem to bother Artie. It certainly didn't bother me. Wasn't I a big authority on the marital musical chairs game? "Oh yes," I said, "I've noticed."

"Well, what do you say, would you mind if I—if we . . .?"

He was asking permission. Like that, I had become his mother. I accepted my new role with pleasure. "Why of course I don't mind," I exclaimed. "Be my guest!"

The relief that swept over me was as sweet as fresh air to a trapped miner, heavenly as the breeze from the plains of Shangri-La. The twenty-ton albatross nestling on my chest got up and flew away. The terrible guilt I carried about because of my poor performance as wife, woman, female, human being, lover, companion, sympathizer, cook, housekeeper, listener when he wanted that, responder when he wanted that. But now, I could make up for it all! What better gift could I give him than a beautiful young thing to have an affair with? And I, oh bliss, the dread was gone, like a straitjacket peeled off, when the covers would rustle in the bed beside me, and a hand reached out. Oh heaven, oh never again!

The warm glow that had been between us in the beginning returned. We liked each other again. Were friends. That word was used a great deal. Oh, we are such good friends! Resentment, harbored ill-will, all shrugged off like raindrops. I went up to Lakeville for a few days, by myself. Did nothing except romp around the house with the dogs, race them to the lake and back, three of us off the leash, reveling in our freedom.

Euphoria lasted nigh onto a week.

Then we were invited by our good friends, the Fred Mortons, to Shepheard's, the "in" discotheque at the time. Not only were they good friends, they were close friends; they had bought property next to us in Bagur, for God's sake! And it was *us* they asked to go with them. But Artie said to me, "Look, Kesi, I think I'll take Marcia instead of you, you've been to those places thousands of times."

"I've never been to Shepheard's," I answered.

"What's the difference, they're all the same. I've never taken her out anywhere—you don't care for nightclubs—"

"Neither do you—"

"But she's a young girl, a dancer, she likes those places—"

Well, I thought, sure I can understand that. God, I've been every-where, done everything, haven't I. Let somebody else have a chance.

Was I so enchanted with my new freedom, my blessed release from responsibility that I was blinded? Or is it that my IQ isn't what it's cracked up to be? It took several more youth-oriented outings, a few more "Ah Kesi, you've-been-seen-done and this child hasn't"'s before an uneasiness began to seep into my feeble brain. Before it finally dawned on me that Artie had somehow relegated me to yesterday's generation when he himself was older! In easing myself out of his bed, had I put myself in the position of being eased out altogether? This was no extracurricular activity, a little playing around on the side the way I had visualized it. He was taking her everywhere. Even to mu-tual friends' homes. *In my place.*

Whoa! Just one bloody minute. I had obviously made a big mistake. He was making it a big deal, a full-blown "romance" yet. No, this would never do.

I waited up for him to come home. He was plenty late, too, about three o'clock in the morning. "Hey! What are you doing up?" He asked almost gaily. I guess he had had a splendid evening. Machito and Garbo, whom I had brought to town, wagged up to greet him.

"I wanted to talk to you."

"What about? God, I'm hungry. What's there to eat?" He headed for the kitchen.

I trailed along. "There's . . . lots of things. Listen. . . ."

He opened the refrigerator door and was rummaging around. "Yeah? Go ahead. I'm listening."

"I'll wait till you're through—"

"I can hear you." He pulled out a pie. He yanked open a drawer for a knife.

"Well look," I said to his shoulder, "I think maybe we have made a mistake. I mean, there isn't going to be any 'us' if you continue this way, I don't want to sit around home all the time while you go out. Marcia wasn't supposed to . . . replace me, she was supposed to . . . you know, be on the side, and now you're taking her everywhere. You can't do that, Artie, no no. We had better back up and start over again and get back to where we were in the beginning. It's you and I who better sleep together, and you'd best forget about Marcia right now before it's too late."

I didn't know how I was going to manage, but I was willing to give it the old college try.

I needn't have worried. Artie wasn't about to touch me with the proverbial ten-foot pole.

Being looked at with pure hatred from eyes that once held tenderness is not easy to take. I was his "friend" who had given him a lollipop, but now I was his enemy who wanted to take it away. "You made sense," he snarled furiously, "and now you're making none. Stop hanging around here, for Christ's sake, making me feel guilty! Go have your own life and leave me alone!" He turned away and began to eat his pie. A pie I had made for him.

I left at dawn for Lakeville with the dogs. It was my favorite time of day. Or used to be. Now there was no studio down the road, nor a grand day's work on a set ahead. Just an absurdly large house, in a foreign place. (It might as well have been called Palacios.)

A fine drizzle sprayed the windshield. The clouds hung low, gray as my thoughts.

Go make your own life, he had said. Without him? Without Artie? Why . . . that wasn't possible, I *was* him. Half of his whole. Had he not labored mightily for six years to achieve just that? Had he not pulled and pushed, molded and yanked and shaped me into his image, made me an integral part of himself, a reflection of his needs and wants? He had even renamed me; wiped out the old, the movie person, the crazy mixed-up kid, and good riddance. *Et voilà!* A brand new person is born! Kesi Shaw. Mrs. Artie. How can Kesi Shaw go have a life of her own. Without Mr. Artie, she doesn't exist.

The albatross returned to sit on my chest and brought not only his family and friends but the entire goddamn albatross colony. . . .

CHAPTER 67...

"Don't get around much . . .

anymore. . . ."

I couldn't breathe. I just bloody well couldn't get air in—or out—of my lungs. Something like running the 10,000 yard dash when you've just run the 20,000 yard dash. It was highly embarrassing. I could understand Artie's annoyance perfectly; who wouldn't be, I was. What a dirty trick my body was playing on me. I told myself asthma wasn't really a sickness.

Meanwhile there it was. And wouldn't go away. The shots didn't seem to help much. "The serum I give you will alleviate some of your suffering," the allergist told me, "but you'll have to get to the root of what's troubling you to have any effective cure. You ought to see a psychoanalyst."

Doc number three. For somebody so healthy I was suddenly up to my ass in doctor bills.

From him—number three—I soon learned to my chagrin that Myrtle had been in charge all along. She knew I couldn't leave a man, that the man had to leave me. She had arranged it all, the sneaky bitch. She was probably arranging this absurd punishment for my body too.

So, what with my busy medical staff necessarily in constant attendance, I was in New York a great deal of the time. Wheezing away. Ms. Primal Scream in person. I was a veritable downpour on Artie's parade and he didn't care for it worth a damn. His new company was swinging, money pouring in from everywhere. He had talked Marcia out of dancing and into being his secretary—success and romance all wrapped up in a neat package—all glorious except for the wheezing remnant from a former life always underfoot. Still playing wife and not knowing how to stop, like a chicken keeps running after its head is cut off, cooking, sewing on buttons, straightening slept-in beds— mine and his. (We were in separate ones finally.)

It didn't add up to a congenial atmosphere. Resentment flourished and ill-temper abounded, monumental arguments set off by the slightest thing. A misplaced *anything* was reason for murder by Artie.

One midnight after I was in bed I heard him come in. I heard him go into the study, presumably to read. The next thing was a bellow. "*Where—the fuck—is—my ashtray!?*"

I shot out of bed. "Isn't it there?" I called out, "I'll get it—" I dashed to the study. I had been well trained.

His eyes blazed at me from his recliner, "Why must I never be able to have things where I want them—"

"The cleaning woman must have—"

"Cop-out, cop-out, the eternal cop-out, everybody's to blame but you—"

"I'll *find* it—" All at once I realized there was an ashtray on the table beside him. "Artie, what's that? Isn't that—"

"*That's—not—my—ashtray!*" he snarled, picked it up and flung it across the room.

Trembling with hatred I picked up the fallen one, saw *his* precious ashtray on a table across the room, retrieved it, took it over and placed it on the table beside his chair while he watched with icy eyes. "You look as if you're smelling shit," he said finally.

"Good night," I said with all the dignity I could muster, and left the room.

Leaving a room before Artie was finished was the greatest crime of all. He stormed after me, furious. "What cute tricks you're pulling here!" he yelled. "Not running, just making sure I'm going to leave, playing the martyr. But you don't fool me, I know you for the monster you are. You set up this whole thing and now you punish me. . . ."

And on and on. Through summer. Through autumn. My analyst heard the instant replay of one of the wranglings once too often. "I'm going to do something I've never done," he said, "but in your case it's necessary. Leave this man. He is too destructive for you."

"But Doctor," I protested, "you are only hearing my side. Perhaps I'm giving you the best of it for me. Artie says we judge ourselves by our intentions and others by their actions. He says I do things in a sneaky ladylike way, when actually I'm a ball-breaker of the worst kind, a monster in the guise of—"

"Believe me." He was impatient. He had heard it many times before. "I know ball-breakers. I know monsters. You are neither."

"But Artie says—"

"Do you know that since you've been coming here—nearly six months—you have spent the major part of your time quoting Artie? It is you we are treating here. . . ."

It was obvious I should clear out. But the execution of the maneuver was beyond me. I, who had traveled so much, couldn't get past the front door. Letting go of a hotshot miracle wasn't the easiest thing in the world. I made it to Christmas. Then the mixture of fear, fury and fuck-up took its toll. I was carted off to the hospital. There I lay during the holiday festivities while experts with their tubes and charts tried to put Ms. Humpty together again.

New Year's Day Artie paid me a duty visit. The TV set was tuned into the Orange Bowl parade. Several pubescent baton twirlers swung into view, their bare thighs, bouncing breasts, even rows of teeth and shapely behinds all flashing in the Florida sun.

The contrast between this display of nubile verve and me was all too sharply defined. Artie stood at the foot of the bed with angry eyes and angry mouth, not deigning to sit nor take off his coat or hat, looking down at this sickly creature who was his wife; who had turned into the biggest spoilsport of all time.

After his departure, a nurse came in to tidy me up, then handed me a comb and brought a mirror so that I could see myself neatening the tangled mess on my head.

While the young ladies pranced on the screen across the room, I stared at the reflection in the mirror before me. Who was this pale, thin-cheeked, dismally sad-eyed . . . *middle-aged* woman!?

Nobody I knew. Obviously a reject of some kind. The one I knew was young! Gorgeous! Adored by one and all! My God, I thought, sitting up a little straighter, you've gone too far, my girl. It's time to stop this nonsense and get yourself together—

"Finished?" asked the nurse, reaching for the mirror.

"Maybe not," I answered. . . .

CHAPTER 68...

"Those were the days, my friend . . .
we thought they'd never end. . . ."

In the year that followed I stopped the silly nonsense and got it together. The first step was to be, most of the time anyway, where Artie wasn't. With this perfectly good house sitting empty in Lakeville, it seemed the logical place to go. Apartheid was not altogether mine; Artie came for weekends, often bringing his girlfriend. We still had this "friendship" marriage going. If you can believe.

In spite of all that, my breathing got back on the proper track—maybe and probably—because an intoxicating thing happened.

It had long been my habit to write things down. Ideas. Happenings. Dreams. These bits of unfinished matter lay in disorderly confusion in my desk. One afternoon I decided to set them right. Hey, I thought, you've got the time to really write now . . . !

The size of the house was ridiculous for one mere woman, two dogs, one part-time man and friend. So we sold it and bought a smaller one. The house on the mountain was so reminiscent of the Spanish one with all its glass front facing south toward a beautiful view that my pulse leaped when I saw it.

I was still clinging, clinging to what was over and done with.

I did it again the next year when I went to see John. I don't really know why I did. Did the times with him seem like the good old days compared to those I had just gone through?

He was a citizen of Ireland now, and had his own castle. An ancient monastery refurbished, its gray stone turrets rising out of the early morning mists like some secret Druid hangout.

He swept down a baronial staircase in a floor-length Japanese robe to greet me. His hair had turned white, the lines in his face deeper, the stoop a little rounder. Was he taking inventory of me? Did I still look like the creature in the hospital mirror?

"How are you, honey?" he said in melted caramel. That hadn't changed. Over Irish coffee polite conversation was exchanged. "Did you have a pleasant trip? The weather isn't at its best." As if I were a perfect stranger who had wandered in out of the bog. I suppose I was. But then, who was this white-haired gentleman in the flowing oriental robe talking to me? Apparently everybody but me knows you can't go home again.

When I got back to Lakeville, Machito was off his feed. It happened once in a while. I didn't think much about it. Nor that some weeks later when a poker game was in progress he insisted on lying right under my feet, sometimes rising to place his chin on my arm. "Machito," I complained, "must you stick so close to me?"

One of the players spoke up. "You ought to put that dog away. He's had it."

I was horrified. "Are you crazy? That's my love!"

"Well, your love is in a bad way."

I looked down at my dog. What I saw chilled me. His muzzle was white. His coat was thin, without luster, his ribs showing. His back legs bent feebly.

When had it happened? When had he grown old? Until that moment he had been the young, beautiful, vigorous dog he had always been, running the length of the terrace in Bagur in the prime of his life.

A wave of tenderness swept over me. I hugged him and scratched his head. But I hadn't understood what he had been trying to tell me.

A wet tongue licked my hand at dawn, nudging me awake. He didn't want to have his heart attack alone.

It was ghastly. Some hideous force, some violent inner explosion hurled him about the room, crashing him into things, finally to knock him to the floor, out cold.

At my outcry he got to his feet and struggled to my side. I held him close and, trying not to tremble, dialed the vet with my free hand. "I was afraid of that," he murmured. "His heartbeat has been irregular for some time. . . ."

"Oh. I didn't realize. Is he . . . in pain?"

"Terrible pain. It would be best if you . . ." The unfinished sentence hovered like an evil spirit in the cool morning air.

I waited two days for the recovery that would never come. My dog didn't eat or sleep. He was in agony.

He watched me pick up the phone, his eyes brimming with trust.

"Please," I said to the vet, "will you come here to do it so Machito won't be upset?"

We made a date for three o'clock.

Did he know? He came over to put his head on my lap. I leaned over to scratch behind his ears. My tears dampened his scruffy coat. So be it, I thought. Another ending. That's what life is, isn't it, a series of endings. "But you," I whispered, "will go out in style, my darling."

I took out a chilled bottle of champagne, opened it, took a glass and a saucer, and went back to Machito.

For him I filled the saucer, for me the glass. When they were empty I filled them again. I let him have as much as he liked. And why not?

By three o'clock if I wasn't ready to meet Machito's Maker, I was at least numb enough to go through with the deed.

A swift needle. It was over. Without even a whimper. The Spanish dream and all its parts—prince, castle and happy-ever-after ending—was finally, irrevocably over. . . .

CHAPTER 69...

"There's no . . . business like show. . . business. . . ."

The dance coach, Victor Griffin, was waiting when I returned to the rehearsal studio. A tall, graceful fellow who turned out to be a fine teacher, forceful, enthusiastic. He quickly reminded me of things I had forgotten. "Lift those ribs! More *strength* in those arms! Keep your shoulders *down*!"

For three days I labored mightily, pulling, pushing, stretching muscles unaccustomed to such endeavor for a very long time, dredging up out of hazy memory a step here, a riff there. With Victor's help I got together a fairly presentable routine.

On the morning of the audition I woke at six o'clock, revved up to go. It didn't help to tell myself it was a minor event and didn't matter. It did. And shouldn't everything you do matter if you're bothering at all? Not to hold on when it's over, that's the trick. . . .

I got out of bed, unfurled my tender, bitterly complaining muscles, and went through the routine once more before I did anything else. Then I showered, trying not to think . . . watched the sun come up . . . rolled my hair . . . listened to the news. . . .

Finally and somehow the moment came to put on makeup, comb out my hair, and slip into the shiny black pantsuit I had decided would be suitable.

And it was countdown time. . . .

We've seen the scene a hundred times: with Ruby herself, Ginger, Joan, Barbra. The darkened theater on its day off, bare stage, upright piano over to one side, the glaring work light, and the watchful eyes down in the seats somewhere, ready with approval or not.

Enter Hopeful. Nervous. A little too eager. Smile too broad. *It's all right for kids, I told myself. Stop that, you ought to thank your lucky stars to still be doing something that is such a turn-on.*

The music begins, and I am on. . . .

I sing. Then I dance and—it is working. It is right. My nervousness dissolves into energy and I dance. Oh, I really am dancing, it feels good, oh it's all come together . . . mmm . . . mmmm . . . till I . . . make you happy too. . . .

Then it was over. Thank you, someone said. Nothing more. But it didn't matter. I went away, elated. I had been good, and I knew it. It was in the bag, and I knew it. . . .

I didn't hear from them for a year. *A year.*

Disappointed? Of course. So what else is new? It wasn't the first time, and with a little luck it wouldn't be the last. You can't be disappointed unless you try something to be disappointed *over.*

But I know about getting on with life. I certainly know all about that. I went home and finished my novel, *I Am a Billboard.* Lyle Stuart published it and when it showed up in Doubleday's window on Fifth Avenue, that made me feel very fine.

The amazement was evident in the agent's voice when he finally got around to calling me the twelve months later. "They want you," he said, not believing his own words, "for the Second National Company of *No No Nanette.*"

So I came down from the mountain and off I went, up and down and around the land, just as in days of yore.

Meanwhile the old world had taken a couple of whirls and there were many changes: Jets whisked us to destinations in the wink of an eye; crowds gathered in theaters to see us instead of in the streets; the men in blue were too busy trying to hold back the mayhem threatening to engulf their inner cities to escort play-actors in and out of town.

But the change in me was the biggest change of all, as I discovered one sweltering night in St. Louis.

It was the Fourth of July. The big number was coming up, and I was waiting in the wings to go on. It was an outdoor theater, and in the dark sky back of the audience I caught a glimpse of the faraway splash of a Roman candle as it burst up over the horizon. Our 1776 Revolution, it appeared, was being celebrated somewhere in the city in time-honored tradition.

But not here on the stage of the Municipal Opera House. Here we nestled snugly in our little empty-headed 1925 stage world, oblivious to the one outside. The boys in their argyle sweaters and knickers were already onstage strumming the ukelele that heralded the beginning of the dance. "I want—to be . . . happy. . . ."

And I was. I would soon be rushing out to join them. Anticipation speeded up my heart, excitement was tugging deliciously at my nerve ends, when all at once it dawned on me—I was doing what I had told my mother I wanted to do when I was fourteen years old back in Atlanta.

I almost burst out laughing. My God, I thought, that was *one hell of a wide detour* you took! I shook my head in disbelief as I recalled how assiduously, how one-track-mindedly, I had followed the signposts along the route. THIS WAY FOR HAPPY ENDING! TURN RIGHT FOR STARDOM! YOUR PRINCE TO THE LEFT! WOMANHOOD STRAIGHT AHEAD!

And who had nailed up these directions with such a knowing hand? The male of our species? Ladies of the Home Journal?

Whichever, one thing was clear; they had been signs pointing to somebody else's Valhalla.

Ah, never mind, I reflected peacefully, I am on my own path at last. Oh, not to go on with this foolish tap dancing, but on my way to being my own person, my own *female* person, who is finally up to listening to the beat of her own drum. Too late? Nonsense. I'm still here, am I not? All this chopping life up into sections and labelling them teen, middle-age and senior citizen is poppycock, I say. Life is one piece, a long silken ribbon, a steady flow of river, a super Interstate to walk and ride and dance and prance along and even crawl if that is the only way, but by God, do it to the end with as much enthusiasm and eagerness as you had at the start.

A few years ago I saw my old friend, Betty Bacall, on "The Tonight Show." And Johnny Carson asked her, "What are you going to do next?"

"Press on," she answered, "press on."

That's about it.

The music swelled up . . . and the spotlight swung my way. . . .

EPILOGUE

Oh yes.

When Artie had his automobile accident, the one I had known was coming, I wasn't in the car. He survived, with thirteen stitches in his forehead.

But the jagged metal from the hood curled back through the car and sliced the passenger seat beside him in half. Kesi Shaw, dutiful wife, going whither thou goest, would have had it.

There was a lesson there somewhere, I was pretty sure. . . .

INDEX